Man & Measure

The Paintings of Tom Wood

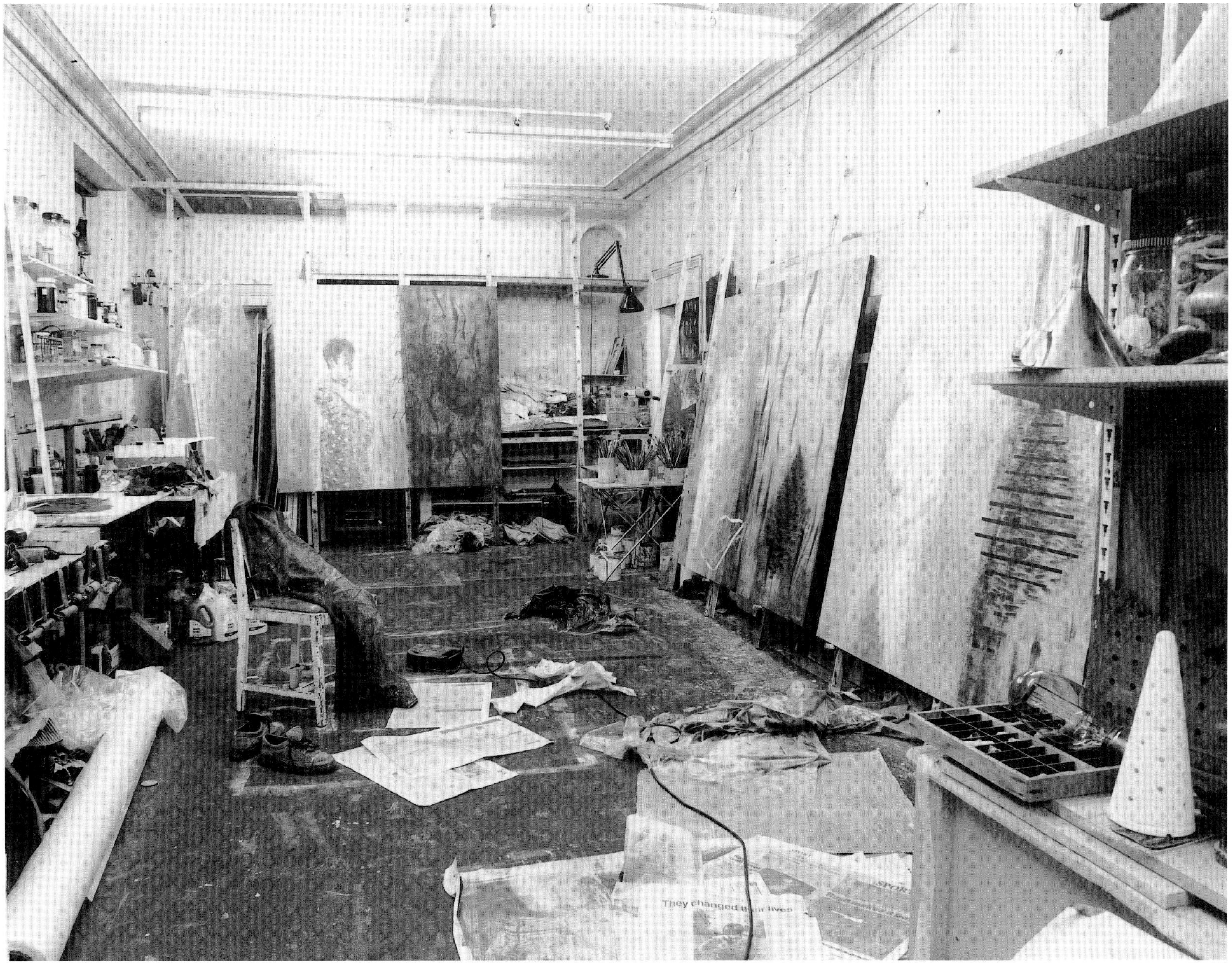

Studio, Dean Clough, Halifax 1995

Man & Measure

THE PAINTINGS OF TOM WOOD

Duncan Robinson

HART GALLERY
London & Nottingham

Cover: **Parable 1993–94. (detail)**
Oil on Panel with Neon
183 × 340 cm (72 × 134 inches)

ISBN: 0-9520759-4-6 Hard back
0-9520759-5-4 Soft back

Photographs: Barry Wood Photography
Richard Littlewood

Previous Publications: *David Blackburn and the Visionary Landscape Tradition*
Sasha Grishin

Forthcoming Publications: *Kenneth Draper*
Roger Berthoud

Designed and printed by Jones & Palmer Ltd. (0121) 236 9007

Paintings 1990 – 1995

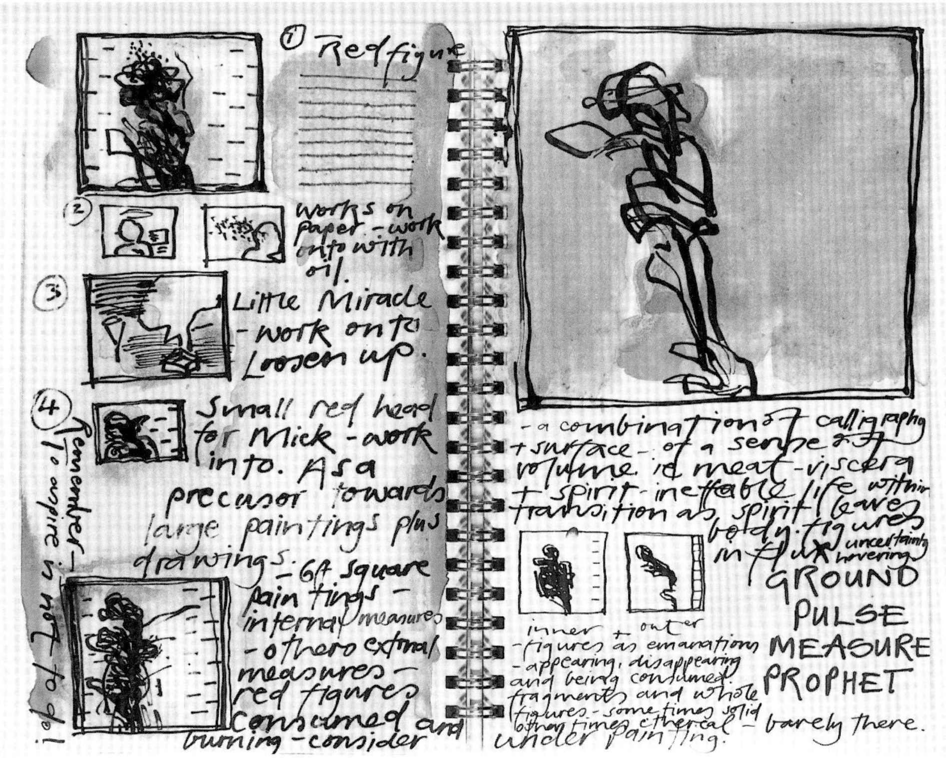

Notebook 1995.

Contents

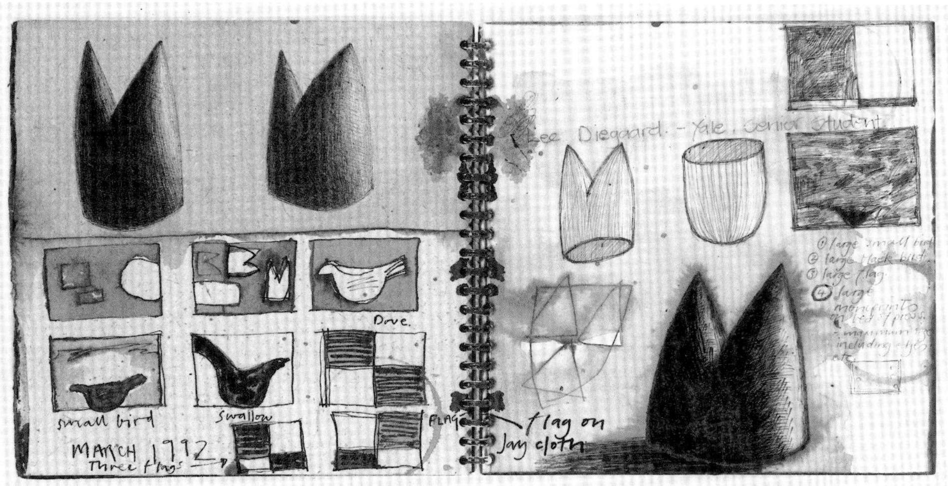

Notebook 1992.

Introduction

In the autumn of 1989, I found myself organising *Crown Pictorial,* an exhibition which set out to give to a North American audience a visual history of the British monarchy from the Tudors to the present day. I was able to do so thanks to the co-operation of my friend and former colleague at Yale, Linda Colley, and of the Curators of the collections at the Yale Center for British Art, from which the exhibits were drawn. Our problems began with the twentieth century, but thanks to the Victoria and Albert Museum, we were able to include a suite of images by that royal photographer *sans pareil,* Cecil Beaton. To our appeals, local royalists responded with offers of coronation mugs, souvenirs of royal visits and other ephemera, and Tony Rushton provided a number of less reverent commentaries from the archives of *Private Eye*. But we lacked any reference to contemporary portraiture, not to mention a grand finale for the exhibition itself. It was then that the cover of *Modern Painters* caught my eye. The caption read *"Tom Wood puts the Prince in the Picture"*, and I determined at once to put both of them into the exhibition.

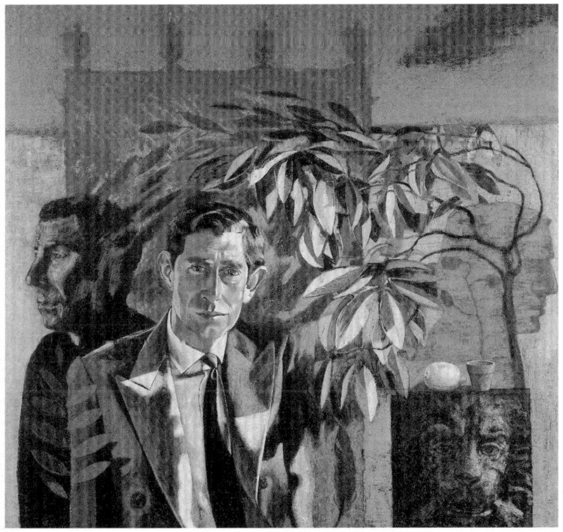

HRH The Prince of Wales.
oil on panel
152.4 × 157.5 cm (60 × 62 inches)
on loan to The National Portrait Gallery

Happily, neither the Prince nor the Painter objected, and just over a year later, in January 1991, the exhibition opened in New Haven, Connecticut. Tom Wood agreed to visit the Center and to give a lecture, which not only confirmed my admiration for his work but introduced me to one of the most thoughtful and articulate of modern painters (a compliment he still refuses to accept). By the time we met, his portraits of HRH The Prince of Wales had attracted a good deal of critical attention, but it is worth dwelling on their success partly as a prelude to the body of work illustrated here and partly because they touch, in their imagery and form, upon the theme of Man and Measure.

Prince Charles met Tom Wood in 1987, during an unscheduled visit to his exhibition of recent work at Dean Clough Art Gallery in Halifax. The Prince's reaction, on the spot, was to say to Wood: "You must do one of me". There followed, rather to Wood's surprise, the necessary preliminaries and then the sittings, which took place at Highgrove House. Several studies resulted, among them the masterful one in oils, the Head Study which is now in the Prince's collection, together with the commissioned portrait, completed in 1989. One of the working drawings became a lithograph, an altogether friendly portrayal in which the head tilts downwards, as if to deny the advantage of rank, towards the eye level of the spectator. Finally Wood elaborated upon his royal subject in a large oil of the heir to the throne as troubled as he is apparent, a branch of olive or bays bent towards his crown, "annihilating all that's made/to a green thought in a green shade". To either side, his left and right profiles fade in and out of focus; a flame-coloured urn-capped façade shimmers in the distance while a dark square, decorated with an antique lion's head, supports a lemon and a flower pot. The pictorial sources for this portrait of Shakespearian dimensions lie in Van Dyke's triple heads of the Prince's ill-fated predecessor, King Charles I, an exercise which history has romanticised to the point of obscuring its original, practical purpose as a visual aid for the great Italian baroque sculptor Bernini. I am also reminded of Titian's much more personal and autobiographical *Three Ages of Man* in the National Gallery in London, a picture in which the great Venetian took stock of his own progress and looked forwards in terms not only of fame but also of family, referring specifically to his son Leone. In taking his measure of the Prince, the painter could not help reflecting upon their common humanity. As he said later of more recent works, "they are all — I suppose — surrogate self-portraits by proxy and as such embody the personal but attempt to express the universal".

Wood's exhibition at Dean Clough in 1987 was meant, in his own words, "to clear the decks" for an exhibition of new work in London the following year. By then, he had reached a stage at which he could begin to withdraw from teaching and arts administration, those necessary props for many a young professional artist with family responsibilities, to devote all of his energies to full-time painting. Another important commission resulted, in 1989, in *Diviner, Mask and Lizard*, designed as a poster for London Transport. Wood's composite of images promoted the British Museum's Museum of Mankind by issuing a compelling visual invitation to everyone who saw it to explore their relationships to cultures past and present, different from their own. The challenge, as he saw it, was in "reflecting a sense of world culture rather than a national one"; a task for which he was better prepared than he knew, as the son of a businessman, from Yorkshire originally, and his Seychelloise wife. They lived in the former British Colony of Tanganyika, where Wood was born and spent the first four years of his life. Then tragedy struck and his suddenly widowed mother left Africa with him and his two older brothers to settle in Liversedge, West Yorkshire.

The sketchbooks Wood took with him to the Museum of Mankind reveal his fascination with everything from tribal masks to a toy aeroplane made of tin plate in Mexico. He approached his task voyeuristically, observing the observer, like his own young daughter "tongue-tied (Elinor) leaning on a case, looking on with bewilderment and awe". At one point, a wonderful golden cockerel, an Oba Cock, was about to dominate the design only to be superseded, overcome by the force of Wood's own argument: "TRY + INCLUDE SOME FIGURES — emblematic, magical, symbolic — another world as real and tangible as this ... Museum allows us for a brief moment to enter that world through the filter of our world — never be the same. We're socialised out of magic — we stand as spectators beyond the glass." At the same time, life goes on, and the sketchbooks double as diaries. There are train times, from Halifax via Leeds to London, addresses, telephone numbers and even directions to a hospital, all measurements in the life of the whole man who keeps appointments, cares for his friends and reminds himself, even as he draws, to buy two litres of white spirit. Eventually, the Diviner emerges, a head within its own profile, a potent symbol of art and artist, together with the X-rayed snake and the four-legged bugs discovered on Mimbres pottery. The sketchbooks abound with references to Braque and Rothko, there is a cutting of Freud's portrait of Bacon alongside rapid drawings, usually in bold, black strokes of the pen, of ethnographical materials. From this wealth of disparate sources Wood's own Museum of Mankind evolved.

In the interview which follows, we begin by talking about a painting which Wood began in 1985 and to which he returned in 1990. *The Family* is his own, brought into the foreground of his art as well as of his life, inscribed as the standard by which he measures both. For Wood either will not or cannot separate the two. I was struck as I read through the notes of our conversations by the elegaic tone which creeps into so many of his comments, and I find it impossible not to relate that note of sadness to the unexpected death of his mother in 1993. He still recalls bitterly the useless platitudes which were recited as condolences by well-meaning acquaintances, and to which his own senseless aphorisms such as "As smoke rises so bees sink" are deliberate, ironic, responses. To suggest that the death of old Mrs Wood, the devout Catholic who, like the *Madonna della Misericordia*, sheltered her brood beneath the ample folds of her faith and love, influenced Wood's work is to miss the point. Faced by the loss of his mother, he had no alternative but to confront in painting the painful contrast between the security of her values and his own lapsed faith. "An ageing thing" without spiritual comfort, he was obliged to recognise his own mortality. Images of desert predominate. Man is shown suffering, not passively, but *"immer strebend"*, like Goethe's Faust. Woman appears as a static, immobile figure, a kind of ageless Eve in an antelapsarian state of impassive pre-awareness. Man and woman together are self-projections by the artist of his own nature, of the dematerialised body and the embodied soul, which describes every one of us, defies measurement and all too often eludes our understanding.

This is not to suggest that the paintings are gloomy. The reproductions of them here are quite sufficient to dispel that notion, although they do not always do justice to the monumental scale of the large canvases. And whatever Wood sets out to paint, he is never constrained by preconceptions. His paintings are journeys of discovery in which chance effects, like encounters on the road, may well determine the outcome. In extreme cases, he is capable of changing direction altogether and will paint himself away from a particular destination. That fate has already overtaken the central figure of *Cathedral*, who is no

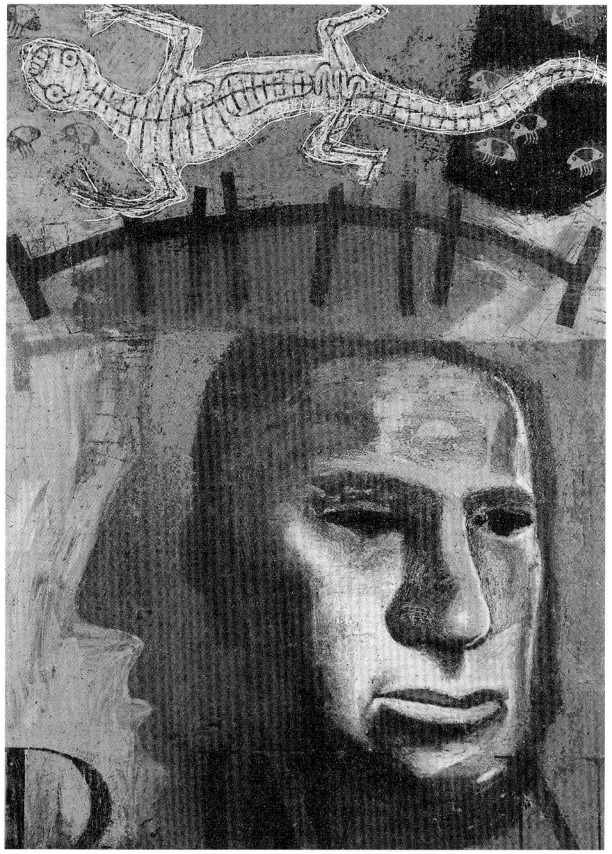

Diviner, Mask and Lizard 1989.
oil and collage on board
136 × 96.5 cm (53.5 × 37.5 inches)
Collection: London Transport

longer discernible as such. I have to confess that I like to think that she might be rediscovered, several centuries from now, and published with photographs of X-rays, to support the theory of some future art historian that artists were so poorly paid in the late twentieth century that even successful ones felt obliged to re-use their canvases!

When I visited Tom Wood in his studio last summer, he was surrounded by works in different media, on paper and on canvas, from rapid sketches and spontaneous explosions of paint on the one hand to carefully developed (and developing) compositions on the other. It was an exhilarating experience, simply to witness the result of his recent visit to Spain and the charge of inspiration he derived from the work of El Greco in particular. It also served to remind me that for the genuinely creative artist there are, happily, many roads to Damascus. Miracles do happen.

It remains only for me to thank John and Kit Hart for inviting me, and Tom Wood for allowing me to ruminate in this way on Man and Measure. I cannot begin to thank them for their patience and forbearance, especially for the past six months when events conspired to distract me, and prevented me from fulfilling my original promises. I take refuge in Tom's own comment that by the time a book appears it is out of date, to which I can only add that images speak for themselves, in a language mercifully independent of words.

Duncan Robinson

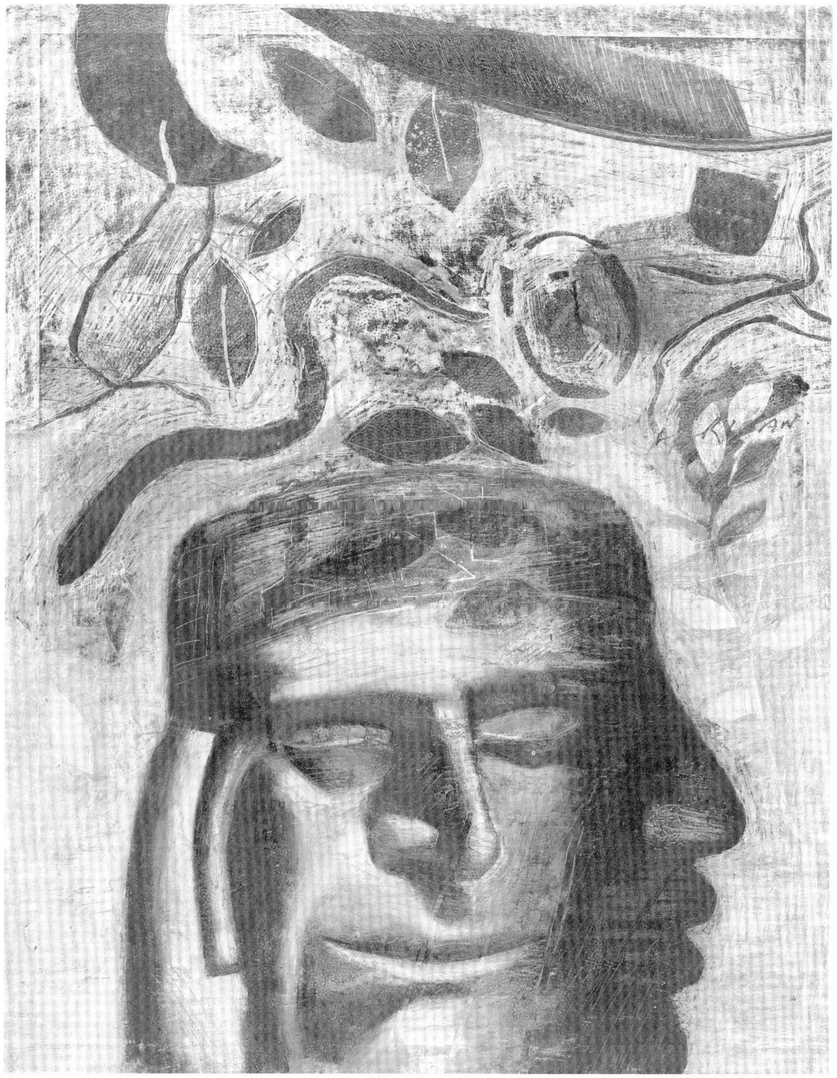

Diviner 1989.
oil on paper
43 × 33.2 cm (17 × 13 inches)
Private Collection

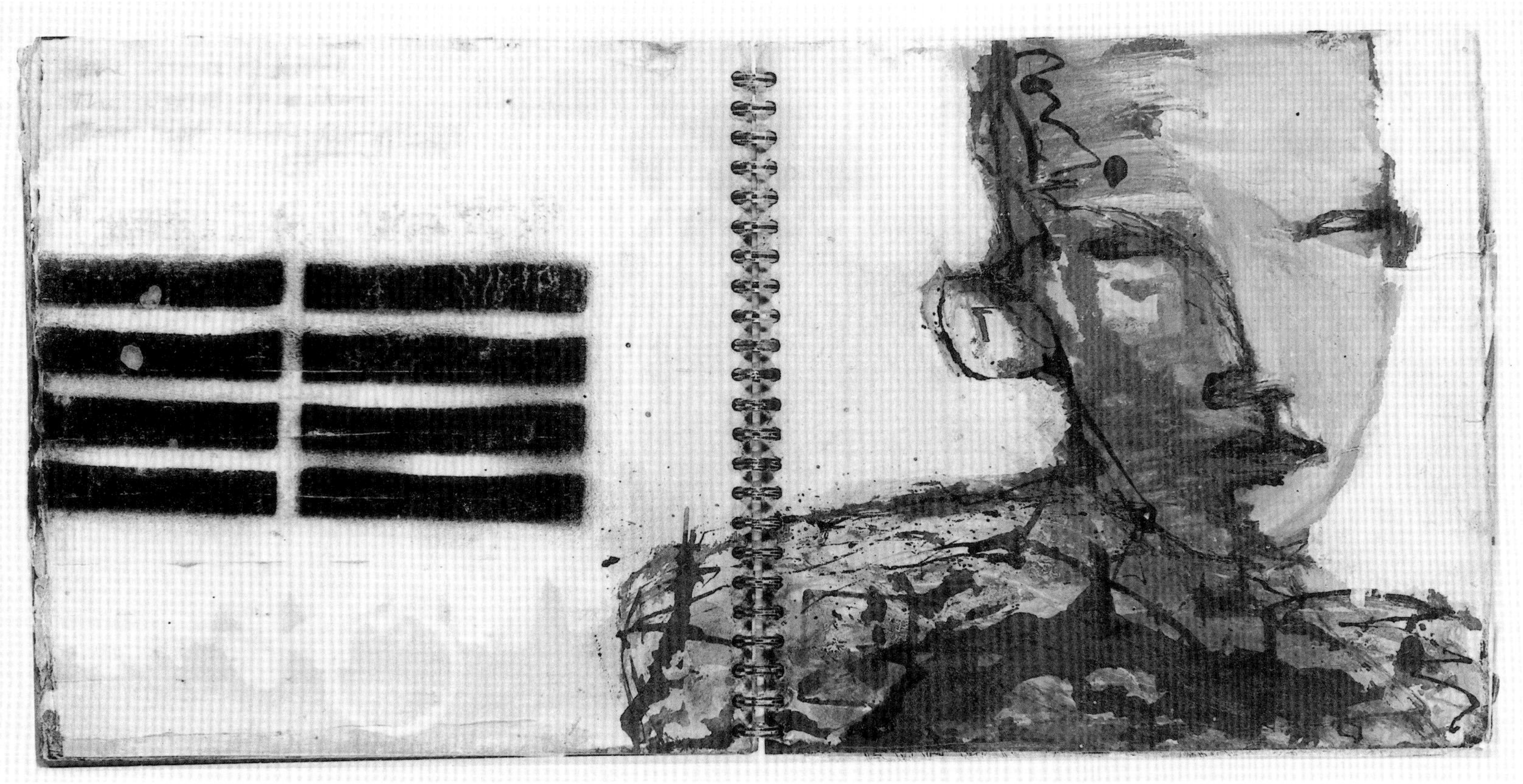

Notebook 1993.

Man & Measure

THE PAINTINGS OF TOM WOOD

'What a work is man, how subtle in faculties,
how infinite in entrails'

Peter Ackroyd
Dan Leno and the Limehouse Golem

DR Tom — I think it was when we were talking about your exhibition at Dean Clough in 1987 that you said it represented a kind of watershed in your career, an opportunity to take stock of what you had achieved before moving on. Is that correct?

TW **Well, yes, for me that exhibition was like that. In all kinds of ways it made me reconsider my assumptions about painting. I think of it like standing on a plateau and being able to glimpse a further horizon thinking I'd like to be there. But exhibitions are often an opportunity to consolidate concerns or to clear the decks and start afresh. I think that's what can be confusing when the show is not a pause but a conclusion and by the time it's seen you're onto another body of work and ideas.**

DR Presumably you feel the same way about books about you?

TW **Yes in a curious way I do but my feelings are more ambiguous where books are concerned.**

DR Perhaps we can come back to that later and you can tell us what to expect from you next?

TW **Books are a strange thing because they will always be in retrospect and they will validate and consolidate things that may have been tentative or fleeting. This to some extent is the issue when work is commissioned. Inevitably it will always be commissioned retrospectively. You're being commissioned, particularly with portraits, on what you've done and not necessarily on what you might do and in that sense it can be difficult, it requires trust and an element of belief.**

DR Now we're talking about retrospection, which is surely a very important element in your work. It seems to me that many of the pictures you paint and the statements that are implied by them are to do with your own past and your immediate surroundings, including the members of your family.

TW **That's true and I find it a struggle to extricate myself from that. I seem to have become obsessive, digging and scratching away at bits of my life. I think it was Kitaj who said that the real purpose of art was to look at the world we live in, whether that's our internal or external world, to look and reflect upon that. To stand outside of ourselves and use the mannerisms of rhetoric will always be hollow, even if the thing we have to say is only a tiny modest thing it will have worth because it has integrity. I don't feel I'm in a position to say I believe *this* or this is important, to make a generalised kind of statement, so what I end up doing is dealing with the specific in a generalised sort of way, by that I mean the works can become layered and obscure so that fairly universal ideas are expressed through specifics like family and friends.**

DR Yes, but to that extent, you're in a great tradition. We need only to recall Rubens painting his wife and child or Titian's Allegory of Time in which he talks of the past, the present and the future not in the abstract but in terms of his own flesh and blood, his son and heir, Leone. Come to think of it, isn't an awful lot of great European painting self-reflective in one way or another, a portrait of the artist in terms of his hopes, ideas and aspirations?

TW **Yes but for me there's a conflict in so far as I have a real resistance to the ideas of the work merely being the artist's ego on display.**

DR Perhaps I am being fanciful, but it occurs to me when I see that you've painted one half only of your face in this picture that by doing so you half admit external reality in the reflection of yourself, but reserve the other half for what you've talked about; the inner life and the life of the mind. In other words, the other half of you lies within the picture. **Plate 1**

TW **That's a wonderful interpretation and I'm sure it's far better than my version which is fairly prosaic and involves the ideas of the painting being formally structured in vertical bands that overlap.**

DR The other thing that strikes me about this picture is the way in which you have represented time and change. I have heard you describe the difficulty of representing flux by means of a static image but that's surely what you have done here. You allow your children to grow visibly in front of the spectator on the canvas by representing them at two different stages in their lives.

TW **Absolutely right. I thought of the painting as a kind of scientific demonstration of growth. The children were painted exactly life size, so much so that I had them stand against the canvas both times and drew around them. The idea being that my paternal subjectivity would not distort the facts. The painting is amongst other things a growth chart.**

DR So you're already measuring?

TW **Yes, absolutely.**

DR Now you're the man with the measure.

TW **That's true. It's curious but you imagine you've got a great breadth of concerns but the truth of it is you can trace a small number of concerns through a large number of works. As David Hill once said to me, "By the time students leave college they've probably already staked out the territory they want to explore for a long time to come. They might enter it from a different place and be equipped differently but the territory stays essentially the same."**

DR Although we're still talking about *The Family*, it seems to me that we are identifying concerns which apply to a number of your pictures. Another

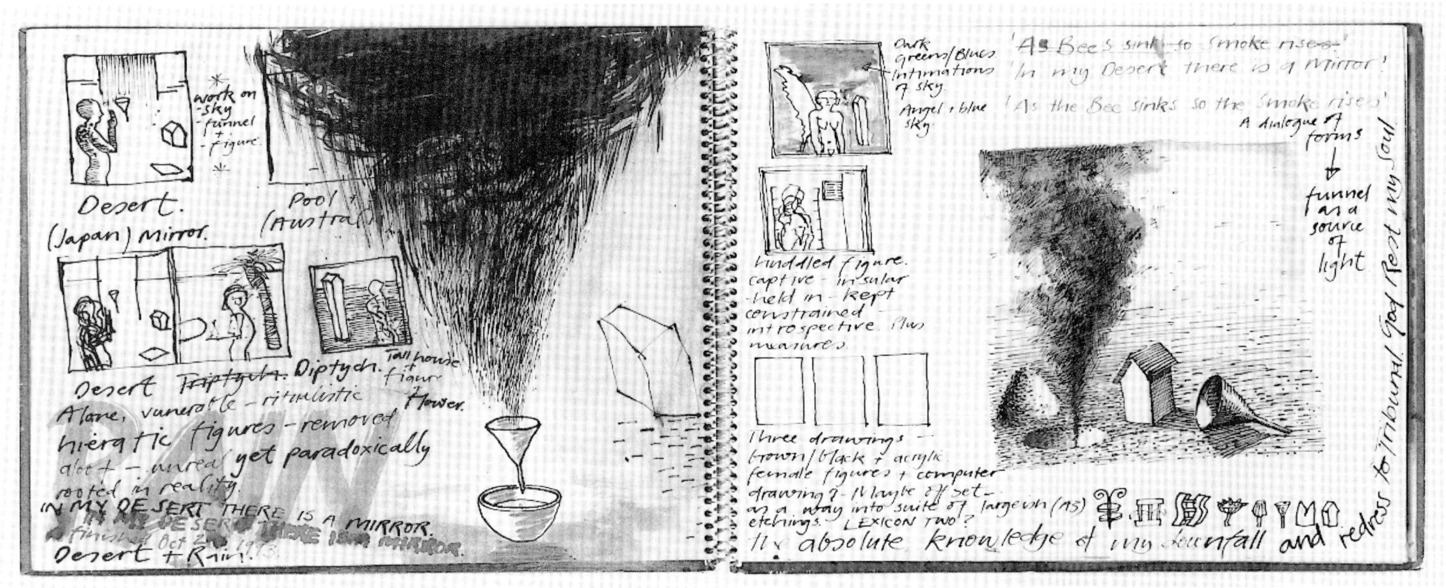

Notebook 1994.

thing that strikes me about the painting is the way in which you introduce different levels of visual representation, as if to indicate different layers of consciousness. You deliberately juxtapose schematic forms which are by implication symbolic: half of a cat here, half of a cat there, ovals and other geometric shapes, lines of connection, the ground itself, all of which engage our eyes and mind in ways different from the almost photographic images of the figures.

TW **I'm very interested in the idea that we can read a painting and read the meanings it might hold across a whole diversity of visual languages, that we can flit easily across these languages and feel sufficiently confident to engage with them on the level of questions. Once a particular mode of representation is established it can just as easily, often within inches of it, be subverted by something else. That all these conventions within painting, like an illusionistic space, or a modernist tilted picture plane, or the diagram which establish their own conventions, can be commodified and selected when necessary, each commenting upon the other. So it's not only what is depicted but also how it's depicted that carries meaning. My ideal of course is to have total freedom to paint across genres with methods that signify total irresponsibility, my 'style' as it were would be to have no 'style'.**

DR Do you think there has ever been a period when artists have been presented with such a wide range of opportunities or options? Yet I suppose that this freedom can be seen as an enormous challenge when so much is available and there are no longer any rules to adhere to.

TW **The establishment of the rules, as you say, are that you should encounter all those different modes of operation or, put another way, make the appropriate choices regardless of personal precedents. It is, I suppose, a post-modernist idea of appropriation and plurality, the idea that all this *mélange* of diverse stuff could hold together in an ironic, self-quoting kind of way. Unfortunately for me this requires a certain distancing. The process engages on a personal level, often in terms of content, but expresses on a disengaged objective level. For me the irony and distancing cancels the affection and close engagement and vice versa. So although I like to work with post-modernism's plurality I struggle with its objectivity.**

DR How do your wife and children feel about the images you produce of them?

TW **They've been surrounded by it for so long now that they feel it's just a part of their lives. It's a bit like Paolozzi's daughter who for long enough thought sculpture was for leaning bicycles against. I like their confidence (or is it apathy?) because it allows me a freedom in the way I choose to depict them. They don't feel precious, so neither do I. It would be awful to think they were being offended in some way. But I also like the idea that the piece of work embodies affection; that it is a kind of small homage or memento of that affection.**

Plate 2 DR I asked you how the members of your family responded to some extent because in the painting of Saskia you have made a museum object out of your daughter.

TW **Yes, I suppose I have really. She fluctuates between mask and face, but still, I hope, reflects affection on my part. From her point of view I think she's just puzzled why I should paint her hair as a mass of yellow stripes.**

DR Is the paint combed?

TW **No, it's a form of stencil that I cut which has been rollered over, moved and rollered over again repeatedly, the stencil being flipped over so that different areas print. I now paint more without conventional brushes than with. To be honest I use anything that will allow me to manipulate the paint physically so that it feels as though it's been evolved rather than applied. When I do apply the paint very obviously I like to do it in such a way that it comments on the application of paint. In other words a brushmark both functions in the context of its mark making status and as a signifier back towards the tradition and implications of the expressive mark in oil paint. And the same is true of the surfaces I make, they emphasise their integrity. There is no sense of trickery or deception but once again we're back to the idea of the plurality but inherent honesty of the visual languages I employ.**

DR So for you the surface is very important. You really work the surface, don't you?

TW **Not as such. I don't 'work' the surface intentionally or separately, not overall anyway. The procedures I use, and I use that word carefully, rather than techniques, which for me implies a certain trickery, results in those surfaces. I seem to work in bursts of energy and enthusiasm where everything is at stake. These phases can last hours or weeks. It's important that I don't get precious about the painting; that the opportunities within the image don't close down. For me the ideal state is one of flux where anything might happen. It's rare that a painting isn't revised, amended and rethought and consequently reworked. There's a certain charge and excitement when all is risked and I employ all manner of strategies to threaten a painting's stability. I know ultimately it will find order but that order may not be conventional and might be all the more precious for the struggles and risks undertaken in order to achieve it. Maybe it's a form of masochism. In this painting of Elinor the struggles are on a more modest scale but they do involve tearing a whole central section out of the painting. It also has bits of linocut, glued and printed onto it, parts of stencils and monoprints, anything in fact is permissible in order to activate the image and surface. I'm trying all the time to generate a dialogue between image, surface and procedure.** **Plate 3**

DR In your talk last month at the Hart Gallery I remember you saying 'I've always been entranced by the head as a vessel, a container', and when you said that I thought at once about this picture because isn't that what you've demonstrated, by juxtaposing Elinor with those wonderful, pot-like forms and shapes, motifs which remind me of your observations of the Museum of Mankind?

TW **I find it difficult to put into words but for a long time now I seem to have made this equation between heads and vessels. I'm aware of all those simplistic analogies where the head is filled as a vessel might fill or a head is a container as a vessel is a container and yet for me there is a greater resonance. It maybe starts with the idea of humility and fragility. The humility of its making, simply and functionally wrought. I'm thinking of a simple, small hand bowl and the fragility of its existence, merely there as long as it's needed. I paint heads and vessels as a shorthand for people and particular faces as a shorthand for a particular life. The heads and bowls equate to the idea of life itself.**

DR I noticed in the sketchbooks that as you jot down observations, some visual and some verbal, there are several which refer to incidents in Museums; incidents involving children running through galleries, intrusions into the Museum world by the irrepressible forces of life outside the display cases. Correct me if I'm wrong, but it seems to me that *Museum Incident* represents a marvellous, a somewhat playful exchange, between art and life. Here I see the fundamental contradiction between art as something which means a great deal to us, as something that we love almost physically but which at the same time is inaccessible, because of the rules which say 'Don't touch'.

Plate 5

TW **What intrigues me about that museum object is that like a rock in a stream it's touched all around by the flow of people, visitors and scholars and as they focus their attention upon it, it comes alive and is reinterpreted and remade in the context of their concerns. We are the catalyst for its life. Its meaning is not immutable. Children looking at ceremonial masks laugh and are amused or struck dumb, awestruck or bewildered; their struggle to apply meaning to this encounter in my mind expands the possible meanings the objects in themselves might hold. It may well break the heart of some curators when confronted by the unilluminated responses of some visitors, the carefully researched labels and contexts ignored. But for me these glancing blows with other lives, other times and other meanings are humbling and provocative.**

DR I hope it doesn't break their hearts, but I know what you mean.

TW **It provokes me in the sense that like the church the calm of museums and the fact that you go in there and confront these extraordinary timeless objects, almost trying to find some sort of secret silent communion with them and then the whole thing is shattered by the arrival of a school group looking to be 'entertained'. This is unfair really but it amuses me to see such sanctity invaded and colonised into something else, such life and exuberance next to something so apparently still. So it is with *Museum Incident*; I think of it as a humorous painting but the humour is concealed beneath layers and layers of obscurity. In the painting I'm shown encountering an exotic naked woman in a museum. I tenderly touch her shoulder as though it were some delicate sexual moment, whereas in truth she is an image derived from an advertisement for thermal underwear and the only charge she represents is not sexual but that from an electric blanket.**

DR But she's been converted into a work of art as well, a statue somewhat in the Egyptian style as David Hockney might have put it. And thanks to your technique here, of painting more in shadow than in light, you as the other figure share her ambiguity as you stretch out, no longer merely the voyeur, metaphorically reaching inside the case and physically touching the object of desire.

TW **Well I suppose I'm moving between a kind of fantasy and an observed thing, between dreamer and witness. But I also like the idea that the painting sits between meanings; that it floats in a middle ground remaining elusive. There are many clues as to what it might mean, but unfortunately all the clues don't add up to the one meaning, you're still left with something of a puzzle.**

DR A moment ago you mentioned sexuality. You must have become acutely aware of it in your encounters with the Museum of Mankind, where so many of the artefacts are not only ritualistic but also explicit in their references to procreation, generation, life and death. Are you being consciously suggestive in your use of certain forms, of amphora, for example, or the spermatozoa — like snakes which wiggle around the canvas?

TW **The snake is a child's toy that has a particularly sensuous and suggestive movement to it. The kind that would provoke all kinds of crude double-entendres or a stoic determination not to see such lewd suggestions. I love the ambiguity and dilemma such a toy provokes and the wriggling dexterity of a parent's embarrassment. In the painting all the marks signs and shapes are to do with sexuality; they are all a code for sex and passion. The open fretwork form is based upon a piece of Korean ironwork representing the flames of passion. I think it's an attractive notion to think that these flames in all their stylised elegance might represent the throbbing urgency of desperate passion.**

DR As we talk another thing occurs to me; that is the way in which you give equal weight to a child's toy or something out of an underwear advertisement and a precious artefact from a museum. Somehow you bring all of these disparate elements together and then you transform them. Stanley Spencer used to say that he was 'always taking something that was rejected and making it the cornerstone' of one of his compositions. Are your everyday objects elevated in a similar way?

TW **Yes they are. The humble, the neglected, the passed over are ideal candidates for an act of transformation. I used to paint little stones collected from the road as if they were jewels.**

DR Yes, I remember reading in one of your notebooks a note about still life, about the importance you attach to a lemon or a teacup.

TW **Maybe the simple fact that they're selected and painted transforms them in some kind of metaphorical alchemy. Some artists consider the fact that an object is selected and its context changed is enough for that act of transformation to occur. I think the painting of it is for me some way of holding it in time, like mummification.**

DR So what goes through your mind when you do occasionally make a sketch of another work of art, of a Doge by Bellini or a Saint by El Greco?

TW **I suppose it's first and foremost an act of homage and possession but it's also my way of trying to connect back into that tradition however obliquely. It's also of, course, a way of slowing down; by drawing it you'll obviously look harder, closer and longer, you make the act of looking work.**

Plate 7 DR Now to turn to *Collage 1991*. I take it that we are looking here at collage?

TW **Yes, most of it is. Occasionally I like to work on a more austere formal level, that is, to make the form the content.**

DR You seem to be very comfortable with it, which I suspect has something to do with your reverence for the surface of a picture, allowing it to work as an actual component rather than as a neutral ground. But to turn our attention to the forms: we encounter more of your seed pods, more cups, more spiky forms. Am I allowed to mention Léger towards the end of his career?

TW **Léger is exactly right — I like the way he made combinations of some things clearly observed and others imagined. The way he transformed them into his own curious forms, in part playful, when flowers look as though they've been constructed from tubing and plasticine but also have a sinister aspect to them as though they could also stab you if you came too close.**

Plate 9 DR This is for the Green Book, I take it, the journal. I must say I like the idea of offering up to the critics a cup full of spikes.

TW **What an idea, I can feel a painting coming on. With the linocuts I sort of suspend my main concerns, take time out as it were. If I think about it, what I've done is to take out all the enjoyable forms, the bits I enjoyed making and put them into the linocuts; so the prints are in a sense a distillation of the pleasure in the paintings. They're also a more immediate way of working with a kind of graphic language, like diagrams, cartoons, script. I can play around with these forms and see what might happen. When you overprint sometimes there are some startling juxtapositions. I think of it as a form of drawing liberating ideas. I'm doing a similar thing at the moment with computers.**

DR Really? As a purely visual exercise, without text?

TW **Yes, no text at the moment — just images and drawings. It's fairly rudimentary; just overlaying layers, adjusting the transparency of each layer, erasing areas, cloning others and drawing back into it. I'm not that skilled but I'm intrigued by that sense of not being entirely in control. Once more I suppose it's an opportunity for images to be in flux but this time retrievable.**

DR Maybe we should talk a little about portraiture and what it takes to persuade you to paint somebody.

TW **Well it began with me making pictures of the people I cared for — as I mentioned earlier, kind of affectionate mementoes. People then started asking me to do portraits for them and as you know I had some success of sorts in this area. Fortunately, things have calmed down and I only do an occasional portrait that I would like to do. It's fairly sporadic which is how I like it. The most enjoyable and, I think, probably most successful portraits are those where I'm working with a sympathetic sitter; someone who feels some personal investment with the portrait and who's aware of my concerns — a kind of partnership I suppose. The portrait of Keith Holmes and Sheila Fairbrass was for me a model of its kind. It was a long, fairly protracted exercise where I made a number of false starts but where their patience and loyalty paid off. Its always an act of faith on the part of the sitter, they must feel vulnerable; my role maybe is to understand that vulnerability, to try and sustain their confidence and at the end of the day to deliver the goods. I have to be honest and say it's not always easy.** Plate 11

DR It's a very formal picture, a diptych, in format.

TW **As a painter of portraits my great hero has always been Holbein and the North European tradition of Van Eyck, Campin, Memlinc and Van der Weyden. That stiffness and Flemish formality along with a kind of Gothic abruptness of forms appeals far more than a southern Renaissance liquidity. By implication I also like the fact that they imply extreme stiffness and that seems to be inherently honest. These paintings are not trying to be anything other than stiff, formally posed tableaux. They don't insinuate movement or the sense of a fleeting glimpse. They tell it as it is, a person has sat or stood there for hours on end aching and sore.**

DR So are we meant to see them like Holbein's Ambassadors?

TW **Yes, for me that has always been a key painting, that and the 'Portrait of George Gisze'.**

DR Well, I can see that Holmes and Fairbrass are self-selected sitters, but you have on some occasions accepted outside commissions. Presumably that was the case with Alan Bennett. Had you met Bennett before you were asked to paint him? Plate 13

TW **No I hadn't met him but, like everybody else, I suppose I thought I knew him. He's a joy to be around and although I didn't spend a great deal of time with him the bit that I did was all pleasure. He had no expectations and gave me total freedom.**

DR I have to admit to a greater preference for the larger painting, the six-footer.

TW **Well I think you're probably right, it's the one I prefer. It's certainly closer to my concerns as a painter but sometimes you're put into a situation where you have to satisfy strong-willed committees and that means offending no one. It's not the ideal scenario.**

DR What is the significance of the chandelier?

TW **The chandelier is meant as a larger than life gesture signifying the theatre in general and the stage production of *The Madness of George III* in particular. The painting is divided into the public and private self, the inner and outer man as I saw it with a kind of fractured and blurred line between the two. Bennett's gaze is for me both timid bashfulness and acute observation.**

DR I think that my preference has to do with the far richer and more textured appearance of the larger painting, and also because of my sense that it portrays the man you got to know. I find it interesting that you refer to him

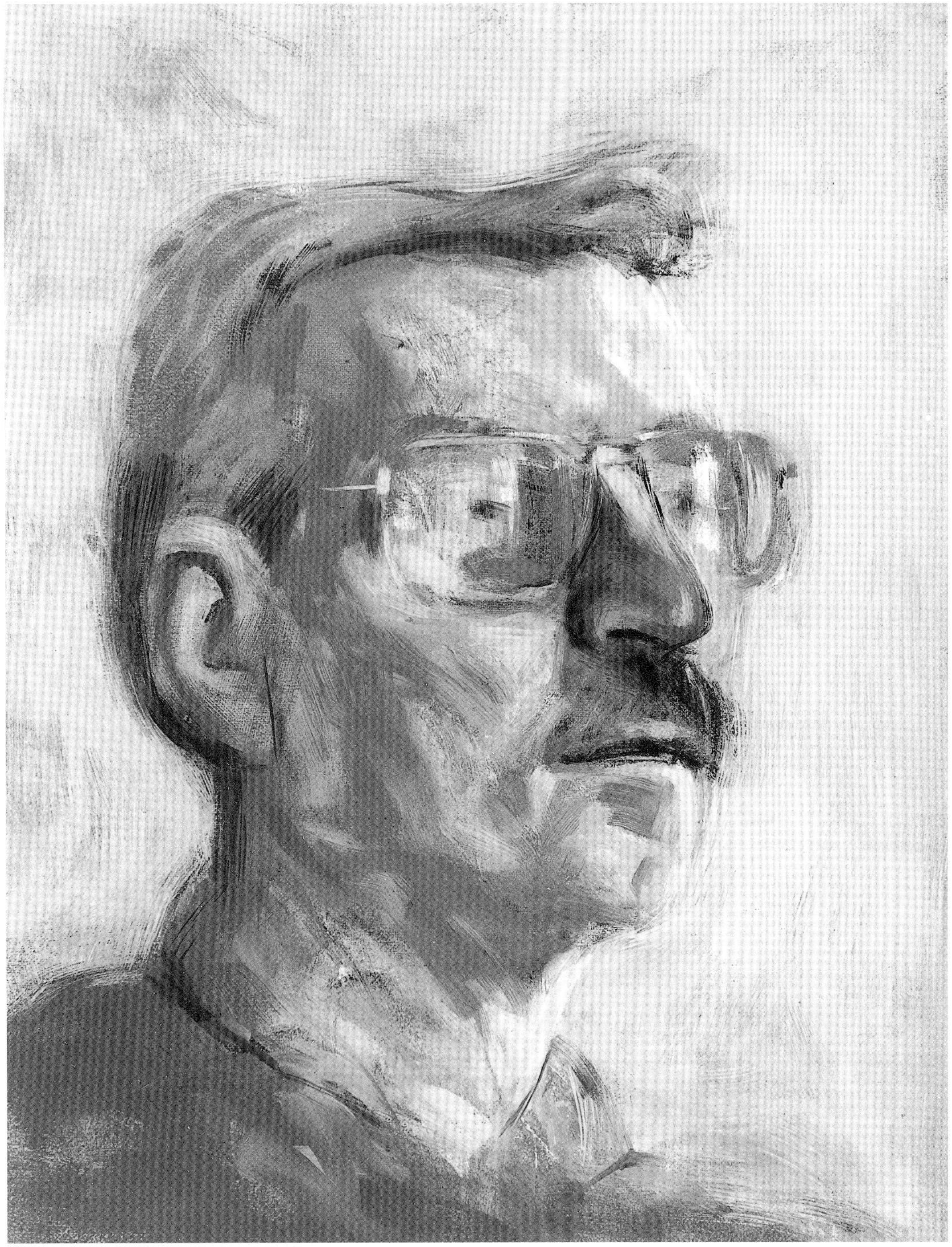

Study of James Fox.
oil on paper
35.5 × 21 cm (14 × 9 inches)
Private Collection

welcoming you into his home because, for me, the larger painting captures
Plate 12 that social encounter, and the quiet communion which followed between you and your sitter. Whereas in the other picture you have concentrated upon the public persona. In that one, Bennett is posed as the distinguished writer, an intellectual looking slightly self-consciously ahead: very much the author posed as opposed to the author unopposed.

Plates 14 & 15 To turn to *Alchemist in Search of The Voice and Standing Alone*: we look back into a much more internal world, into deeply introspective figures. There's something sombre and meditative . . . sombre is the best word I can find to describe the mood of these paintings. At the same time they are very clear about what they are not about. This is painting. Isn't it?

TW **Absolutely and in a sense they've set the agenda for all the work since then. They embody, however crudely, my attempts to manifest externally those hopes, ambitions, dreams and desires that we hold internally. I've tried to use various strategies to communicate this, but primarily it's an image of the body or the head usually in conjunction with some external forms. The forms although often ambiguous, provoke a dialogue with the contorted body. Inevitably there are questions but these can only be answered in the context of the viewer's own hopes, ambitions, dreams and desires. The first painting is very dramatic with the figure desperately stretching upwards as though yearning to break free of some invisible bonds.**

DR In a way it goes back to the Diviner, doesn't it? But whether it's the Diviner, the Alchemist or the Angel, the figure standing alone is also you?

TW **Well yes, I suppose it is really.**

DR I find it very moving in a way because the Alchemist carries as his baggage, so to speak, meshed into his figure, your familiar symbols, the cone, the pod, the rod.

TW **They're maybe an aspect of my internal world being realized externally. It's only a glimpse, a fragment, not the whole story so to speak. If I were to think hard about it, *Standing Alone* is probably a painting about someone hitting middle age and feeling isolated, frustrated and disappointed; yearning for the dreams he had as a young man, standing on a hill in Halifax and seeing the world he was going to conquer slipping away; a sad, romantic, elegiac poem to the death of hope.**

DR Halifax never looked better. Forgive me, that was flippant. As you have pointed out to me, these could easily have become rather self-indulgent figures but emphatically they are not. When I said earlier that they are clear about what they are not about, I didn't mean to sound enigmatic. I was referring to your dematerialisation of the figure, detached from the substance of flesh and blood. We're not talking about Holbein here, are we? And yet I detect a certain ambiguity. You're not denying totally the physicality of the figure but nor do you want to dwell upon it; you literally dissolve parts of the figure into the ground.

TW **Again the procedure has contributed. The way I'm painting has evolved and maybe that is something to do with the bigger scale giving me greater freedom. I'm trying to make the means and methods of applying the paint somehow directly embody, or become the equivalent of, the feelings and emotions that they're trying to describe. So the idea of things being pushed, pulled, pressed, moved, scraped and scratched directly relates to feelings of being pushed, pulled, pressed, moved, scratched and manipulated. The paintings have a physicality that carries its own meaning beyond its overt figurative content.**

DR Yes.

TW **I find these works very hard to talk about in so far as they're unresolved in my own mind. I can't easily categorise them.**

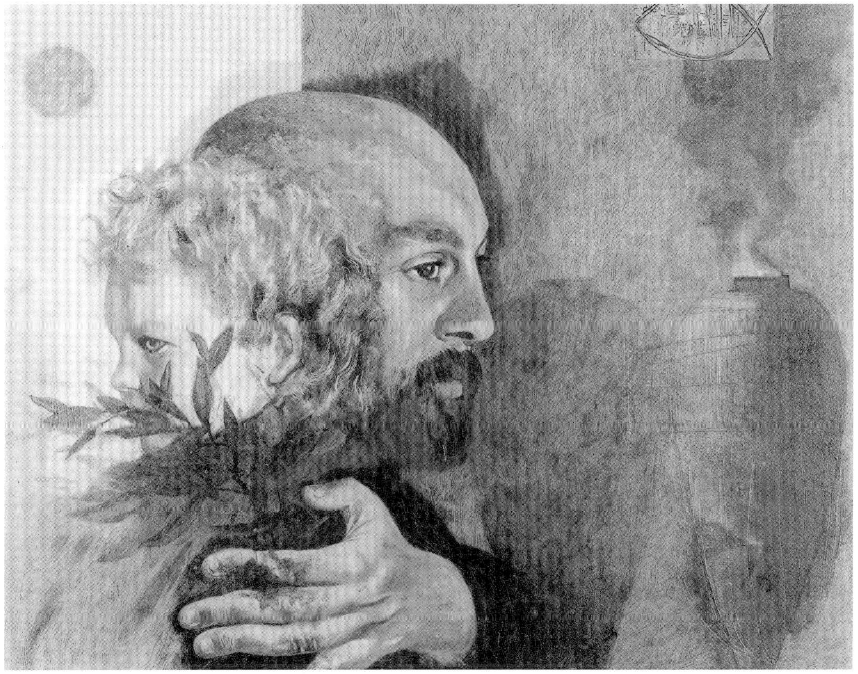

Self-Portrait with Saskia.
oil on board
61 × 91.5 cm (36 × 24 inches)
Private Collection

DR But that's why you painted them. After all, you are a painter. Paint is your medium, and although I've always maintained that you talk about your paintings better than anyone writes about them, in the end they stand or fall as painted objects, expressed in your chosen medium.

I doubt if anyone looking at *Standing Alone* would fail to make the connection with you as both artist and subject. On the other hand, when we
come to the *Soldier/Grill* pictures, I wonder if you are trying to stand back Plate 16
from yourself by creating a more objective series of figures with whom you identify less?

TW **The problem for me with *Standing Alone* is that it could easily be**

seen as a pathetic figure saying 'listen to me, I'm suffering, can't you see'. It could be just seen as a wallowing in male self-pity, i.e. "I work so hard and nobody appreciates me" syndrome. But the problem with that is that if it is me, or even an aspect of me, it's not entirely true. I've got a very supportive wife, an understanding family and really no reason to feel neglected and self-pity. But deep down there is a trait, and I'd like to think that this is a fairly universal condition but it might not be the case, a tendency towards self-pitying, macho-martyrdom, a veering towards self-dramatisation, an unhealthy introspection. But maybe that's integral to being a solitary artist. The 'Soldier' paintings, although derived from a small bronze of General Gordon by Hamo Thorneycroft, are just as you've said a way of distancing myself. I'm dealing with the same issues but now at arm's length. The soldier as
Plate 17 **I represent him is a stern figure, driven to extremes, no longer in control of his own destiny.**

DR Am I right in thinking that the Soldier refers back in your work to the Warrior Heads or the Leopard Man you painted around 1980? Then too you seemed to be fascinated by martial figures, helmeted heads with cast and welded features and fixed, metallic gazes.

TW **Yes, I think it does, the antecedents of *Soldier/Grill* are certainly *Leopard Man* and *Warrior* in spirit if not in form.**

DR And again, it's a very sombre picture. He's not simply the obedient soldier; you've managed to invest him with a kind of reflectiveness. As you say, he isn't in charge of his own destiny to the extent that the rest of us like to feel we are. Even the grill, with its very clearly painted black lines which take on an abstract life of their own on the surface of the painting, suggest all kinds of things from prison bars to military barracks. They are elements of control and anticipate the later pictures of measure.

TW **And the idea of repetition, things being relentlessly and solidly repeated — a kind of thumping in the brain. I feel it's quite threatening to be confronted by something such as this, something that's out of your control.**

DR I do think that 'Man and Measure' is a brilliant title which applies to this entire phase of your career and is susceptible to a wide range of interpretation. In one sense, you are the one doing the measuring, as you did at the beginning in *The Family*, but you also introduce the measure as an external constraint, threatening to subject the individual, making him a victim of the measure.

TW **That's exactly right. The whole notion of measurement, of being measured, of being confronted by the results of that measurement is a kind of threatening aspect to our lives. I think often we don't feel up to it, we don't conform to some ideal standard and as we get older that ideal seems to conspire even further against us. To an extent all the paintings of this time carry these ideas in one form or another. Sometimes it's very obvious and the notion of measurement predominates, at other times it resonates as a kind of distant drumbeat marking a rhythm and pace within the painting.**

DR You're using military terminology again . . . but it's internal as well as external, isn't it? By which I mean that in addition to the kind of measuring that irritates us, frustrates and possibly threatens us, as when we feel we're being reduced to meaningless statistics, or when we're admitted to the hospital ward and assigned a number, there is also the measuring of oneself. I get the strong impression that some of your measuring is self-inflicted, a form of self-criticism. In other words, it's not just that you don't like E.U. regulations.

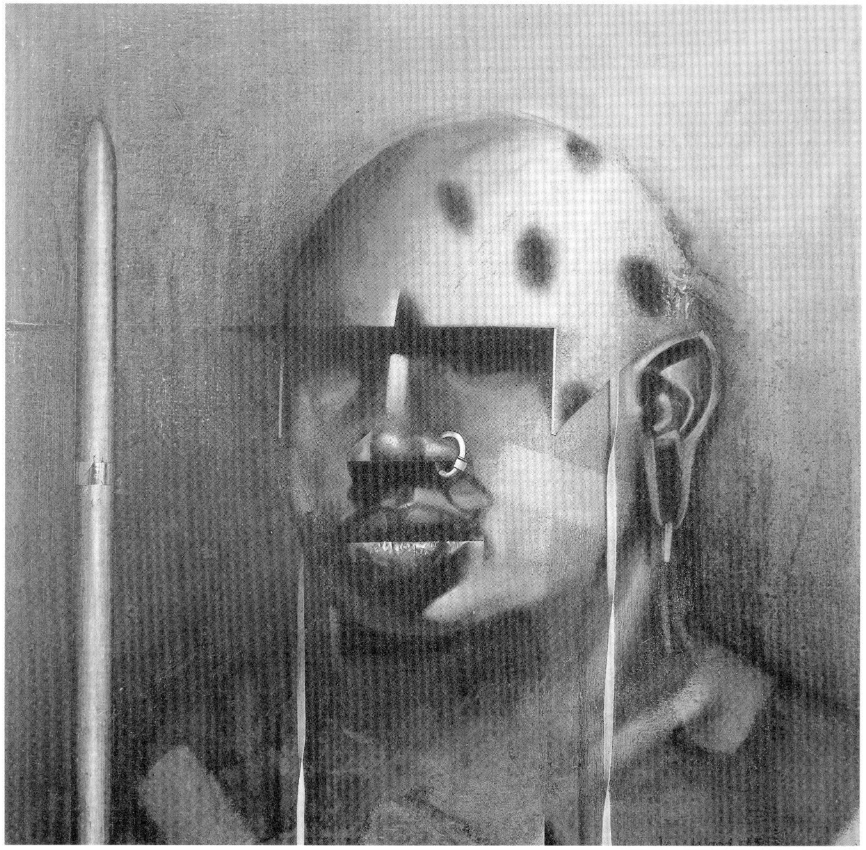

Leopard Man 1980.
acrylic on canvas
76.2 × 76.2 cm (30 × 30 inches)
Private Collection

TW **No, no it's not just that, and it's not just a sort of self-flagellation either. But it's something to do with being an artist, a painter who finds himself endlessly being compared and measured on a scale over which he has no control and often not knowing who is doing the measuring. I suppose it's simply an idea of vulnerability, a universal idea of insecurity which is also embodied in the conditional nature of the paintings. They function more as provocations, questions rather than answers or conclusions. So a** **Plate 18**
painting like *Fossil Man and Lyre* is full of ambiguities; it is tenuous, vaporous, the image, I hope, only just there.

DR No, it's very intangible. You're resisting resolution and yet at the same time you're building up the surface from the ground to some kind of resolution in the final glazes. Why on earth am I speaking in terms of old master techniques when in fact the impression you give here is the reverse, of excavating downwards from the surface of the picture. It turns you into a kind of archaeologist of the image, the discoverer of the final residue of painted form found on the wall of a cave.

TW **Or scrapings in the earth, as though all you're left with is a stain where once a body was lain. The painted surface might be the equivalent to such ambiguous residue, its poignancy might lie in the enigma of a past event leaving the barest of marks. I found it interesting at this time to work with very little, to see if I could make a surface resonate from the most minimal of scratchings and adjustments. Yet I was still working with the figure but trying to remake it somehow so that it would obey the conventions but give the appearance of being barely there. For me the figures in *Fossil Man and Lyre* and *Tomorrow, Tomorrow and Tomorrow* are really both sides of the same coin. Whilst one resists resolution and feels abraded, worn and excavated, the other forms itself out of the surface, fitting fairly and squarely within a tradition of depicting the figure. One could be seen as the stage prior to the decay of the other or conversely one could be an imaginative reconstruction of how the other might have been.**

DR I'm interested to hear you say that the themes go back to these two paintings, because it strikes me that here we are facing another of your preoccupations; the theme of the Doppelganger, or the reflected image which haunts the subject and undermines the unities of time and space. Not that your reflections are mirror images. You differentiate between them by the way in which they are painted, so that one becomes a shadow of the other, a recollection or a premonition of time past or time to come.

Plate 19 **TW** **Well, again *Tommorrow, Tommorrow and Tommorrow* is a painting that carries a certain insecurity within it, it's a question rather than an answer. I'm not sure myself what's going on. I know there are two figures and these two figures have some kind of relationship between them but what that is precisely I don't know. I feel it's appropriate that I shouldn't prescribe the nature of their relationship.**

DR Yes, because they're not mirror images, their limbs are in different positions.

TW **And the curious thing about this ambiguous figure on the right is that it is often interpreted as a man carrying a scythe like some representation of the Grim Reaper.**

DR Father Time?

TW **Yes, Father Time. But in truth it's based on a photograph of a Sound man carrying a boom microphone. I thought at one point that he might represent an idea of the modern world intruding into a timeless tragedy, not to help but just to record, to objectively witness as though that in itself was constructive, which I suppose it is sometimes. No one else has ever seen it in that way.**

DR I certainly hadn't. Yet there is a feature in the painting which fascinates me; it is the strange headdress, almost like a fool's cap in a medieval mystery play. In general, I wonder if you are prepared to accept the fact that images like this can evoke all kinds of readings? Can you also bear the thought of interpretations which had never occurred to you?

TW **Oh yes, I enjoy other people's views and ideas. In a sense we're back to the museums again, their dialogue is a kind of catalyst to breathe life into these slumbering objects. The paintings go through a lot of stages. The figures in *Tomorrow, Tomorrow and Tomorrow* have been miners showering after a hard days work, to soldiers having their wounds washed and dressed, to the helpless patients of a mental hospital being showered to prisoners being cleansed prior to being gassed. For me the figures carry the residue of all those associations and more; once I considered one figure witness and the other victim. At one point there were actual shelf brackets screwed onto the surface of the painting from which wire hung as a kind of grisly threat. When these were discarded, they left the holes and marks of their being there and the painting, which is on panel, seemed to me to transform itself into a wall. And the wall like a daguerreotype may well carry the shadowy memory of all that it has witnessed.**

DR We're introduced here to something you develop in the pictures which follow. I can only describe it as deliberate distortion of the features, as if the figures have been pushed and pulled up against a sheet of glass. Do you think in terms of distortion or not?

TW **No I don't think so. I don't ever deliberately distort but I do sometimes lose control. What I mean by that is, I allow more intuition than premeditation into my processes and consequently the images do contort and I just accept that as inherent within the procedures.**

DR What is the procedure you use?

TW **I make an image and then I use rollers and my hands to press other materials into it, these can be bits of carpet, paper, corrugated cardboard, underlay and polythene — anything, in fact, that might lift and transfer the image. Then there is a long process of constantly making, lifting, transferring, adjusting and remaking the image; this goes on for a long time and as I said before it's more intuition than planning. It's at this stage that the image can change and alter radically, everything is in complete flux. So when you see a figure, that figure has probably been moved ten times around the painting and what you're often seeing is the fragmentary residue of previous decisions. Finally it arrives at some kind of resolution and I suppose it's just an extension to what Bacon did with his figures, but more particularly what he did with his head triptychs.**

DR I wondered if you would mention Bacon because, as you know, he always denied the idea of distortion in his work and seems to have been genuinely surprised when people referred to it.

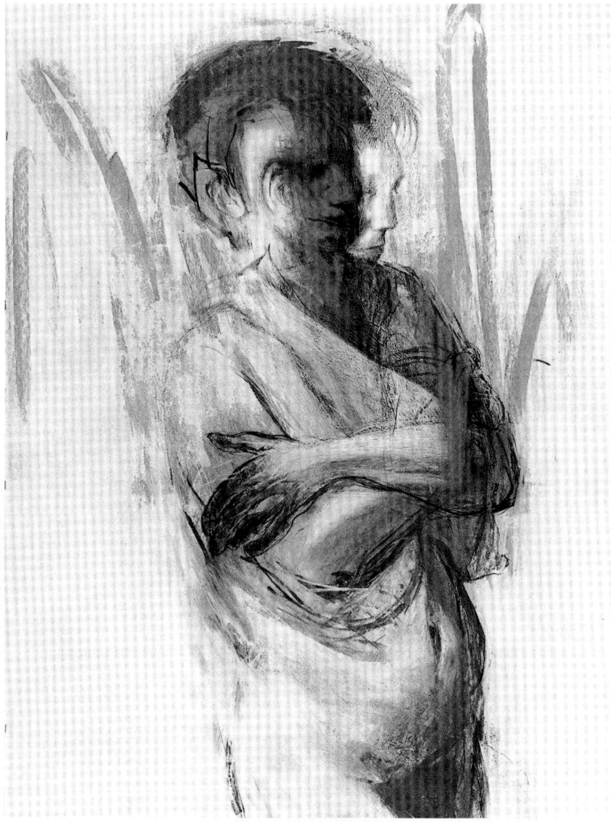
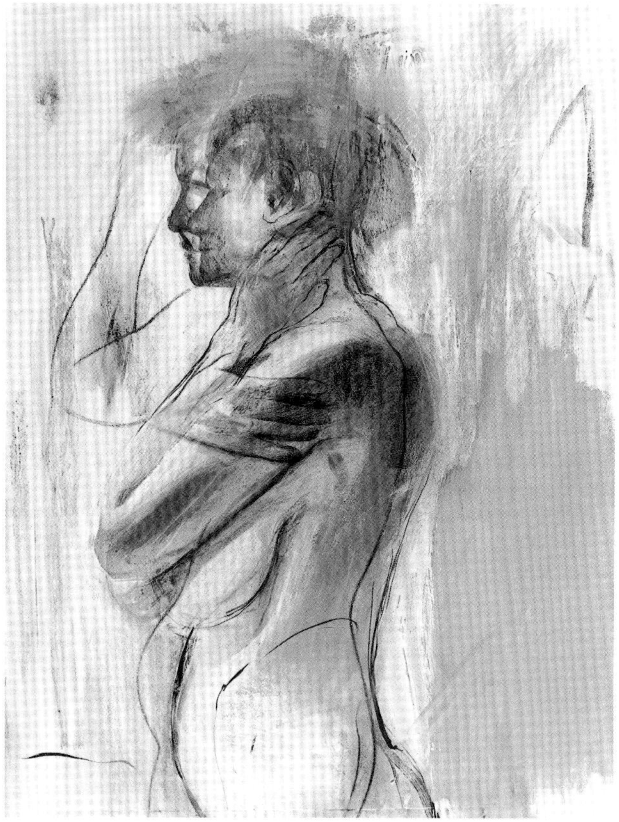
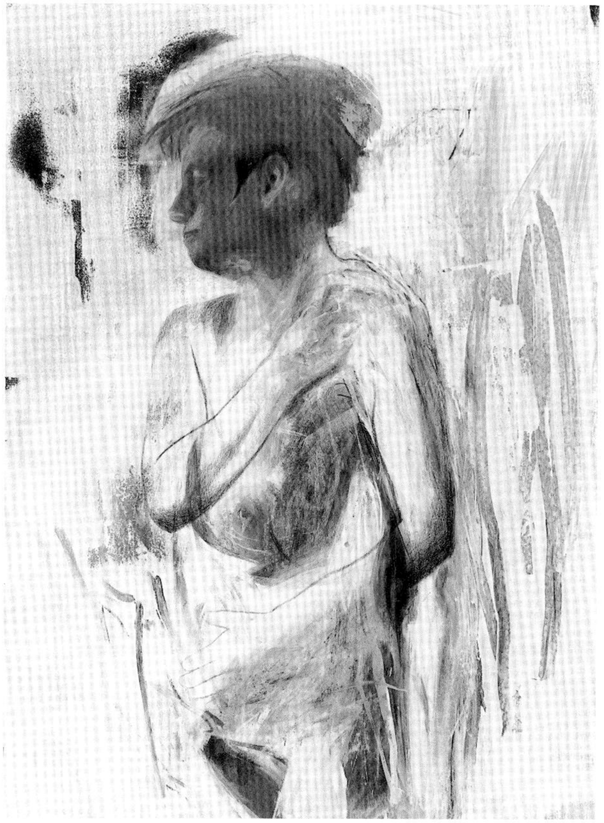

From Life I, II and III 1995
mixed media on paper
each 110 × 80 cm (43.5 × 31.5 inches)
Private Collection

TW **Well the word 'distortion' seems to imply a certain wilful manipulation of something recognizable for no other end than to add a kind of superficial style. What I'm trying to do is to find some sort of resonance and meaning in the image by its constant change and movement which implies a state of flux as though the image is always in transition, its meaning conditional. The ambiguity inherent within it speaks, rather than an imposed ambiguity or purposeful obfuscation. So the paintings struggle towards lucidity rather than suffocate beneath imposed obscurity.**

DR It's interesting that people react so strongly to this picture. It seems to elicit very specific interpretations, almost as if it invites us to make connections with precise, historical events. Do you think it has anything to do with the fact that among this series of figures, this one is the most highly finished and individualised, the closest to portraiture? And does it strike you as relevant that all the interpretations you have mentioned are essentially painful, with implications of suffering, even unto death? Is suffering something you are trying to come to terms with here?

TW **I don't really set out to make paintings that display suffering. Sometimes I find suffering in the images without putting it there. Maybe my Catholic upbringing has given me a predisposition towards images of suffering.**

DR But as we look at them, are we in a Vale of Tears?

TW **Well yes, I suppose we are, although I am trying to avoid self-pity but possibly not very successfully. When I look at *Into the Ether to Dissolve*, I wish I could do more because it seems to me to naturally progress from the Soldier paintings and *Tomorrow, Tomorrow and Tomorrow*. There's a man in a room which has the feel of a bare cell and in his solitude and isolation he melts away, dissolving into the walls.** Plate 20

DR Definitely a Man of Sorrows.

TW **He'll eventually evaporate and become the merest stain and once again the wall will be the witness. I suppose it's a fate waiting for all of us, it's terribly gloomy really.**

DR And this is what is left of the overhead light?

TW **Yes, that's all that's left, an ellipse of light unable to illuminate anything, just sitting there hovering in space. There's also a small black grill and, for a while, I had a dilemma as to whether the grill should be black or white. In the end I decided on black because white implied hope, as though there was a light beyond the room. The deadness of the black reinforced the relentless pessimism of the image.**

DR Now why *The Night Museum*?

Plate 21 TW **I think *The Night Museum* is a kind of oblique homage to Stephen Farthing's work and via him to Rembrandt. It's in the title rather than the form of the work. Farthing did a wonderful painting called *The Nightwatch* which is now at Cartwright Hall in Bradford. His title is a witty pun on Rembrandt's painting and my title refers to Farthing's painting.**

I feel sometimes that maybe the paintings change too abruptly and they become too obscure.

DR No, I don't feel that at all. I see a definite continuity from *Standing Alone* to *'Redemption'*. For me, *Tattoo Man* is a direct descendent of *Diviner* because both are heads which combine the real and the symbolic. Incidentally, talking of 'Vales of Tears', there's something distinctly painful about these tattoos and scars.

TW **In this instance I think the title, *Redemption*, is important in so far as it indicates a looking up and outwards. Previously these figures have been insulated in their own pain but now they are looking beyond seeking hope, and in that, redemption. The figure in *Redemption* is trying to become an angel. He's got a wing and a celestial trumpet of sorts and sits beneath some form of gauze-like canopy. At one point I thought this might be too theatrical and I did the painting *Angel III* in response to it. Now I feel each represents their own version of events, and each is valid.** Plate 25 Plate 24

DR In different ways each is effective as far as I am concerned. There is a vulnerability here, an admission that 'Naked came I'. At the same time, the idea of the human quest and the longing for something beyond material existence comes across very strongly in this picture. Are you fond of the poetry of Yeats?

TW **I haven't read any.**

DR Well, there may be no direct connection, but some of your images remind me of the way in which Yeats used his poetry to attempt a reconciliation between art and life. He does so using as symbols the assorted fragments of other civilisations, "such forms as Grecian goldsmiths make", which "come from the holy fire, perne in a gyre. And become the singing masters of my soul." You too seem to want to purify by fire and gyrate towards an "artifice of eternity", in search of consolation in this life and belief in something more enduring beyond.

TW **It's a wonderful summary and seems to be what I'm trying to do.**

DR *Sailing to Byzantium*. Now, your *Parable* is a painting on a very ambitious scale. Perhaps because the figure is a woman. You seem to have stepped back and separated yourself from the protagonist. The symbols are yours, your cones of fire, this little . . . Plate 27

TW **. . . House, beach hut, I don't know, a sign for home maybe.**

DR The habitations of men.

TW **Yes. In a way the paintings for me are more ambitious. To paint a woman and to identify or be identified with this woman was a challenge. It's not in my eyes an act of appropriation, not intentionally at least. It's more an attempt to universalise an idea about the human condition. It aspires in a way to Kitaj's painting, *Self Portrait as a Woman*, with all its ambivalences, open questions and contentions. The title *Parable* is a comment back in on itself in so far as in the painting all the elements exist with which to construct a story or parable but they aren't necessarily cohesive or logical. The parable constructed may well undermine its own**

purpose. This painting is part of that body of work I've made and am still making in response to my mother's death in May 1993. At that time I felt robbed and violated, unbearably sad and angry at her sudden death. All around me stories and words of consolation were being offered. I felt humbled by the generous and honest concern of others but also angry at our need to rationalise such personal tragedies. At that time I felt there was no good, no parable to be drawn from such a thing and in a way I saw the painting *Parable* as a kind of beautiful painting that seethes with anger.

DR Yet there's no savagery in here, although at times you have depicted anger in your work, or even brutality. But not here, not at all.

TW **Well, I was talking through clenched teeth when I made this painting, although it doesn't appear so. I think of it as shouting. As though I'm shouting, 'So this is what you want, so these are the stories you told me, now look at them, now tell me their meaning' and for me there is no meaning, it's hollow, it's empty and the painting carries that idea.**

DR Railing against fate. But then how does the picture evolve from your desire to express those feelings which none the less are somehow transmuted into what you yourself have described as serene; an image which, in its own way is rather more optimistic than some of the others we have looked at?

TW **I suppose, in a sense, I shoot myself in the foot because the beauty and serenity within the painting, the quiet inner light that glows, is meant ironically. But you're right, if I look objectively it doesn't look that way. If it is a parable at all and a consolation, then that consolation is for others and not for me. Maybe it's true place is as part of a series with *Drowning in a Desert* and *West Coast Deluge*, the individual parts making a greater whole.**

Plates 37 & 59 DR But I still find *Parable* unusual in terms of what has gone before, of the paintings in which we've seen the figure isolated, threatened and struggling. Here the naked woman appears to accept everything placidly, in a trance — like state of contemplation. Thanks to the house, there is a sense of refuge in the picture. We may be a long way from traditional spiritual values, from the idea of salvation, but at least there is shelter, protection from the elements, or perhaps from our emotions.

TW **Really these paintings should be seen in relation to the desert paintings, they're probably the real heirs to these paintings.**

Plate 28 DR You would say some of the same things about *Red Angel*, wouldn't you?

TW **Yes, these figures looking into their hands, these figures who in a way are blind. They're searching for something and, even though there are clues all around, they'll never find it. The desert paintings are primarily about loss. In the barren landscape these figures inhabit, their slim hopes are pinned on these obscure tokens from which, they might divine some meaning, but it's unlikely.**

DR What is the significance of looking into your hand apart from the fact that it casts a shadow upon the face?

TW **It's that you're unable to see anything except inwards, towards yourself. Your view is so obscured that there is only introspection.**

DR So it's a kind of modern Vanitas, with the sitter's hand in place of the mirror, the *memento mori.*

TW **Well, yes undoubtedly. It is a reminder and reflection upon our own mortality but in some way this is bound up with a sense of loss and anger at that loss.**

DR Well, yes, but in spite of the much more livid colour, it is hard not to see the figure in a sympathetic light.

TW **I know and I struggle with that, the inherent stillness and cohesive surface and mood somewhat undermines my position. I can only think that my ambivalence allows me to straddle both anger and sympathy simultaneously if uncomfortably. I think I'm probably too kind to the figures, I let them off the hook.**

DR Now what about *As Smoke Rises So Bees Sink*? Where does the phrase come from? Plates 34 & 35

TW **Both titles, *As Smoke Rises So Bees Sink* and *In My Desert there is a Mirror* are inventions, my own phrases meant to sound like quotations.**

DR I thought for a moment you were a bee-keeper, because bee-keepers use smoke, don't they?

TW **Yes they do, but the idea is held in the words. At times of crisis we seem to offer one another consolation in the form of little aphorisms, such as, 'It was probably for the best,' and 'Time is a great healer' and 'Tomorrow brings a new dawn'.**

They're meant to plug the gap when in truth words are wholly inadequate but silence would be even more painful.

DR So in looking into the hole in the ground, are we looking at nothing again?

TW **She's peering into a void. In this post-nuclear holocaust landscape all she has to protect herself is a flimsy veil.**

DR A bee-keeper's net?

TW **Maybe a net and maybe the regular dashes in the smoke represent bees but it's not a painting about bees.**

DR Again, it's important to look at the actual painting, because it makes you very aware of the surface. You talked earlier about not wanting to leave traces of your brush on the panel, here you have really flattened the paint on to the surface. How?

TW **Well, it's been rollered, scraped, pressed, I've probably pushed it around with cloths, polythene, sprayed onto it; anything really. Everything's allowed. I want the painting to show quite clearly the evidence of its making. That evidence might well be some form of record or code displaying my relationship physically to that surface. By that I mean the larger paintings may well function as some kind of mirror. When I'm working with the life size figures there comes a point when they seem to have acquired the weight, substance and presence of a real figure in the room. It's at that point it feels like I'm dancing in front of a mirror.**

DR But you're also denying yourself your imprint, the mark of your hand.

TW **Its the autograph, the signature, the ego-filled gesture I want to avoid. As I've mentioned earlier the image should evolve, it should coalesce rather than be applied. It doesn't relentlessly march forward towards a conclusion, it veers backwards and forwards, it's stalked rather than chased. As a consequence I probably lose as much as I retain, so for me the paintings are always fragmentary. Even the big paintings seem to me to be fragments of a larger whole. I always imagine that they carry on beyond their edges. When I painted a few landscapes as a student the problem was always where the edge should be. How to contain all that visual and sensory information into that small rectangle. So when I painted *West Coast Deluge*, which is a large work, I imagined it as a kind of view through a narrow slot. I was thinking of the American painter Neil Jenney as well as work nearer to home.**

Plate 37

DR It's a wonderful picture; everything from Turner's *Fifth Plague of Egypt* to John Martin's *Deluge*.

TW **I was thinking of John Martin and his apocalyptic visions, but also lots of other things from Frederick Church's panoramas to Caspar David Freidrich to Coppola's final scenes in *Apocalypse Now*.**

DR Why 'West Coast'?

TW **It was because I'd visited Los Angeles a few weeks before the large earthquake struck. When I saw the images on television of all that devastation and I remembered how it had felt on the beach at Malibu and walking in the gardens of the Getty Museum with views towards that extraordinary blue Pacific Ocean, then I'd felt for a brief moment how paradise might be. After the earthquake there were lots of interviews with survivors. In the midst of all this chaos and wreckage it seemed to me people were trying to rationalize, trying to find some sense in it all. There was talk of the awesome power of nature, talk of nature revenging herself as though the people of Los Angeles were themselves in some way to blame and by implication would be better people for the lesson they had learnt.**

DR Isn't that a rather Biblical idea, of a stern God?

TW **But don't you think that the whole of Biblical teaching is to do with rationalizing tragedy. It's trying to find meaning in these terrible incidents we're endlessly being confronted by. Using tragedy as a way of testing our beliefs and ultimately finding our fundamental selves. I suppose what I'm doing is, as you said earlier, I'm railing against that, I'm saying "there is no rationale, there are no worthwhile lessons", that it is all ultimately bleak, empty, hollow and banal. Nihilism, I suppose.**

DR Another striking feature of *West Coast Deluge* is its strong sense of landscape, which seems to me to be more pronounced than in many of your other paintings. For instance, there is a definite horizon line which runs across the full width of the painting.

TW **Yes, this seems to define the space in the painting. It was the first time for a long time that I'd actually acknowledged a traditional deep narrative space. Previously when I'd depicted space it was always knowingly and selectively, as though in quotation marks, this is a whole-hearted embrace of traditional perspective.**

DR It's very useful having such a good detail of the painting because once again it brings us back to the surface and to the way in which you treat it. In this case, in that sweeping gesture, there is clear evidence of your brushstroke. **Plate 36**

TW **That's appropriate in this painting where there's a direct reference back to Martin or Turner even. The use of a signatory mark seems to me to be one way of making that connection. In 'Looking at El Greco' and 'Miracle' in formal terms there's a similar use of that kind of mark. Only this time the figures have the feel of apparitions, there's an insecurity about their presence.**

DR In the title *Looking at El Greco* you're once again inviting us to think about your relationship to the art of the past. **Plate 38**

TW **I went to Toledo where I saw El Greco's monumental *Burial of Count Orgaz*. I think it's probably one of the most memorable, extraordinary paintings I've ever seen. My painting is really about me looking at that painting; how it felt. The painting went through so many stages that really all we're left with is the residue of the memory of that experience.**

DR Most of us have to be content with our memories, but you've been able to translate them into a painting which exists in its own right.

TW **But it's the memory of the feelings felt whilst looking at the painting that I'm trying to evoke rather than the memory of me sitting there, standing outside of myself watching me, watching the painting. I hope that makes some kind of sense.**

DR And the marks of measurement are part of this?

TW **Well the measures, in this case marks or dashes, always come back as a kind of plea for rationality, or maybe even an acknowledgement of the rational world. They act as a counterweight when things have become too ecstatic or emotional. It's sort of saying 'calm down', 'take it steady', that idea.**

DR Now that's an act of self-discipline. By your own admission, there are times when you resent the intrusion of reason, which you regard as inhibiting or even threatening, yet here you are imposing it upon yourself.

TW **I am but you must remember the paintings are no different to life; full of contradictions, and various shades of meaning. *Miracle* might be seen in this light. It depicts a strange incident when something inexplicable happens. It could be a small miracle and only later can we rationalise it and give it significance. Of course that significance is contingent upon our own context. The facts of the miracle are then transformed, they become shadowy, moveable, convenient, not unlike our belief in reliquaries. The idea that these fragments achieve their potency due to the beliefs they embody is fascinating. It's not a million miles from the Turin** **Plate 39**

Shroud to a Beuys Vitrine. In formal terms *Miracle* is not so dissimilar to the Bees painting, many of the elements are the same.

DR Would you agree that there is an optimism here that is absent from *As Smoke Rises So Bees Sink*? Apart from anything else, the title suggests hope, if not belief.

TW **Well it's not that optimistic. If its saying anything, then it's saying that we're all hoping for a miracle.**

DR With flame and fire again, the Burning Bush, all of it emanating from a strange little box.

TW **It's just an empty little box that bursts into life, that's all. I'm almost tempted to say it happens every day if you look. But the paintings are also a chance to do something particular with paint. In *Miracle* I wanted to paint a large, fiery, vaporous kind of form appearing to escape the bounds of its confinement and I wanted to paint it in a particular kind of way, this painting allowed me to do that. *Burning up* is another painting where I wanted to apply paint in a particular kind of way to obscure the figure. It was exhibited and, I thought, finished but then reworked, it's on it's second life. The title is taken directly from an early Tony Bevan painting, an act of homage I suppose.**

Plate 41

DR I don't think that your painting could be more different from Bevan's. Characteristically, you're dissolving your forms, whereas I think of him as an assertive, almost acerbic, draughtsman.

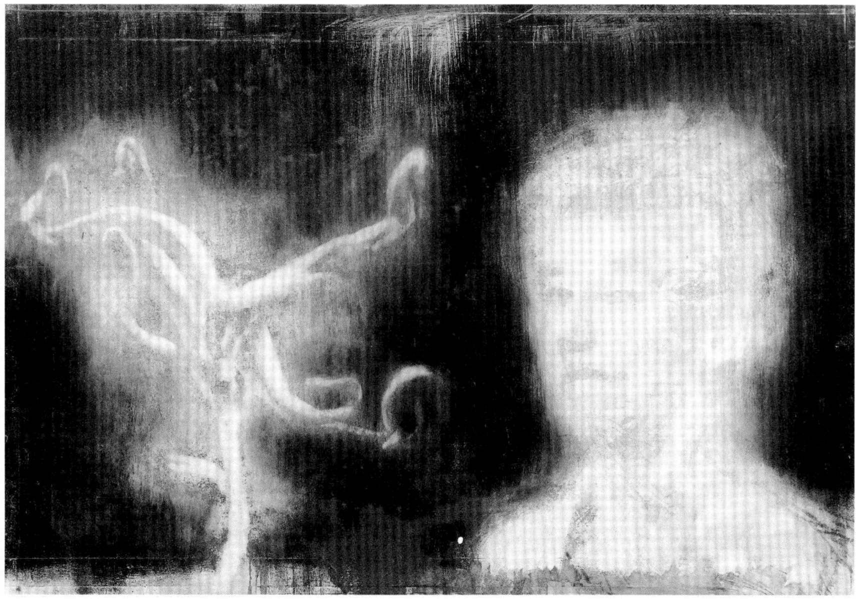

Study 1995
oil on paper and board
45.7 × 58.4 cm (18 × 23 inches)
Private Collection

TW **I like that assertiveness, the large scale and combination of sophistication and blunt crudity. His figures, for me, have a feeling of timeless inevitability more like Rembrandt than the Tudor portraits they were once shown with. In his certainty there are questions. My work at the moment seems far more uncertain, elusive and ambiguous.**

DR Yes, they appear as marks on the wall, scratches in the sand.

TW **Flickering flames. The intensity of her gaze, the internal compression of her questioning self cause her to combust.**

DR Now where was it, was it in *Furnace* that you began to apply your measures as concrete, geometrical shapes? Those are in relief aren't they?

TW **They're sprayed onto the perspex so that they're always slightly apart — in other words it's an external measure being applied from elsewhere.**

DR Turning now to your *Old Science* series. I cannot help invoking the name of William Blake. I'm thinking of his Newton, with his calipers, measuring out the Universe. He is Blake's symbol of man's ability to measure, to map, to plot the physical world and yet, at the same time, to fall victim to his own earth-bound science. **Plate 42 & 43**

TW **It is that Newtonian view of the world where everything is available to be measured and consequently understood. It's also thinking about those early pseudo-sciences like Eugenics and Phrenology.**

DR But there's something deeply compassionate about them. Surely they are not based upon those nineteenth century photographs which are distinctly cruel, unfeeling in the way in which people are lined up as scientific specimens.

TW **That's right, but they inspired this series where the inside was judged by the outside. These terribly sad people are being ruthlessly measured, as you say held up as specimens. The measures are engraved onto the perspex and metaphorically engraved into the subjects, they're permanent. They are uncomfortable paintings, even harsh.**

DR Clearly.

TW **But I am on the side of the specimens. It may well be just a knee-jerk reaction to always side with the underdog but beyond the superficial harshness I think there is a sort of sympathy.**

DR At the same time you are testing and challenging. You do it to yourself all the time, but you are doing it here to our assumptions. I am reminded again of your attitude towards painting still life, when you say that you've taken a simple object and transformed it by the act of painting it. Similarly the *Old Science* paintings cover very sensitive territory. They challenge not only the nineteenth century and its attitudes to medical research, but many of our other ideas which are residual legacies from that time.

TW **Absolutely, the title *Old Science*, probably should have been *Old Science/New Science*. The key image for me is the first Man and Measure painting, *Man and Measure I*. It summarizes all these ideas. The figure stands stretching upwards, yearning.** **Plate 44**

DR *Standing Alone*.

TW **Yes as in *Standing Alone* and he's being measured, confined into a shallow space. The perspex which holds the measures is both a literal and metaphorical screen behind which the figure is compressed. For me there is something medical about the measures as though on the glass of an X-ray machine. A small perforated cone, whose unknown function is troubling, also occupies the space. The medical connotations probably give it an air of unease, a sense of vague threat and ultimately sadness.**

DR But it's interesting also that you're encasing your work, placing a physical barrier between us and the painting.

TW **I like to glaze works for two reasons. One being as you've said, a distancing device; its a means of excluding, a way of reinforcing the notion of the viewer, the watcher, the outsider looking in as witness. And also as a formal resolution to the work, the glazing acts like a varnish unifying the whole surface. Bacon did something similar.**

Plate 45 DR What about *History Painting*?

TW **It's a painting that came from me thinking about the work of George Catlin and his pictures of native Americans. I suppose they're examples of early ethnography. They exemplify that need to study, record and categorize. I felt uneasy about the kind of evaluations such a study would arrive at. There seems to be a need to either condemn or cherish. *History Painting* was going to be the first of a long series of works considering that notion but it never got beyond the one painting.**

DR But whereas he regarded his function as documentary, to make an accurate record of the different Indian tribes, you are inventing, relying upon the power of your imagination.

TW **I find it necessary to invent around an idea rather than attempt to record. The figure is painted as though it might once have been a sepia-toned photograph. Maybe an American Indian with a headdress, dignity still intact.**

Plate 46 & 47 DR No, I see that. I also see that you're still measuring, which brings us, finally, to the *Man and Measure* paintings, in which the measures are attached to the stretcher but comprise a separate element, part of the overall picture but not within the painted field.

TW **The measures sit alongside the painting as you say, not in it. But they've always been separate, imposed from the outside. Now they're entirely unyielding, solid geometric forms, to me they feel quasi-industrial.**

DR They could have been factory-sprayed.

TW **Exactly. These figures have no escape, no opportunities for sympathy, they're the complete victims of their measures. As such they're vulnerable and uncomfortable. In *Man and Measure II* there is the remnant of a dial, one method of measurement. In *Man and Measure III* the appearance of a small mask may well represent some loss, a deterioration in identity, one part of the fracturing of the self. A text comprising of orders, shouted exhortations is written beneath the surface. These are like the commands barked at the victim, of which only incoherent fragments remain to be seen. One such fragment says 'no hair' as though this was a category he would be placed in. A category that in itself is meaningless but may provide comfort for others as one more form of establishing a spurious hierarchy.**

DR As a matter of interest are you basing these figures on a model?

TW **I work with a number of people. I draw in order to understand and remember the figure, I rarely paint from the drawings. I take lots of photographs and use these but the procedures I use means the image inevitably deviates dramatically from the photographs. The photograph is more of a reminder than anything else. I really enjoy the opportunity to exploit those accidents and coincidences inherent in the procedures.**

DR You talk about writing on, or in, the canvas, but the characters we find here are graffiti-like marks.

TW **My taste is fairly catholic, I go from the ascetic classicism of Ben Nicholson through to the overblown rhetoric of John Martin and the New York angst of Ross Bleckner. I veer from one extreme to another, I like extremes. In this piece, *Reflection,* there is for me the feel of a meeting between Nicholson and Matisse. Although it's called *Reflection* the two heads are quite dissimilar.** Plate 49

DR This head is very Nicholson-like. You must know those paintings of his from the 1920s, the landscapes he produced in Cumbria and in Cornwall, some of them night scenes in which the view is outwards, from a darkened room, through the windows and into the night.

TW **Yes, I know the ones you mean and although looking at the visual evidence it probably seems unlikely, Ben Nicholson has been quite an influence. If anything he did too many paintings, but the best of them make that transition from picture to object. They have that feel of having been arrived at through a process of subtraction as though they were excavated out of the surface not painted onto it.**

DR I like the depth here which seems to be a depth which has more to do with colour than with space.

TW **A lot of that comes from the way in which they've been worked. I've used pastels with oil paint and ink so they sit somewhere between drawing and painting, it's all fairly intuitive and immediate. I hope they retain something of the energy of a spontaneous drawing. These calligraphic lines and splashes which abruptly intrude are for me like the crackle of unleashed energy.**

DR Now what about the shrine within the enclosure? I'm fascinated by your enclosures, those refuges which begin as little houses then become . . . Plate 48

TW **. . . Tabernacles.**

DR Yes, that is just the right word because now the building has taken on a quasi-religious significance. Back to 'the holy city of Byzantium', perhaps.

TW **Possibly, certainly the Mediterranean, a roadside chapel perhaps. All these pieces, *Shrine*, *Reflection*, *Blind Man* and *Shadow* I think of as a series. They all have heads, horizons indicating landscapes and enclosures of one form or another. The blind man is in the enclosure of his own blindness and he negotiates the world through counting amongst other things. For him numbers, and by that I mean measuring, is vital.** Plates 52 & 53

DR I also get a strong sense that you're giving notice to us that in some respect we are all blind.

TW **Well I think Richard Deacon got it right with his sculpture *For Those who have Ears*. In other words it's there if you choose to see it. Blindness doesn't only afflict the eyes.**

DR The *Toledo* series. I think you were working on these when I came to see you in your studio in Dean Clough last summer?

Plate 54 – 57 TW **Yes, that's right, these and the *Looking at El Greco* painting. The one constant that runs through them all is the silhouette of my head. I act as a witness travelling in the footsteps of the pilgrims, the works record that journey. They are also an attempt to expand my vocabulary of forms, to find a way of notating things seen and felt without resorting to my own conventions. They're about inventing and exploring motifs and trying to invest them with significance.**

DR There are hints of mazes, architectural drawings, attempts to solve spatial problems.

TW **As in a plan. The difference between reading the journey in a map and walking the same route. They're two very different experiences of space and time.**

DR Where did the trip to Toledo lead you?

TW **It led me back to an interest in Catholicism, the version exemplified in the contorted Baroque visions of El Greco. Not as a practising Catholic but more a spectator trawling for images.**

Plate 59 DR *Drowning in a Desert* seems to belong to the pre-Toledo series. It's a vast picture, and a deeply impressive one in its physical presence, when you see it on the wall as I did on one occasion at the Hart Gallery.

TW **It does have a sort of presence about it.**

DR You don't sound too convinced!

TW **No it's not that I'm not convinced, it's just that I'm trying to find some words to put with it. It's such a seemingly simple painting on such a large scale it's hard to know where to begin. I imagined it as an enormous barren landscape, a desert where you could die, drown, disappear or literally dissolve leaving only a stain. The Icarus-like figure is sliding down, liquefying into the sand leaving only an open barren landscape. Maybe the two panels make one scene or maybe they are a kind of before and after. Either way, as a whole they represent a figure on the brink of catastrophe seeming to endure a fearsome loneliness.**

DR That rings very true. I'm told that one of the most striking experiences in a desert is the loss of scale. I suppose there is no standard of measurement in the seemingly endless space of the desert, extending as far as you can see to the ends of visible distance. Ultimately, you are forced to question your own powers of perception.

TW **And also your own relevance and mortality. It must be a terrifying experience — endless solitude.**

DR I see that we are winding up. I was just going to add, provocatively I admit, that in the context of uncertain space, measuring might be something of a comfort, a means of restoring certainty and scale. Man was never more confident than in the Renaissance when he became the centre of the known universe, and the measure of all things. To that, and after I have thanked you for dealing so patiently with my questions, I insist that you must have the last word.

TW **Last year I wrote on a painting, "Bring no truths, Tell no lies", I still hold by that.**

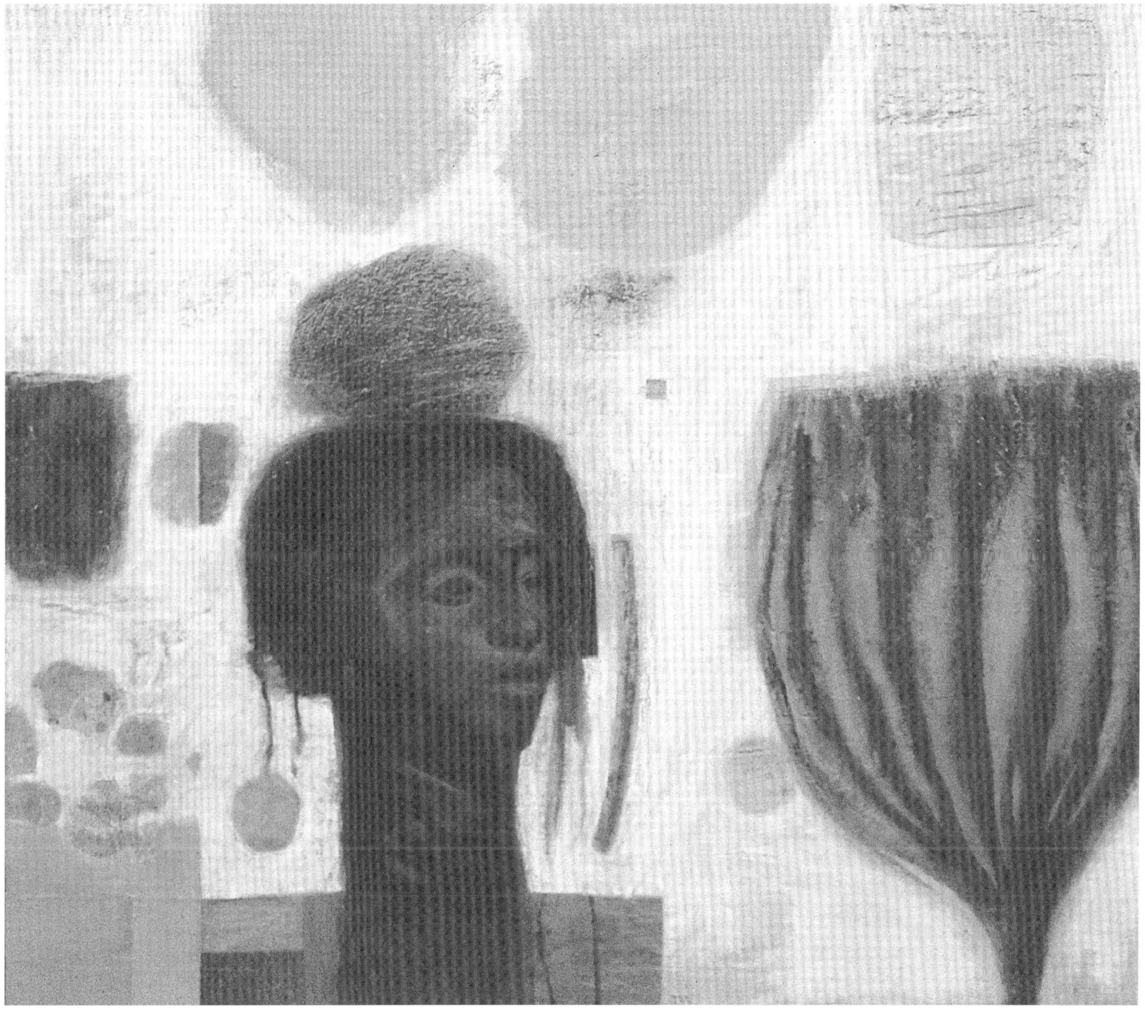

Untitled (Still life) 1991
oil on board
80 × 90 cm (31.5 × 35.5 inches)

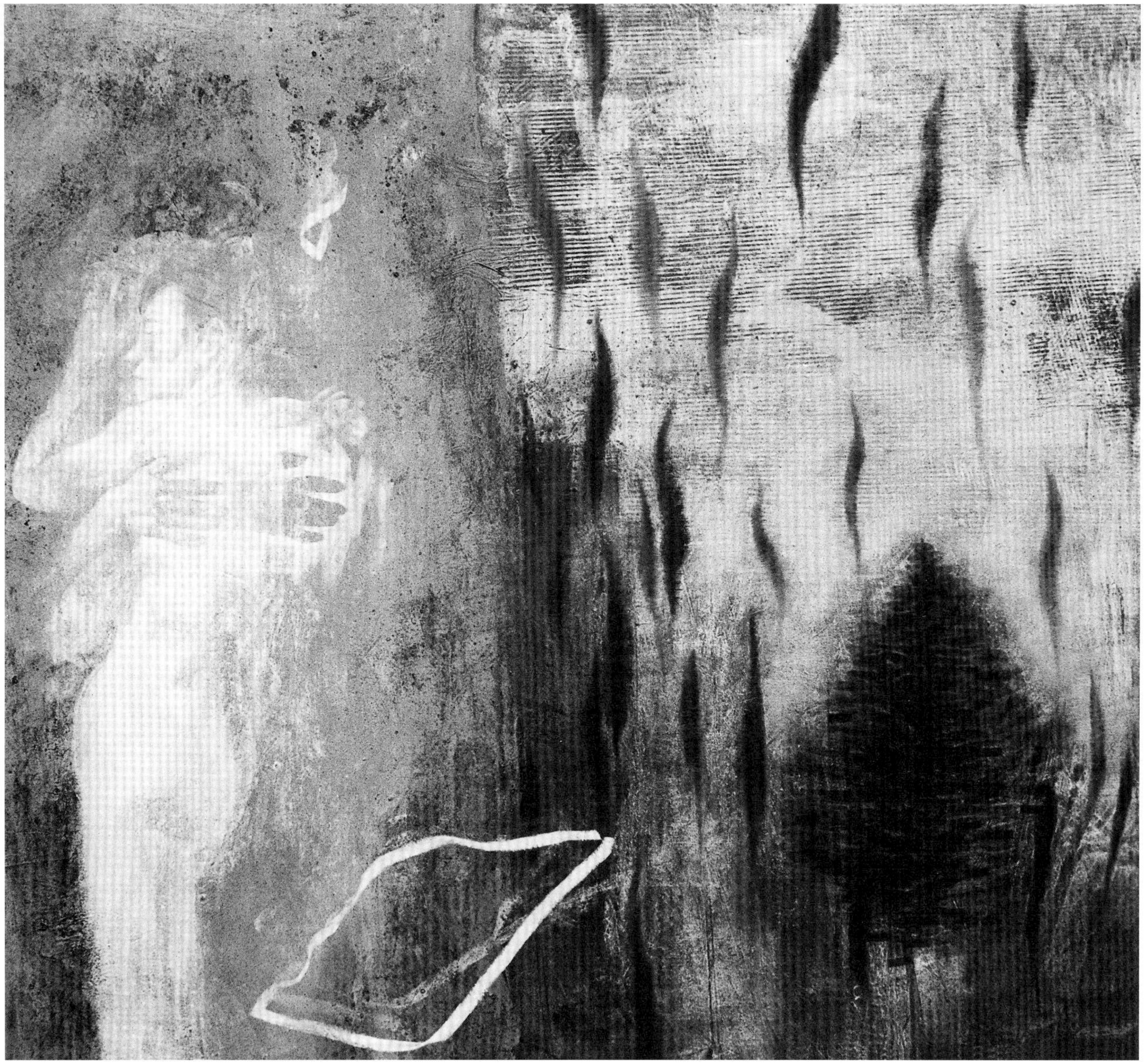

Possession 1995
oil on board
170.2 × 182.8 cm (67 × 72 inches)

L 'homme et la Mesure

LES PEINTURES DE TOM WOOD

"Quel chef d 'oeuvre est l'homme; avec quelle subtilité de pensée, quelle profondeur d 'emotion dans ses entrailles. "

Peter Ackroyd

Dan Leno and the Limehouse Golem

DR Lorsque nous étions en train de parler, Tom, de ton exposition à Dean Clough en 1987, je crois que tu disais qu'elle représentait une sorte de grand tournant dans ta carrière, un point de repère où tu pouvais te rendre compte de ce que tu avais fait avant de poursuivre C'est vrai?

TW Eh bien, oui; pour moi, c'était ca, l'exposition. De plusieurs manières, elle m'a fait reconsidérer mes idées sur la peinture. C'etait comme si je me tenais sur un plateau, capable d'apercevoir un horizon plus lointain que j'aurais voulu atteindre. Mais les expositions nous donnent souvent la possibilité de consolider nos préoccupations, de déblayer le terrain, et commencer de nouveau. Je crois que ce qui peut être déroutant, c'est quand l'exposition ne constitue pas une pause, mais une conclusion, et, lorsqu'on arrive à ce point, on est déjà lancé sur un autre chemin, en train de faire d'autres oeuvres, d'avoir d'autres idées.

DR Je pense que tu as les memes idées sur les livres à ton sujet?

TW Oui C'est bizarre, mais vrai. Cependant, j'ai des sentiments ambigus en ce qui concerne les livres. Les livres sont bizarres parce-qu'ils parlent toujours rétrospectivement. Ils confirmeront et consolideront ce qui n'a pu être que fugace ou provisoire. Dans un certain sens, c'est le cas lorsque le travail est commandé. Inévitablement, la commission sera toujours rétrospective. On me commissionne, particulièrement quand il s'agit de portraits, sur la base de ce que j'ai fait et non pas sur la base de ce que je pourrais faire - dans ce sens, il ya de la difficulté; l'affaire demande de la foi et un élément de confiance.

DR On parle, donc, maintenant, de la rétrospection, cette rétrospection qui est certainement un élément important de ton oeuvre. Il me semble que beaucoup de tes peintures et ce qu'elles disent ou impliquent ont quelque chose à voir avec ton passé, ton environnement et les mémentos de ta famille.

TW C'est vrai, et je trouve dificile d'échapper à tout ça. Je suis devenu obsédé; je creuse et je gratte dans des morceaux de ma vie. Je crois que c'était Kitaj qui à dit que le but principal de l'art était de regarder le monde où nous habitons, intérieur ou extérieur, de regarder et de réfléchir. De nous mettre en dehors de nous-mêmes et de nous servir des affectations de la rhétorique sera toujours un acte vain; meme si ce que nous avons à dire est une toute petite chose, cette chose aura une valeur à cause de son intégrité. Je n'ose pas dire si telle ou telle chose est importante, ou prononcer d'une façon généralisée; je veux dire qu mes oeuvres peuvent finir en couches et obscures de sorte qu'elle expriment des idées universelles à travers des caractéristiques comme la famille ou les amis.

DR Oui, mais là, tu suis une grande tradition. Nous n'avons qu'à nous rappeler Rubens qui a peint sa femme et son enfant, ou "*L'Allégerie du Temps*" de Titian ou il parle du passé, du présent et de l'avenir, non pas dans l'abstrait mais à travers sa propre chair, son propre sang, dans la personne de son fils et héritier, Leone. Quand on y pense, ne pourrait-on pas dire que beaucoup de la grande peinture européenne reflète le peintre: dans un sens ou dans un autre, le tableau montre l'ambition, un portrait de l'artiste lui-même, de ses espoirs, ses idées, ses aspirations.

TW Oui, mais, pour moi, il y a un conflit, dans le sens que je n'accepterais jamais que les idées de l'oeuvre soient une démonstration du soi de l'artiste.

DR Peut-être suis-je un peu fantaisiste, mais il me semble que quand tu n'as peint que la moitié de ton visage dans ce tableau, qu'en ce faisant tu admets à moitié l'extrême réalité dans le reflet de toi-même, mais que tu réserves l'autre moitié dans ce dont tu as parlé, la vie intérieure et la vie intellectuelle, autrement parlant - l'autre moitié de toi dans le tableau.

TW C'est une interprétation merveilleuse et je suis sûr qu'elle est préférable à la mienne qui est assez prosaïque et comprend les idées que la peinture est structurée formellement avec des bandes verticales qui se chevauchent.

DR L'autre chose qui me frappe lorsque je regarde cete peinture est la façon dont tu as représenté le temps et le changement. Je t'ai entendu décrire la difficulté de représenter le flux par une image statiquc. mais c'est surement ce que tu as fait ici. Tu permets à tes enfants de croître visiblement devant le spectateur de la toile en les représentant à deux points différents de leur croissance.

TW Absolument. Pour moi la peinture était une sorte de démonstration seientifique de la croissance. J'ai peint les enfants de taille naturelle exacte, jusqu'au point où je les ai fait se tenir contre la toile les deux fois, et j'ai dessiné leurs silhouettes, l'idée étant d'empêcher ma subjectivité paternelle de déformer les faits.

Entre autres choses, la peinture est un graphique de croissance.

DR J'ai remarqué que, dans les cahiers de croquis, tu as fait quelques observations visuelles et verbales; il y en a qui parlent d'incidents dans des musées; des incidents avec des enfants qui courent à travers les galeries, des intrusions dans le monde des musées faites par les forces irresistibles de la vie qui se trouvent en dehors des vitrines d'exposition. Corrige-moi si j'ai tort, mais il me semble que *"L'incident au Musée"* représente un merveilleux échange, quelque peu badin, entre l'art et la vie. Je vois ici une contradiction fondamentale entre l'art qui a beaucoup d'importance pour nous, et que nous aimons presque physiquement, mais qui est, à la fois, inaccessible, à cause des règles qui disent "Défense d'y toucher."

TW Ce qui m'intrigue de l'objet qu'on trouve dans un musée est qu'il ressemble à un rocher dans un ruisseau, car le courant de la foule de gens, visiteurs, intellectuels, savants, y touche; à cause de leur attention, il prend vie; il est réinterprété, refait dans le contexte de leurs préoccupations. Nous sommes les catalyseurs pour sa vie. Sa signification n'est pas immuable. Des enfants qui regardent des masques cérémoniaux rient, les trouvent drôles, ou sont rendu muets, stupéfaits ou perplexes. Leur lutte pour trouver une signification dans cette rencontre multiplie pour moi les significations possibles possédées par les objets eux-mêmes. Les réponses naïves, le manque de compréhension de quelques-uns des visiteurs sont bien capables de briser le coeur de certains conservateurs de musée qui s'aperçoivent que leurs étiquettes, produit d'une recherche soigneuse pour montrer le contexte de l'objet, n'ont aucun effet. Mais, pour mois, ces heurts obliques contre d'autres vies, d'autres époques, eh bien, je les trouve provocateurs, et les accepte avec humilité.

DR Pendant cette conversation, je pense à une autre théorie, c'est la façon dont tu attaches une importance égale à un jouet d'enfant ou quelque chose qui fait partie d'une publicité pour la lingerie et à un artefact précieux trouvé dans un musée. Tu as une façon de réunir tous ces éléments disparates, et puis de les transformer. Stanley Spencer disait qu'il "prenait toujours un objet abandonné et en faisait le fondement" d'une de ses compositions. Est-ce que tu élèves des objets de tous les jours de la même façon?

TW Oui. Ce qui est humble, négligé, abandonné est un candidat idéal pour l'acte de transformation. Dans le temps, je peignais de petits cailloux ramassés au bord de la route, comme si c'étaient des bijoux.

DR Oui, je me souviens d'avoir lu dans un de tes carnets une note que tu avais faite sur la nature morte, sur l'importance que tu attaches à un citron ou à une tasse à thé.

TW C'est, peut-etre, le simple fait d'être sélectionnés et peints qui les transforme - une sorte d'alchimie métaphorique. Il y a des artistes qui croient que l'acte de sélectionner un objet et de changer son contexte est suffisant pour résulter à cette transformation. Pour moi, le fait de le peindre le fixe dans le temps - une sorte de momification.

DR Si je tourne à *"Collage 1991"*. Ici c'est vraiment du collage?

TW Oui, pour la plupart. Parfois, j'aime travailler sur un niveau plus austère, plus formel, c'est à dire où je rends la forme en contenu.

DR Tu parais très à l'aise avec ce genre, et je soupçonne que c'est peut-être à cause de ta révérence pour la surface d'un tableau, le fait que tu la laisses fonctionner en partie constituante de l'image, plutôt qu'en fond neutre pour le tableau. Mais, si nous regardons maintenant les formes, nous voyons davantage de tes cosses, de tes tasses. des formes hérissées de pointes. Est-ce que je peu mentionner Léger vers la fin de sa carrière?

TW Oui, exactement, Léger - J'aime la façon dont il combinait des choses clairement vues et d'autres imaginées, la façon dont il les a transformées en ses propres formes bizarres, en partie badines, où les fleurs ont l'air d'être construites de tubes et de plasticène, mais ont, hélas, un aspect sinistre comme si elles pourraient te poignarder si tu t'approchais de trop près.

DR Celui-ci est pour le Livre Vert, j'imagine, la revue. Il faut que je te dise que j'aime l'idée d'offrir une tasse remplie d'épines aux critiques.

TW Avec les gravures sur linoléum, je laisse tomber ce que je fais pour le moment. Si j'y pense, ce que j'ai fait c'est d'en extraire toutes les formes qui me font plaisir, les morceaux qui m'ont plu lorsque je les ai faits, et je les ai mis dans les gravures sur linoléum; ainsi les estampes sont, dans un sens, une distillation du plaisir qui se trouve dans les peintures. Elles sont aussi une façon plus immédiate de travailler avec une sorte de langue graphique, comme des diagrammes, des caricatures, de la calligraphie. Je peux jouer avec ces formes et voir ce qui en est le résultat. Quand on surimprime, il y a parfois des juxtapositions surprenantes. Je le considère comme une sorte de dessin qui libère les idées. A présent, je fais quelque chose de semblable avec les ordinateurs.

DR Vraiment? Comme exercice purement visuel, sans texte?

TW Oui, pas de tête pour le moment - juste des images et des dessins. C'est assez rudimentaire; on fait chevaucher des couches, on ajuste la transparence de chaque couche, on efface des parties, on clone d'autres, et puis on redessine sur le résultat. Je ne suis pas très doué, et l'idée de mon manque de contrôle m'intrigue. Je suppose que c'est encore une possibilité d'avoir des images en flux mais que cette fois on peut retrouver.

DR On devrait peut-etre parler de l'art du portrait et de ce qui te persuade de peindre le portrait de quelqu'un.

TW Eh bien, j'ai commencé en faisant des images des gens que j'aimais comme j'ai déjà dit, des mémentos affectueux. Puis, les gens ont commencé à me demander de faire des portraits, et, comme tu sais, j'ai eu un certain succès. Heureusement, maintenant il y a un peu de calme, et je ne fais que les quelques rares portraits que j'aime faire. C'est une occupation assez sporadique et je l'aime comme ça. Les

portraits que j'aime mieux faire sont ceux où le sujet est sympathique, quelqu'un qui offre un investissement personnel dans le portrait, et qui est sensible à mes soucis à moi - c'est, je suppose, une sorte d'association. Le portrait de Keith Holmes et de Sheila Fairbrass était pour moi un modèle de son genre. C'était un exercice assez prolongé où j'ai fait un nombre de faux démarrages, mais où leur patience et leur loyauté ont triomphé. C'est toujours un acte de foi de la part du sujet; il doit se sentir vulnérable; mon rôle est de comprendre cette vulnérabilité, d'essayer de maintenir sa confiance, et, del, finalement, de livrer le produit. Pour etre honnête, ce n'est pas toujours facile.

DR Bien, je peux voir que Fairbrass et Holmes sont des sujets sélectionnés par toi, mais tu as, parfois, accepté des commandes de l'extérieur. Je pense que c'était le cas avec Alan Bennett. Est-ce que tu avais fait la connaissance de Bennett avant qu'on t'ait demandé de faire son portrait?

TW Non, je ne l'avais pas rencontré, mais, comme tout le monde, il me semblait le connaître déjà. Etre avec lui est une vraie joie, et, bien que je n'aie pas passé beaucoup de temps dans sa compagne, le peu de temps oû j'étais avec lui était un plaisir total. Il n'avait pas d'idées conçues du résultat et m'a accordé une liberté complète.

DR Je dois admettre que je préfère le plus grand tableau, celui de deux mètres.

TW Et tu as probablement raison; c'est celui que j'aime mieux. Il est certain qu'il s'approche davantage de mes soucis de peintre, mais quelquefois on se trouve dans des situations oû il faut saffsfaire des comités peut-etre un peu têtues sans offenser personne. Ce n'est pas un scénario idéal.

DR Je pense que ma préférence a quelque chose à voir avec l'apparence plus riche, plus texturé du plus grand tableau, et aussi à cause de mon idée qu'il montre l'homme dont tu as fait la connaissance. Le fait que tu parles de lui en train de t'acceuillir chez-lui m'intéresse, parce que, pour moi, le plus grand tableau capte cette rencontre sociale, et le rapport paisible qui a suivi entre ton sujet et toi; pendant que, dans l'autre tableau, tu as mis l'emphase sur la PERSONA publique. Dans celui-ci, on voit Bennett qui pose en écrivain distingué, intellectuel, qui regarde droit devant lui, tout à fait l'auteur posé, comme quelqu'un avec le monde contre lui, en contraste avec l'auteur qui ne ressent pas cette opposition. Les planches numéros 14 et 15 sont rétrospectives et regardent dans un monde intérieur, dans des figures prfondément introspectives. Il y a quelque chose de sombre et de méditatif-sombre est le meilleur mot que je puisse trouver pour décrire l'atmosphère de ces tableaux. En même temps, ils montrent clairement ce qui n'est pas leur sujet. C'est de la peinture, n'est-ce pas?

TW Absolument, et, dans un sens, ils forment la base de tout le travail depuis. Ils comprennent, quelque peu crûment, mes efforts d'extérioriser les espoirs, ambitions, rêves et désirs que nous avons intérieurement. J'ai tenté de me servir de diverses stratégies pour communiquer ceci, mais c'est, avant tout, une image du corps ou de la tête, en conjonction avec quelques formes extérieures. Les formes sont souvent ambiguës et provoquent un dialogue avec le corps tordu. Inévitablement, il reste quelques questions, mais on ne peut y répondre que dans le contexte des espoirs de celui qui regarde, de ses ambitions, rêves et désirs. Le premier tableau est très dramatique, avec le personnage qui s'étire désespérément vers le haut, comme s'il luttait pour rompre quelques liens invisibles.

DR Dans un sens, il revient au Sourcier n'est ce pas? Mais Sourcier, Alchimiste ou Ange, celui qui se tient seul, c'est toi aussi ?

TW Oui, je suppose que c'est ça.

Ils sont, peut-être, un aspect de mon monde intérieur, réalisé extérieurement. Ce n'est qu'un aperçu, une bribe, pas toute l'histoire pour ainsi dire. Si je le considérais sérieusement, "Debout et Seul" est probablement une peinture de quelqu'un qui arrive soudain et brutalement a un certain age, et qui se sent isolé, fruste et déçu, qui cherche ses rêves de jeun'homme qui se tient sur une colline de Halifax et qui voit que le monde qu'il voulait conquérir est en train de disparaltre peu à peu; un triste poème romantique, élégiaque à la mort de l'espoir.

DR C'est une introduction à quelque chose que tu développes dans les tableaux qui suivent. Ma seule façon de le décrire et de dire que c'est une distortion faite délibérément des traits, comme si les figures ollt été poussées et tirées contre une plaque de verre. Est-ce que tu penses à une "distortion" ou non ?

TW Non, je ne crois pas.

Je fais une image et puis je me sers de rouleaux et de mes mains pour y introduire, en poussant, d'autres matières; des morceaux de moquette, de papier, de carton ondulé, de thibaude, de polythène - n'importe quoi, en effet qui puissent soulever et transférer l'image. Puis vient un long procédé de fabriquer, transférer, ajuster et refaire l'image; ceci continue pendant assez longtemps, et, comme j'ai déjà dit, c'est plutôt une question d'intuition que de plan. C'est à ce point que l'image peut changer radicalement; tout est en flux total. Donc, quand tu vois une figure, cette figure a probablement changé de place dix fois autour de la peinture, et ce que tu vois est le résidu fragmentaire de décisions prises auparavant. Finalement, on arrive à une sorte de résolution, et je suppose que c'est seulement une extension de ce que faisait Bacon avec ses figures, mais plus particulièrement de ce qu'il faisait avec ses triptyques de têtes.

DR Mais tu te prives de ton empreinte, la marque de ta main.

TW C'est précisément l'autographe, la signature, le geste rempli de moi que je veux éviter. Comme j'ai déjà dit, l'image doit évoluer; elle doit se fondre ensemble plutot que d'être appliquée. Elle n'avance pas implacablement vers une conclusion; elle tourne et retourne. Elle est poursuivie plutôt que chassée. Par conséquent, je perds probablement autant que je retiens; ainsi, pour moi, les peintures restent toujours fragmentaires. Même les grands tableaux me

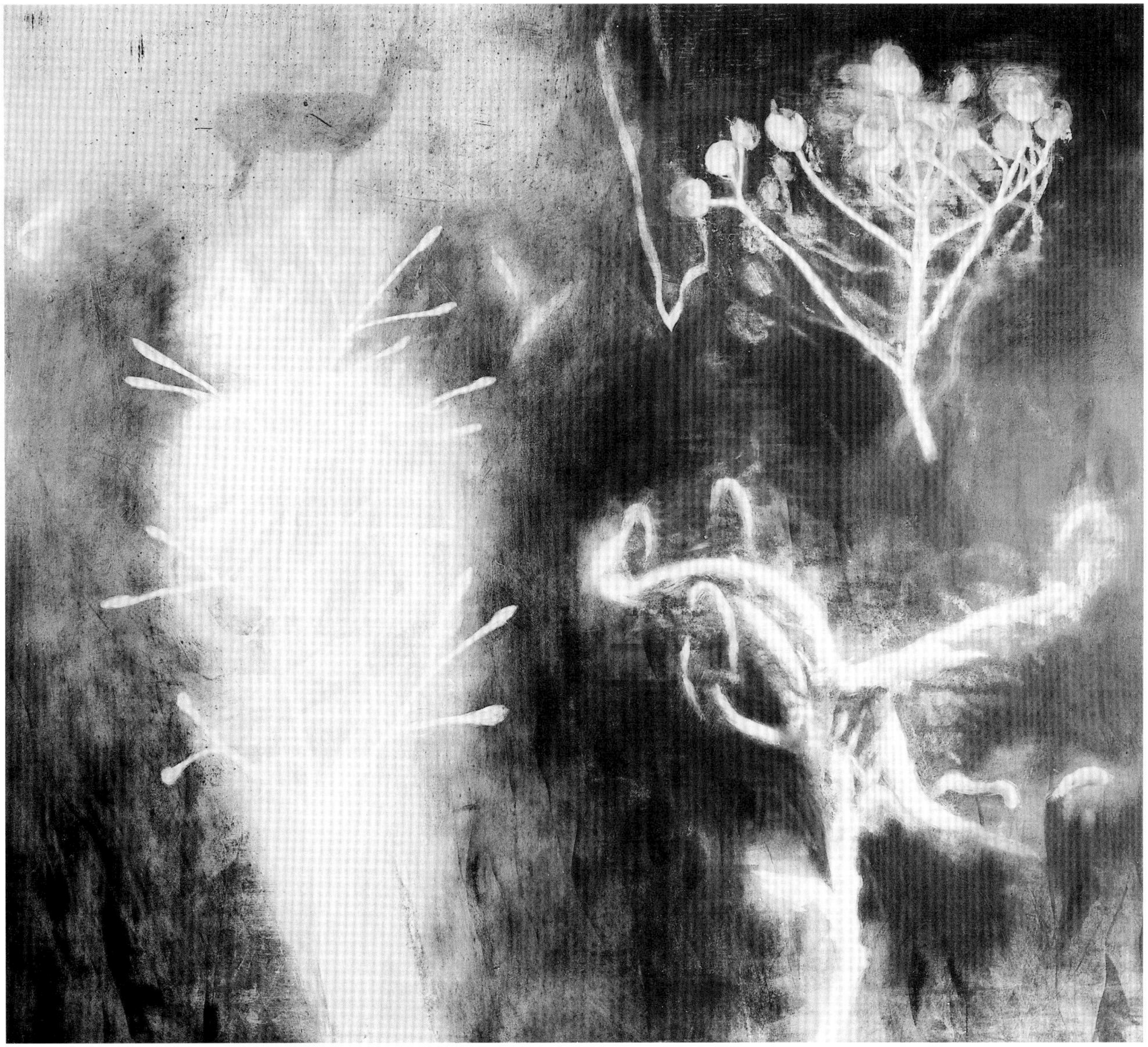

Thorny Annunciation 1995
oil on panel
170.2 × 182.8 cm (67 × 72 inches)

semblent être des morceaux d'un tout plus grand. Je les vois toujours en train de continuer plus loin que leurs bords. Quand, étudiant, j'ai peint quelques paysages, le problème était toujours où devrait être le bord. Comment contenir toute cette information visuelle et sensorielle dans ce petit rectangle. A cause de ça, quand j'ai peint "*Déluge sur la Côte occidentale*", qui est un grand tableau, je l'ai vu comme une sorte de vue à travers une petite fente. Je pensais a John Martin et à ses visions apocalyptiques, mais aussi à toutes sortes d'autres choses - les panoramas de Frederick Church, Caspar David Friedrich, et aux scènes finales de "*Maintenant l'Apocallypse*" de Coppola.

DR Alors - "*Pendant que la fumée monte, les abeilles descendent*". D'où vient cette phrase?

TW Les deux titres "*Pendant que la fumée monte, les abeilles descendent*" et "*Dans mon Désert il y a un Miroir*" sont des inventions, mes phrases à moi; je veux qu'elles ressemblent à des citations.

Lorsque nous passons à travers des crises, nous nous cosolons avec de petits aphorismes, tels que "C'était probablement pour le mieux" et "Le Temps guérit tout" et "Demain apportera une nouvelle aube."

DR Ainsi, en regardant dans le trou dans la terre, encore nous ne voyons rien ?

TW Elle essaie de voir dans un vide. Dans ce paysage post-nucléaire d'holocauste, pour se protéger elle n'a rien qu'un voile fragile.

DR Un filet d'apiculteur?

TW Peut-être un filet et peut-etre que les tirets qu'on voit dans la fumée représentent des abeilles mais ce n'est pas une peinture à propos des abeilles.

DR Tu dirais les mêmes choses au sujet de "*l'Ange Rouge*", n'est-ce pas?

TW Oui, ces personnages regardent dans leurs mains; ces personnages qui sont, dans un sens, aveugles. Ils cherchent quelque chose, et, même s'il y a des clés partout, ils ne vont jamais le trouver. Les peintures du désert concernent surtout la perte. Dans le paysage stérile que les personnages habitent, leurs maigres espoirs sont attachés a ces gages obscurs, dont, s'ils étaient capables de les trouver, ils pourraient deviner quelque signification, mais ce n'est pas probable.

DR Et "*Peinture de l'Histoire*"?

TW C'est une peinture qui m'est venue quand je pensais à l'oeuvre de George Catlin et ses tableaux des indigènes d'Amérique. Je suppose que ce sont des exemples des débuts de l'ethnographie. Ils montrent le besoin d'étudier, d'enregistrer, et de catégoriser. Je me sentais inquiet sur la question des évaluations où une telle étude pourrait arriver. Il semble exister un besoin ou de condamner ou de chérir. "*Peinture de l'Histoire*" devait être le premier d'une longue série d'oeuvres qui considéreraient cette idée, mais je n'ai jamais fait plus d'une peinture.

DR Mais, pendant qu'il voyait son travail comme documentaire, celui d'enregistrer d'une façon précise les tribus indiennes, tu inventes, en comptant sur la puissance de ton imagination.

TW Je trouve que j'ai besoin d'inventer autour d'une idée plutot que d'essayer d'enregistrer. Le personnage est peint comme si, dans le temps, c'était une photographie en sépia; peut-être un Indien américain coiffé de plumes et de sa dignité.

DR Non, je vois ça Je vois aussi que tu es toujours en train de mesurer, ce qui nous mène, finalement, à la série "*L'Homme et la Mesure*" dans lesquelles les mesures sont attachées au cadre mais comprennent Ull élément séparé, une partie du tableau qui ne se trouve pas dans la superficie peinte.

TW Les mesures se trouvent à côté de la peinture comme tu dis, et pas à son intérieur. Mais elles ont toujours été séparées, imposées de l'extérieur. Maintenant elles sont des formes géométriques solides, qui ne bougent pas; pour moi, elles sont quasi-industrielles.

DR Elles auraient pu être appliquées avec un pulvérisateur d'usine.

TW Exactement. Ces personnages ne peuvent pas s'évader, ne recevront pas de pitié; ce sont les victimes complètes de leurs mesures. Comme telles, ils sont vulnérables et inconfortables. Dans "*L'Homme et la Mesure II*", il y a ce qui reste de la face d'une pendule, une des méthodes de mesurer. Dans "*L'Homme et la Mesure III*", l'apparition d'un petit masque peut bien représenter quelque perte, une détérioration d'identité, une partie de la fracturation du soi. Un texte composé d'ordres, d'exhortations criées, est écrit sous la surface. Ils ressemblent aux ordres aboyés à la victime, dont ne restent à être vus que quelques bribes incoherentes. Un de ces fragments dit "pas de cheveux" comme si c'était une catégorie où on le mettrait; une catégorie qui, en elle-même, manque de signification mais qui peut réconforter les autres parce qu'elle contribue à établir une fausse hiérarchie.

DR Il m'intéresserait de savoir si tu bases ces personnages sur un modèle.

TW Je travaille avec plusieurs personnes. Je dessine pour comprendre et me rappeler du personnage. Je ne peins que rarement après des dessins. Je prends beaucoup de photographies, et les utilise, mais les procédés dont je me sers font que l'image dévie dramatiquement de la photographie. La photographie est plutôt un pense-bête qu'autrechose. J'aime beaucoup la possibilité d'exploiter ces accidents et coincidences qui sont inhérents au procédés.

DR Tu parles d'écrire sur ou dans la toile, mais les personnages qu'on trouve ici ressemblent à des graffiti.

TW Mon goût est assez catholique. Je pars du classicisme ascètique de Ben Nicholson, et je continue à travers la rhétorique exagérée de John Martin et l'angst NewYorkais de Ross Bleckner. Je passe d'une

extrême à une autre; j'adore les extrêmes. Dans ce morceau "*Reflet*", il y a pour moi le sens d'une rencontre entre Nicholson et Matisse. Bien qu'il ait pour titre "*Reflet*", les deux têtes ne se ressemblent pas du tout.

DR J'aime ici la profondeur qui semble être une profondeur qui a davantage à voir avec la couleur qu'avec l'espace.

TW Ca s'explique par la méthode dont ils ont été travaillés. Je me suis servi de pastels avec de la peinture à l'huile et de l'encre; on peut donc dire qu'ils sont à mi-chemin entre le dessin et la peinture; c'est intuitif et immédiat. J'espère qu'ils gardent quelque chose de l'énergie d'un dessin spontané. Ces lignes et taches calligraphiques qui empiètent abruptement sont pour moi comme le crépitement d'une énergie lachée.

DR Maintenant, que dirais-tu apropos du reliquaire dans la clôture? Tes clôtures me fascinent, ces réfuges qui commencent en étant de petites maisons et puis deviennent . . .

TW . . . des Tabernacles.

DR Oui, c'est bien le mot juste, car maintenant le batiment a pris une signification quasi-religieuse. On revient à la "ville sainte" de Bysance, peut-être.

TW Possiblement - certainement la Méditerranée - une chapelle au bord de la route, peut-être. Tous ces morceaux: "*Reliquaire, Reflet, l'Aveugle et Ombre*" forment une série pour moi. Ils ont tous de têtes, des horizons qui indiquent des paysages et différentes sortes de clôtures. L'aveugle est dans la clôture de sa cécité, et il négocie le monde à force de compter, entre autres choses. Pour lui, des chiffres, et je veux dire la mesure, sont surimportants.

DR Il y a des allusions aux labyrinthes, des dessins architecturaux, essais de résoudre des problèmes spatiaux.

TW Comme dans un plan. La différence entre la préparation du voyage sur une carte et traverser la même route à pied. Ce sont deux expériences différentes de l'espace et du temps.

DR La série "*Tolède*". Je crois que tu y travaillais quand je suis venu te voir dans ton atelier à Dean Clough, l'été dernier.

TW Oui, tu as raison, ceux-là et la peinture qui s'appelle "*Regarder El Greco*". Ce qui est commun à tous, c'est la silhouette de ma tête. Je fonctionne comme témoin qui suit les pas des pélerins; les oeuvres enregistrent ce voyage. Elles représentent aussi un effort d'agrandir mon vocabulaire de formes, de trouver une façon de faire une notation de choses vues et senties sans revenir à mes propres conventions. Il s'agit d'inventer et d'explorer des motifs, et d'essayer de les investir de signification.

DR Jusqu'où t'a mené ce voyage à Tolède?

TW Il m'a fait revenir à un intérêt au Catholicisme tel qu'on le voit dans les visions Baroques et torturées d'EI Greco. Pas comme un catholique pratiquant mais plutôt un spectateur qui cherche des images.

DR "*Se noyer dans le Désert*" semble appartenir a la série pré-Tolède. C'est un tableau énorme qui est très impressionant en ce qui concerne sa présence physique quand on le voit au mur comme je l'ai vu une fois dans la galerie Hart.

TW C'est vrai qu'il a une certaine présence.

DR Tu n'as pas l'air convaincu!

TW Non, ce n'est pas que je ne sois pas convaincu; c'est juste que j'essaie de trouver d'autres paroles pour l'accompagner. C'est une peinture qui paraît si simple sur une si grande échelle qu'il est difficile de savoir par où commencer. Je la vois comme un paysage énorme, stérile, un désert où l'on pourrait mourir, se noyer, disparaitre ou se dissoudre litéralement, en ne laissant qu'une tache. Ce personnage qui ressemble à Icare glisse en bas, se liquéfiant dans le sable et ne laissant qu'un paysage ouvert et stérile. Peut-etre que les deux panneaux ne fassent qu'une seule scène, ou peut-être sont-ils une sorte d'avant et après. N'importe, le tout représente quelqu'un sur le bord d'une catastrophe qui semble souffrir une solitude effroyable.

DR Ça sonne très vrai. On me dit qu'une des expériences les plus frappantes dans un désert, cest la perte d'échelle normale. Je suppose qu'il n'y a pas de standard pour mesurer dans cet espace qui semble sans fin qu'est un désert qui 'étend aussi loin qu'on peut voir aux frontières de la distance visible. Finalement, on est forcé de douter de ses propres pouvoirs de perception.

TW Et aussi de sa propre pertinence et de sa mortalité. La solitude sans fin doit constituer une expérience vraiment effroyable.

DR Je m'aperçois que nous arrivons à la fin de notre conversation. J'étais sur le point d'ajouter, peut-être d'un esprit provocateur, je l'admets, que, dans le contexte d'un espace incertain, pouvoir mesurer pourrait être un confort en quelque sorte, un moyen de restaurer la certitude et l'échelle. L'homme n'a jamais eu plus de confiance que pendant la Renaissance lorsqu'il est devenu le centre de l'univers connu, et la mesure de tout ce qui existait. Quand je t'aurai remercié de répondre avec tant de patience à mes questions, je te demanderai de dire le dernier mot de réponse.

TW L'année dernière, j'ai écrit sur une peinture: "Ne venez pas à moi avec des vérités. Ne dites pas de mensonges." Je tiens encore à ça.

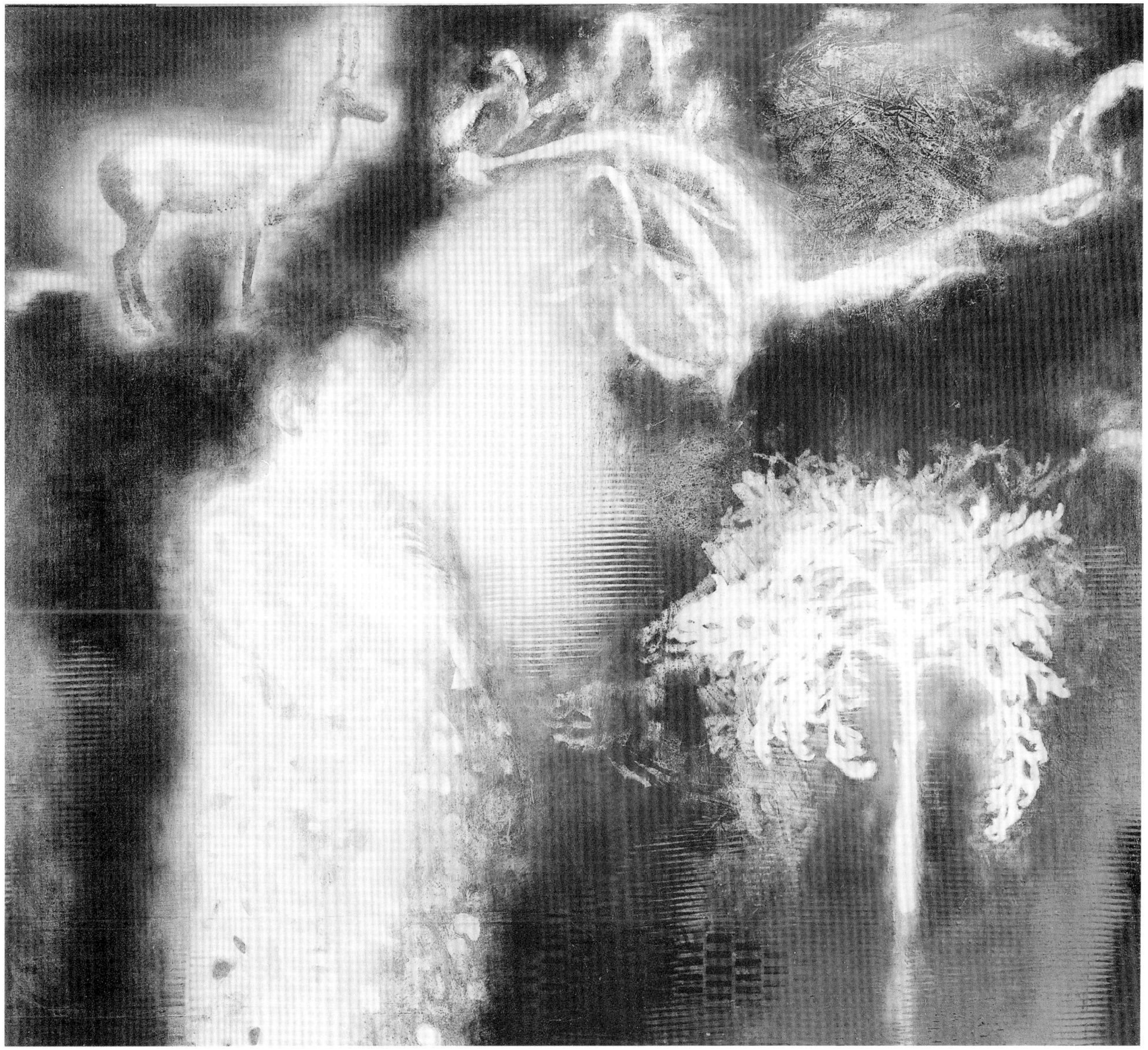

In the Garden of the Hesperides 1996
oil on panel
170 × 183 cm (67 × 72 inches)

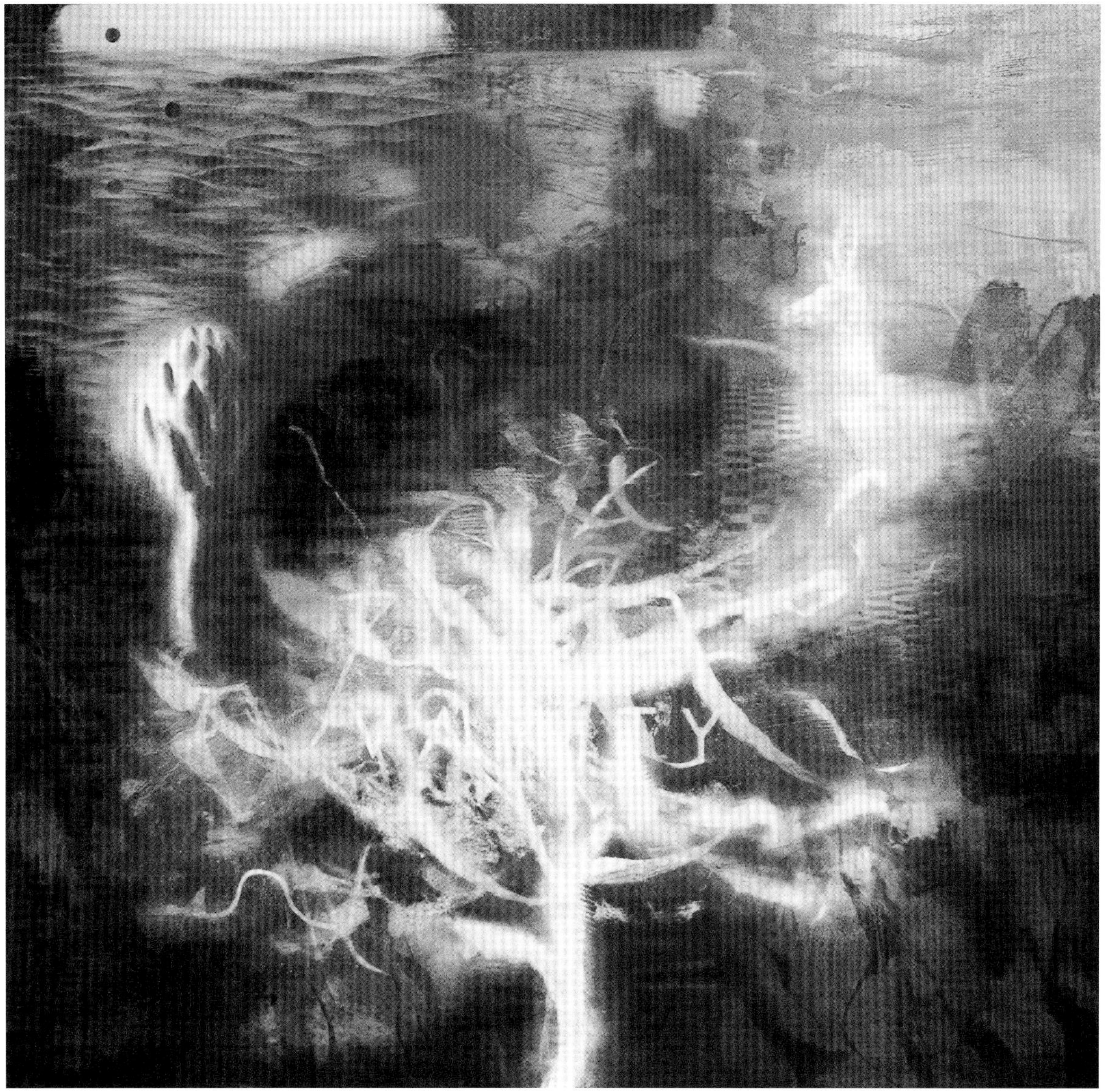

The Coil of Vanity or In and Out of Favour 1996
oil on panel
183 × 183 cm (72 × 72 inches)

Mensch und Maß
Die Gemälde Von Tom Wood

"Was für eine Schöpfung der Mensch doch ist, wie fein in seinen Fähigkeiten, wie unbegrenzt in seinem Innern"

Peter Ackroyd

Dan Leno und der Limehouse Golem

DR Tom, ich glaube es war, als wir 1987 über Ihre Ausstellung in Dean Clough sprachen, daß Sie sagten, daß sie eine Art Wendepunkt in Ihrer Karriere darstellte, eine Gelegenheit Inventur zu machen von dem, was Sie soweit erreicht hatten, ehe Sie Ihre nächsten Schritte unternahmen. Stimmt das?

TW Ach ja, für mich hatte diese Ausstellung diese Bedeutung. Auf unterschiedliche Weise veranlaßte sie mich, meine Theorien über das Malen noch einmal zu überdenken. Ich denke daran, als ob ich auf einem Plateau stehe und einen weiteren Horizont erblicken kann und denke, daß ich gern dort sein möchte. Aber Ausstellungen bieten oft die Gelegenheit, Anliegen zu konsolidieren oder alles aufzuräumen und von Neuem zu beginnen. Ich glaube, daß dies verwirrend sein kann, wenn die Ausstellung nicht eine Pause ist, sondern ein Abschluß, und daß man sich schon inmitten anderer Arbeit und anderer Ideen befindet, wenn sie angeschaut wird.

DR Ich nehme an, Sie denken genau so auch über Bücher die über Sie geschrieben werden?

TW Ja, das stimmt wohl auf eine eigentümliche Art, aber meine Gefühle sind weit vieldeutiger, soweit es Bücher betrifft.

Bücher sind eigenartige Dinge, da sie immer rückblickend sind und sie bewerten oder konsolidieren Dinge, die vielleicht nur unverbindlich oder flüchtig waren. Dies trifft auch in gewissem Maße zu, wenn ein Kunstwerk in Auftrag gegeben wird. Es ist unvermeidbar, daß es rückblickend in Auftrag gegeben wird. Ich erhalte einen Auftrag, besonders für ein Porträt, aufgrund dessen, was ich getan habe und nicht notwendigerweise aufgrund dessen, was ich vielleicht tun werde und so kann es schwierig sein, es erfordert Vertrauen und einen gewissen Glauben.

DR Nun sprechen wir also über Rückblick, der doch sicherlich ein wichtiges Element Ihrer Arbeit ist. Für mich sieht es so aus, als ob viele der Bilder, die Sie malen, und die darin angedeuteten Aussagen etwas mit Ihrer eigenen Vergangenheit und Ihrer unmittelbaren Umgebung, einschließlich ihrer Familienerinnerungen, zu tun haben.

TW Das stimmt, und es ist für mich schwierig, mich diesem zu entziehen. Es scheint, als ob ich davon besessen bin, an Teilen meines Lebens herumzugraben und herumzukratzen. Ich glaube es war Kitaj, der sagte, daß der wirkliche Zweck der Kunst wäre, sich die Welt, in der wir leben, anzuschauen, gleich ob es unsere Außen- oder Innenwelt sei, sie anzuschauen und darüber nachzudenken. Außerhalb sich selbst zu stehen und die Mannerismen der Rhetorik zu gebrauchen, wird stets hohl klingen. Selbst, wenn das, was wir auszusagen haben, nur klein und bescheiden ist, wird es dennoch wegen seiner Integrität wertvoll sein. Ich fühle, daß ich nicht in der Lage bin, zu sagen, daß ich glaube, daß dieses oder jenes wichtig ist, also eine Art von verallgemeinernder Aussage zu machen. Was ich daher schließlich tue, ist, mich mit dem Spezifischen in einer verallgemeinerndeden Art zu befassen; damit meine ich, die Arbeiten können vielschichtig und undurchsichtig werden, so daß ziemlich universale Ideen durch Spezifisches wie Familie und Freunde ausgedrückt werden.

DR Ja, aber was das betrift, befinden Sie sich in einer großen Tradition. Wir brauchen uns hier ja nur an Rubens, der seine Frau und sein Kind malte, zu erinnern oder an Titians Allegorie der Zeit, in der er von der Vergangenheit, der Gegenwart und der Zukunft nicht im Abstrakten spricht, sondern durch sein eigenes Fleisch und Blut, durch seinen Sohn und Erben Leone. Wenn man darüber nachdenkt, ist denn nicht ein sehr großer Teil europäischer Malerei selbstreflektierend, auf die eine oder andere Art Ehrgeiz, ein Porträt des Künstlers, bezüglich seiner Hoffnungen, Ideen und Aspirationen?

TW Ja, aber für mich besteht hier ein Konflikt, insofem als ich der Idee, daß das Werk lediglich das Ego des Künstlers ausstellt, wirklich widerstehe.

DR Vielleicht bin ich hier ein bißchen zu phantasievoll, aber wenn ich sehe, daß Sie in diesem Gemälde Ihr Gesicht nur zur Hälfte gemalt haben, kommt mir der Gedanke, daß Sie damit, die äußerste Realität der Reflektion Ihrer selbst halb zugestehen, aber zugleich die andere Hälfte dessen, worüber das Sie gesprochen haben, zurückhalten-nämlich das Innenleben und das Geistesleben. Mit anderen Worten, die andere Hälfte von Ihnen liegt im Inneren des Bildes.

TW Das ist eine wunderbare Interpretation und ich bin sicher, sie ist bei weitem besser als meine eigene Version, die ziemlich prosaisch ist und auf der Idee beruht, daß das Gemälde in senkrechten Bändern aufgebaut ist die sich überlagern.

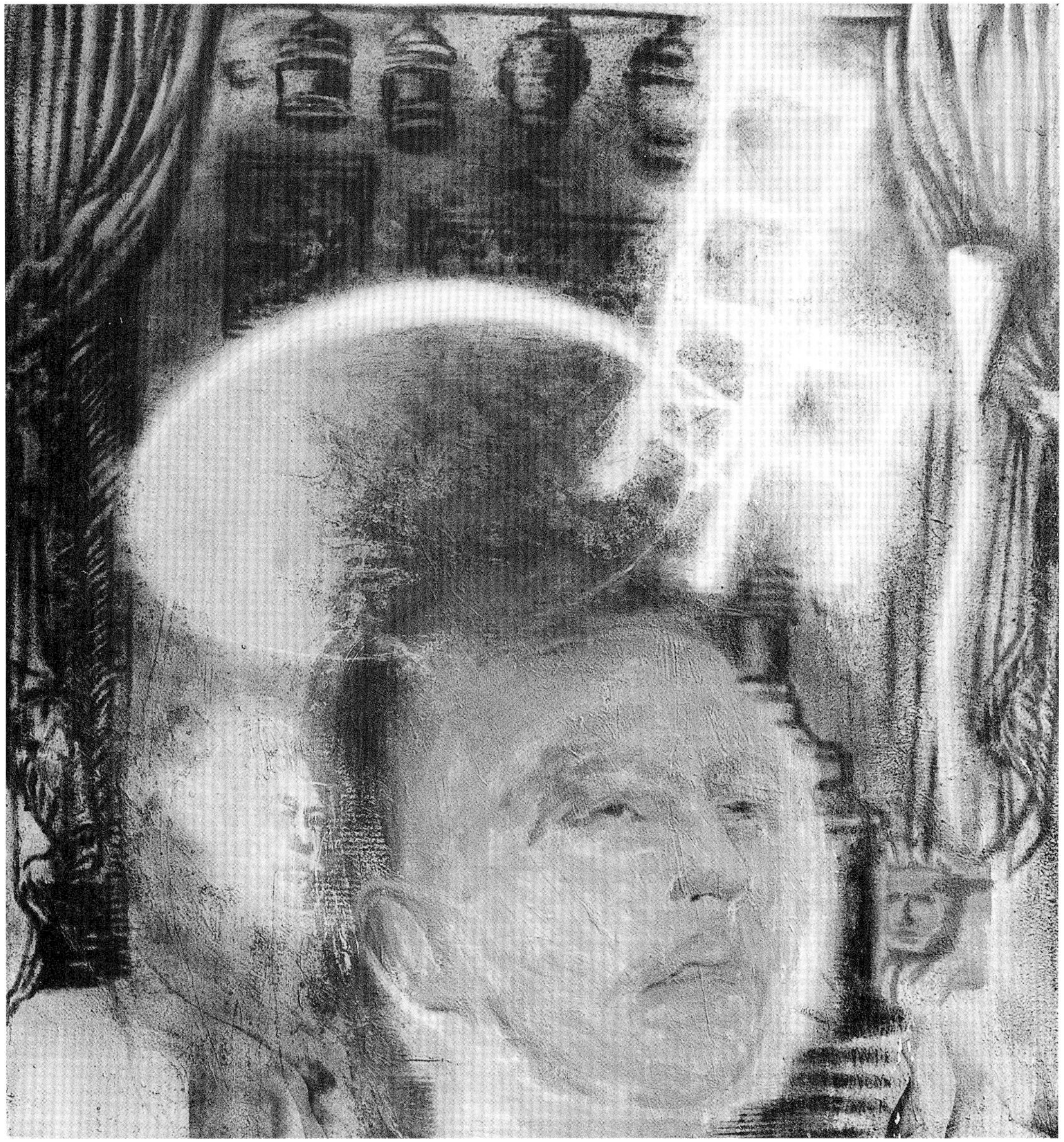

St Anselm Forsees the Method of his Martydom 1995–96
oil on panel
182.8 × 170.2 cm (72 × 67 inches)

DR Was mir auch an diesem Bild auffällt, ist die Art und Weise, in der. Sie Zeit und Wechsel darstellen. Ich habe gehört, wie Sie die Schwierigkeit, ständigen Wechsel mittels eines statischen Bildes darzustellen, beschreiben; aber Sie haben hier doch gerade dieses getan. Sie ermöglichen, daß Ihre Kinder sichtbar vor den Augen des Zuschauers auf der Leinwand wachsen, indem Sie sie an zwei verschiedenen Zeitpunkten ihres Lebens darstellen.

TW Sie haben vollkommen recht. Ich dachte an dieses Gemälde als eine Art wissenschaftlicher Demonstration des Wachsens. Die Kinder wurden in genauer Lebensgröße gemalt, ich ließ sie sogar vor der Leinwand stehen und habe beide Male um sie herum gezeichnet Die Idee war, daß meine väterliche Sujektivität nicht die Tatsachen verfälschen sollte. Unter anderem ist dieses Bild ein Wachstumsdiagramm.

DR Ich habe in den Skizzenbüchern bemerkt, daß, wenn Sie Beobachtungen — festhalten manche visuell und manche schriftlich — es mehrere gibt, die sich auf Ereignisse in Museen beziehen, Ereignisse in denen Kinder durch die Galerien rennen, das Eindringen von nicht unterdrückbbaren Kräften des Lebens außerhalb der Schaukästen in das Museum. Sagen Sie bitte, wenn ich unrecht habe, aber mir scheint, daß das *Museumsereignis* ein wunderschönes, etwas verspieltes Wechselspiel zwischen Kunst und Leben darstellt. Hier sehe ich den fundamentalen Widerspruch zwischen Kunst, die uns so viel bedeutet als etwas, das wir fast körperlich lieben aber welches gleichzeitig wegen der Vorschriften, die 'Nicht berühren!' sagen, unzugänglich ist.

TW Was mich an diesem Museumsstück fasziniert, ist, daß es wie ein Felsen in einem Bach von allen Seiten vom Fluß der Leute, Besucher und Wissenschaftler berührt wird und daß es lebendig und neu interpretiert und im Rahmen ihrer Anliegen neu gestaltet wird, wenn sie ihre Aufmerksamkeit darauf lenken. Wir sind der Katalysator für sein Leben. Seine Bedeutung ist nicht gesichert. Kinder, die sich zeremonielle Masken ansehen, lachen und sind belustigt oder ihnen ist die Sprache verschlagen, sie sind von Schrecken ergriffen oder verwirrt: ihr Bemühen, dieser Begegnung einen Sinn zu geben, erweitert die möglichen Bedeutungen, die die Gegenstände selbst halten. Manchem Kustos mag es wohl beinahe das Herz zerreißen, wenn sie der unwissenden Reaktion mancher Besucher begegnen, wenn alle ihre sorgfältig und bedacht erforschten Etikette und Zusammenhänge ignoriert werden. Aber für mich ist es demütigend und herausfordernd, von diesem anderen Leben, anderen zeiten und anderen bedeutungen gestreift zu werden.

DR Da kommt mir auch eine andere Theorie in den Sinn: Es handelt sich darum, wie Sie einem Kinderspielzeug oder etwas aus einer Unterwäscheanzeige dasselbe Gewicht geben, wie einem wertvollem Artefakt eines Museums. Irgendwie bringen Sie alle diese verschiedenen Elemente zusammen und gestalten sie um. Stanley Spencer pflegte zu sagen, daß er 'immer etwas, das verworfen worden war, nahm, und es zum Grundstein einer seiner Kompositionen machte'. Werden Ihre Alltagsgegenstände in ähnlicher Weise erhoben?

TW Ja, das ist so. Das Bescheidene, das Verworfene, das Mißachtete sind ideale Kandidaten für eine Tat der Umformung. Ich pflegte kleine, auf der Straße aufgelesene Steine zu malen, als ob sie Edelsteine wären.

DR Ja, ich erinnere mich daran, in Ihrem Notizbuch eine Bemerkung über Stilleben gelesen zu haben, und zwar über die Wichtigkeit, die Sie einer Zitrone oder einer Kaffeetasse verleihen.

TW Vielleicht werden sie durch die einfache Tatsache, daß sie ausgewählt und gemalt werden, in einer Art metaphorischer Alchemie umgestaltet. Einige Künstler meinen, daß die Tatsache, daß ein Objekt gewählt wird und sein Kontext verändert wird, genug ist, um der Akt der Umgestaltung stattfinden zu lassen. Ich glaube, es zu malen, ist für mich eine Art und Weise, es in der Zeit festzuhalten, eine Art Mummifizierung.

DR Nun wende ich mich zur *Collage 1991*. Ich nehme an, daß wir uns hier eine Collage anschauen?

TW Ja, zum größten Teil ist es das. Gelegentlich arbeite ich gern auf einem strengeren, mehr formellen Niveau, das heißt, die Form zum Inhalt zu machen.

DR Anscheinend fühlen Sie sich dabei ganz wohl. Ich nehme an, das hat etwas mit Ihrer Ehrfurcht für die Oberläche eines Bildes zu tun, wenn sie es ihr gestatten, als tatsächliche Komponente und nicht nur als neutraler Hintergrund zu fungieren. Aber wenden wir uns doch jetzt den Formen zu: wir treffen mehr Ihrer Samenschoten, mehr Tassen, mehr stachlige Formen. Darf ich Léger am Ende seiner Karriere erwähnen?

TW Leger stimmt genau — mir gefällt es, wie er Kombinationen von klar beobachteten Dingen und von vorgestellten Dingen erschafft. Die Art und Weise, wie er sie in seine eigenen seltsamen Formen verwandelt hat, teilweise spielerisch, wenn Blumen aussehen, als ob sie aus Schläuchen und Plastilin konstruiert wären, aber sie haben dennoch eine unheimliche Seite, als ob sie dich stechen könnten, wenn du zu nahe kommst.

DR Ich nehme an, dies ist für das Grüne Buch, das Journal. Ich muß sagen, mir gefällt die Idee, den Kritikern eine Tasse voller Dornen anzubieten.

TW Bei den Linolschnitten setze ich meine Hauptanliegen aus, ich gehe sozusagen auf Urlaub. Wenn ich darüber nachdenke -was ich eigentlich getan habe, ich habe alle angenehmen Formen herausgenommen, alle die Dinge, deren Schöpfung mir Spaß machte und habe sie dann in Linolschnitte gebracht: die Drucke sind auf eine Art eine Destillation des Vergnügens an den Gemälden. Sie sind auch eine unmittelbarere Art, mit einer Art

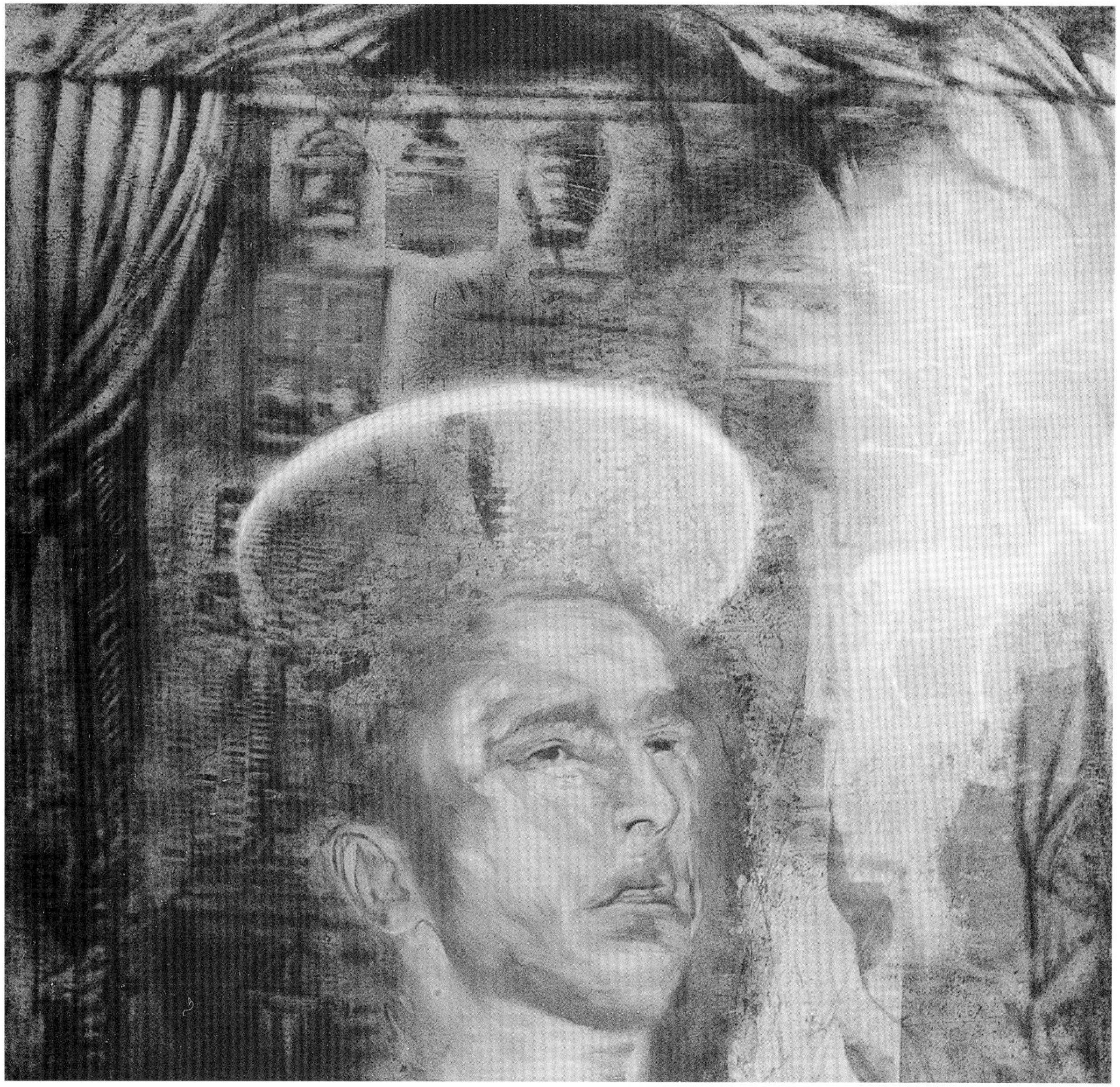

St Jerome Considers the Fate of Animals 1996
oil on panel
182.8 × 182.8 cm (72 × 72 inches)

grafischer Sprache, wie Diagrammen, Karikaturen, Schrift zu arbeiten. Ich kann mit diesen Formen herumspielen und sehen, was geschieht. Wenn man überdruckt, gibt es oft erstaunliche Nebeneinanderstellungen. Ich betrachte sie als eine Form des Zeichnens befreiender Ideen. Augenblicklich tue ich ähnliche Dinge mit Computern.

DR Wirklich, als rein visuelle Übung, ohne jeglichen Text?

TW Ja, augenblicklich kein Text — nur Bilder und Zeichnungen. Es ist ziemlich rudimentär; lediglich überdeckende Schichten, die sich der Transparenz jeder Schicht anpassen, Flächen ausradieren, andere klonen und sich dann wieder zurückziehen. Ich bin nicht so geschickt und von dem Gefühl, nicht ganz in Kontrolle zu sein, fasziniert. Wiederum meine ich, es ist eine Gelegenheit, daß Bilder im Fluß sind, diesmal jedoch umkehrbar.

DR Vielleicht sollten wir über Porträtmalerei sprechen und wie Sie dazu überredet werden können, jemanden zu malen.

TW Es begann damit, daß ich Bilder von Leuten, die mir etwas bedeuteten, anfertigte — wie ich früher erwähnte — eine Art liebevolle Andenken. Dies entwickelte sich und Leute baten mich, für sie Porträts zu malen, und wie Sie ja wissen, war ich auf diesem Gebiet ganz erfolgreich. Glücklicherweise haben sich die Dinge nun beruhigt und ich male nur das gelegentliche Porträt, das ich malen möchte. Es geschieht ziemlich sporadisch, und so ist es mir am liebsten. Die angenehmsten und ich glaube die erfolgreichsten Porträts sind diejenigen, bei denen ich mit einem sympathischen Modell arbeite; mit jemandem, der etwas Persönliches in das Porträt investiert hat und sich meiner Anliegen bewußt ist — eine Art Partnerschaft, meine ich. Das Porträt von Keith Holmes und Sheila Fairbrass war für mich ein Modell dieser Art. Es war ein langer, ziemlich ausgedehnter Vorgang, bei dem ich eine Anzahl falscher Anfänge unternahm, aber wo sich Geduld und Treue bezahlt machten. Es ist stets ein Glaubensakt auf Seiten des Modells, sie müssen sich verletzbar fühlen. Meine Rolle besteht vielleicht darin, diese Verwundbarkeit zu verstehen, zu versuchen, ihr Vertrauen zu erhalten und am Ende des Tages die Ware zu liefern. Ich muß ehrlich sein und zugeben, daß dies nicht immer leicht ist.

DR Na gut, ich kann sehen, daß Holmes und Fairbrass selbst-gewählte Modelle sind, aber gelegentlich haben Sie Aufträge von außen angenommen. Vermutlich war das mit Alan Bennett der Fall. Hatten Sie Bennett getroffen, ehe Sie gefragt wurden, ihn zu malen?

TW Nein, ich hatte ihn vorher nicht getroffen, aber wie jedermann, habe ich ihn wohl gekannt. Es ist eine große Freude, ihn bei sich zu haben und obwohl ich nicht viel Zeit mit ihm verbrachte, war die kurze Zeit, in der ich mit ihm zusammen war, ein reines Vergnügen Er hatte keinerlei Erwartungen und gab mir totale Freiheit.

DR Ich muß zugeben, daß ich die größeren Porträts bedeutend lieber habe, die zwei Meter großen.

TW Ja, ich glaube Sie haben vielleicht recht, diese gefallen auch mir am besten. Es liegt meinem Anliegen als Maler bestimmt näher, aber manchmal kommt man in eine Situation, wo man ein eigenwilliges Komitee zufriedenstellen muß und das heißt, niemanden zu beleidigen. Es ist nicht das ideale Szenarium.

DR Ich glaube, daß meine Vorliebe sich auf das bei weiten reichere und mehr texturierte Aussehen des größeren Gemäldes bezieht und auch in meinem Gefühl, daß es die Menschen, die man kennengelernt hat, porträtiert, begründet ist. Für mich ist es interessant, daß Sie sich darauf beziehen, daß er Sie in seinem Hause willkommen heißt, denn für mich fangen die größeren Gemälde gesellschaftliche Begegnung und die stille Zwiesprache zwischen Ihnen und Ihrem Modell ein. Während Sie sich in dem anderen Bild auf die Persönlichkeit des öffentlichen Lebens konzentriert haben, wird in diesem Bennett als hervorragender Schriftsteller dargestellt, ein Intellektueller, der leicht befangen vor sich hin schaut: deutlich dargestellt als der posierende Autor im Gegensatz zum Autor, der entspannt ist. Wenden wir uns den Platten 14 und 15 zu: wir schauen hier in eine bei weitem mehr innere Welt, in introspektive Figuren hinein. Hier gibt es etwas Feierliches und Beschauliches . . . Feierlich ist das beste Wort, das ich finden kann, um die Stimmung dieser Gemälde zu beschreiben. Auf der anderen Seite zeigen sie sehr deutlich, was sie zeigen wollen. Das ist Malerei, nicht wahr?

TW Absolut, und in gewisser Hinsicht haben sie das Programm für alle späteren Arbeiten bestimmt. Sie verkörpern, wenn auch in grober Form, meine Versuche, jene Hoffnungen, Ambitionen, Träume und Wünsche, die wir innerlich beherbergen, äußerlich darzustellen. Ich habe versucht, verschiedene Strategien zu benutzen, um dieses mitzuteilen, aber vor allem ist es ein Bild des Körpers oder des Kopfes, gewöhnlich zusammen mit einigen äußeren Formen. Obwohl diese Formen mehrdeutig sind, fordern sie einen Dialog mit dem verzerrten Körper heraus. Unvermeidlicherweise gibt es da Fragen; aber diese können nur im Zusammenhang mit den Hoffnungen, Ambitionen, Träumen und Wünschen des Betrachter selbst beantwortet werden. Das erste Gemälde ist sehr dramatisch, die Figur streckt sich verzweifelt nach oben, als ob sie sich danach sehnt, sich von unsichtbaren Fesseln zu befreien.

DR Auf eine Art geht das/dies auf den Wahrsager zurück, nicht wahr Aber gleich, ob die Figur der Wahrsager, der Alchemist oder der Engel ist, die alleinstehende Figur sind auch Sie?

TW Ja, ich glaube, das ist wirklich so. Viele Aspekte meines Innenlebens werden in der Außenwelt realisiert. Es ist nur ein flüchtiger Blick, ein Fragment, nicht die ganze Geschichte, sozusagen. Wenn ich darüber sehr nachdenken würde, *Allein stehend* ist wahrscheinlich ein Gemälde von jemanden, der seine mittleren Jahre erreicht hat

und sich isoliert, frustriert und enttäuscht fühlt, der sich nach den Träumen, die er als junger Mann hatte, als er auf einem Hügel in Halifax stand, sehnt und der die Welt, die er erobern wollte, entweichen sieht; ein trauriges, romantisches elegisches Gedicht über den Tod der Hoffnung.

DR Uns wird hier etwas vorgestellt, das Sie in den folgenden Bildern weiterentwickeln. Ich kann das nur als bewußte Verzerrung der Züge beschreiben, als ob die Figuren gegen eine Glasscheibe gestoßen und von ihr wegezogen würden. Denken Sie in Begriffen der Verzerrung?

TW Nein, so denke ich nicht. Ich stelle ein Bild her und dann benutze ich Rollen und meine Hände, um andere Materialien hineinzudrücken, da kann es sich um Stückchen von einem Teppich, Papier, Wellpappe, Teppichunterlagen und Plastik handeln, tatsächlich alles, was das Bild erheben und übertragen kann. Dann gibt es das lange Verfahren des dauernden Machens, des Hochhebens, des Übertragens, des Abstimmens und der Neuerschaffung des Bildes. Dies dauert eine lange Zeit und wie ich schon sagte, es ist mehr intuitiv als geplant. Zu diesem Zeitpunkt kann sich das Bild ändern und radikal umformen, alles ist vollkommen in Fluß. Wenn man da eine Figur sieht, dann ist diese Figur vielleicht zehnmal im Bilde herumbewegt worden und was man sieht, ist der fragmentarische Rest früherer Entscheidungen. Schließlich erreicht es eine Art Resolution und ich nehme an, es ist nur eine Erweiterung dessen, was Bacon mit seinen Figuren unternahm, aber spezifischer, was er mit seinem Kopftriptychon tat.

DR Aber Sie versagen sich auch Ihren bleibenden Eindruck, das Unverwechselbare Ihrer Hand.

TW Ich möchte das Autogramm, die Unterschrift, die ich-bezogene Geste vermeiden. Wie ich früher erwähnte, das Bild sollte sich entwickeln, sollte zusammenkommen und nicht aufgetragen werden. Es marschiert nicht unerbittlich vorwärts, der Vollendung zu. Es schwenkt rückwärts und vorwärts, es wird eher angepirscht als gejagt. Demzufolge verliere ich wahrscheinlich so viel, wie ich behalte, meine Gemälde sind für mich daher immer fragmentarisch. Selbst die großen Gemälde scheinen mir Fragmente eines größeren Ganzen zu sein. Ich stelle mir immer vor, daß sie über ihre Ränder hinausgehen Als ich als Student einige Landschaften malte, war für mich immer die Schwierigkeit, wo die Ränder sein sollten. Wie man all die visuellen und sinnlichen Informationen in solch einem kleinen Rechteck einfassen konnte. Als ich *Überschwemmungan der Westküste* malte, das eine große Arbeit ist, habe ich es mir als eine Art Blick durch einen engen Schlitz vorgestellt.

Ich dachte an John Martin und seine apokalyptischen Visionen, aber auch an viele andere Dinge von Frederick Churchs Panoramen zu Caspar David Friedrich bis hin zu Coppolas Schlußszenen in *Apocalypse Now*.

DR Und wie steht es mit *So wie der Rauch aufsteigt, sinken die Bienen?* Woher kommt dieser Satz?

TW Beide Titel *So wie der Rauch aufsteigt, sinken die Bienen und In meiner Wüste gibt es einen Spiegel* sind Erfindungen, sind meine eigenen Sätze, die wie Zitate klingen sollen. In Krisenzeiten sprechen wir uns Trost in Form von Aphorismen zu, z.B. 'Das war vielleicht am besten' oder 'Die Zeit heilt alles' und 'Morgen ist ein neuer Tag'.

DR Da sehen wir also in ein Loch im Boden und wir sehen wiederum nichts?

TW Sie schaut ins Leere. In dieser Landschaft nach einem Atominferno besitzt sie nur einen dünnen Schleier, um sich zu be schützen.

DR Das Netz eines Imkers?

TW Vielleicht ein Netz und vielleicht stellen die regelmäßigen Striche im Rauch Bienen dar, aber es handelt sich nicht um ein Gemälde über Bienen.

DR Sie würden wohl Ähnliches über das Werk *Roter Engel* sagen, nicht wahr?

TW Ja, diese Figuren schauen in ihre Hände, sie sind auf eine Art blind. Sie suchen nach etwas, und obwohl es überall Hinweise gibt, werden sie es nie finden. Bei den Wüstenbildern handelt es sich vor allem um Verlust. In der öden Landschaft, die diese Figuren bewohnen, hängt ihre Hoffnung an diesen verworrenen Zeichen, von denen sie etwas erfahren könnten, falls sie sie nur finden könnten, aber das ist unwahrscheinlich.

DR Und was läßt sich über *Geschichtsgemälde* sagen?

TW Es ist ein Gemälde, das seinen Ursprung darin hat, daß ich über die Arbeiten von George Catlin und seine Bilder von den eingeborenen Amerikanern nachdachte. Ich nehme an, sie sind Beispiele früher Ethnographie. Sie veranschaulichen die Notwendigkeit zu studieren, aufzuzeichnen und zu kategorisieren. Ich habe ein unangenehmes Gefühl dabei, zu welchen Bewertungen eine solche Studie kommen würde. Da scheint es notwendig zu sein, entweder zu verdammen oder zu loben. *Geschichtsgemälde* sollte eines einer langen Reihe von Arbeiten sein, die diese Erwägung in Betracht ziehen, aber es blieb bei dem einen Gemälde.

DR Aber währender seine Aufgabe als dokumentarisch ansah, genaue Aufzeichnungen über die verschiedenen Indianerstämme anzufertigen, erfinden Sie, verlassen sich auf die Kraft Ihrer Phantasie.

TW Ich halte es für notwendig, um Ideen herum zu erfinden, anstatt zu versuchen aufzuzeichnen. Die Figur ist so gemalt, als ob sie einmal eine sepiafarbene Fotografie war. Vielleicht ein Indianer mit seinem Kopfschmuck, mit seiner noch unverletzten Würde.

DR Nein, das sehe ich. Ich sehe auch, daß Sie noch messen, und dies bringt uns schließlich zu den 'Mensch und Maß' — Gemälden, in denen die Maße am

Rahmen befestigt sind, aber sie bilden ein gesondertes Element, Teil des ganzen Bildes, aber nicht in der bemalten Fläche.

TW **Diese Maße sind neben den Gemälden, wie Sie sagen, nicht in ihnen. Aber sie sind immer gesondert, von außen her aufgezwungen, Jetzt sind sie ganz und gar unnachgiebige, massive, geometrische Formen, für mich haben sie ein quasi-industrielles Gefühl.**

DR Sie könnten in einer Fabrik lackiert worden sein.

TW **Genau. Diese Figuren können nicht entkommen, sie haben keine Gelegenheit für Mitgefühl, sie sind die vollkommenen Opfer ihrer Maße. Als solche sind sie verwundbar und unbequem. In *Mensch und Maß II* befindet sich der Rest eines Zifferblattes, einer Art des Messens. In *Mensch und Maß III* mag das Erscheinen einer Maske wohl einen gewissen Verlust darstellen, eine Verschlechterung der Identität, ein Teil des Zerbrechens des Selbst. Ein Text von Befehlen, schreienden Ermahnungen ist unterhalb der Oberfläche geschrieben. Sie sind wie Befehle, mit denen das Opfer angebellt wird, von denen nur unverständliche Fragmente gesehen werden können. Ein solches Fragment sagt 'kein Haar', als ob dies eine Kategorie sei, in die er eingeordnet würde. Eine Kategorie, die in sich selbst bedeutungslos ist, aber sie bietet vielleicht anderen Trost, da sie eine Art von unechter Hierarchie begründet.**

DR Interessehalber, beruhen diese Figuren auf einem Modell?

TW **Ich arbeite mit einer Anzahl von Leuten. Ich zeichne, um die Figur zu verstehen und mich an sie zu erinnern. Ich male sehr selten nach den Zeichnungen. Ich nehme eine Menge Fotografien und benutze sie, aber die Verfahren, die ich benutze, bedeuten, daß das Bild unvermeidlicherweise dramatisch von den Fotografien abweicht. Die Fotografie ist mehr eine Gedächtnisstütze. Ich habe wirklich viel Spaß an der Möglichkeit, diese Unfälle und Zufälle, die zu diesen Verfahren gehören, auszunutzen.**

DR Sie sprechen darüber, daß Sie auf oder in die Leinwand schreiben, aber die Schriftzeichen, die man hier findet, sind graffitiähnliche Zeichen.

TW **Mein Geschmack ist ziemlich vielseitig. Ich bewege mich von der aszetischen Klassik des Ben Nicholson bis zur geschwollenen Rhetorik des John Martin und der New York Angst des Ross Bleckner. Ich weiche von einem Extrem zum anderen. Extreme gefallen mir. In diesem Stück *Reflektion* befindet sich für mich das Gefühl eines Treffens von Nicholson mit Matisse. Obwohl es *Reflektion* heißt, sind die beiden Köpfe ganz verschieden.**

DR Mir gefällt hier die Tiefe, die eine Tiefe zu sein scheint, die man mehr, der Farbe als dem Raum zu verdanken hat.

TW **Das kommt zum großen Teil von der Art der Bearbeitung. Ich habe Pastell mit Ölfarbe und Tinte benutzt, so daß sie sich zwischen Zeichnung und Gemälde befinden. Es ist alles ziemlich intuitiv und unmittelbar. Ich hoffe, daß sie etwas von der Energie einer spontanen Zeichnung behalten. Die kalligrafischen Linien und Spritzer, die schroff eindringen, sind für mich wie das Knistern ausgelöster Energie.**

DR Und was bedeutet der Schrein innerhalb der Einfriedung? Ihre Einfriedungen faszinieren mich; jene Zufluchtsorte, die als kleine Häuser begannen, werden dann . . .

TW **Tabernakel.**

DR Ja, das ist genau das richtige Wort, denn das Gebäude hat nun eine quasi-religiöse Bedeutung angenommen. Vielleicht zurück zur 'heiligen Stadt von Byzanz.

TW **Vielleicht, bestimmt mittelmeerländisch, vielleicht eine Kapelle am Straßenrand. Alle diese Stücke *Schrein, Reflektion, Blinder Mann* und *Schatten* sehe ich als eine Serie. Sie haben alle Köpfe, Horizonte, die Landschaften andeuten und Einfriedungen, dereiner oder anderen Art. Der blinde Mann ist in der Einfriedung seiner eigenen Blindheit und findet sich in der Welt unter anderem mittels Zählen zurecht. Für ihn sind Zahlen, und damit meine ich Messen, lebenswichtig.**

DR Da gibt es Andeutungen von Labyrinthen, architektonischen Zeichnungen, Versuche, räumliche Probleme zu lösen.

TW **Wie in einem Plan. Der Unterschied zwischen dem Lesen einer Reise auf der Landkarte und dem Wandern desselben Weges. Sie sind zwei verschiedene Erlebnisse von Raum und Zeit.**

DR Die Toledo Serie. Ich glaube, Sie arbeiteten daran, als ich Sie im vergangenen Sommer in Ihrem Studio in Dean Clough besuchte.

TW **Ja, das stimmt, an diesen und am Gemälde *Anschauen El Grecos*. Die eine Konstante, die durch all diese läuft, ist die Silhouette meines Kopfes. Ich diene als Zeuge, der in den Fußstapfen der Pilger reist, und die Werke zeichnen die Reise auf. Sie sind ebenfalls ein Versuch, mein Vokabular der Formen zu erweitern, einen Weg zu finden, die gesehenen und gefühlten Dinge zu notieren, ohne auf meine eigenen Konventionen zurückgreifen zu müssen. Sie handeln vom Erfinden und Erforschen von Motiven und den Versuch ihnen Bedeutung zu verleihen.**

DR Wohin hat sie die Fahrt nach Toledo geführt?

TW **Es hat mich zum Interesse am Katholizismus zurückgeführt, an der Version, die in den verrenkten Barockvisionen El Grecos veranschaulicht ist. Nicht als praktizierender Katholik, sondern mehr als Zuschauer, der nach Bildern fischt.**

DR *Ertrinken in der Wüste* scheint zu den Serien vor Toledo zu gehören. Es ist ein sehr großes Bild, und es ist sehr eindrucksvoll in seiner physischen

Gegenwart, wenn maln es an der Wand hängen sieht, wie ich es einmal in der Galerie Hart sah.

TW **Ja, es hat eine Art Gegenwart.**

DR Sie scheinen nicht zu überzeugt?

TW **Nein, nicht, daß ich nicht überzeugt bin, ich versuche nur einige Worte zu finden, die dazu passen. Es ist scheinbar ein so einfaches Gemälde in solch einem großen Maßstab; es ist schwierig zu wissen, wo man beginnen soll. Ich habe es mir als eine ungeheuer große, öde Landschaft vorgestellt, eine Wüste, in der man sterben, ertrinken, verschwinden oder buchstäblich sich auflösen könnte und nur einen Fleck zurückließe. Diese Ikarus-ähnliche Figur gleitet herunter, verflüssigt sich im Sande und hinterläßt nur eine offene, öde Landschaft. Vielleicht bilden diese beiden Tafeln eine Szene oder vielleicht sind sie eine Art Davor und Danach. Auf alle Fälle, als Ganzes stellen sie eine Figur am Rande einer Katastrophe dar, die scheinbar eine furchterregende Einsamkeit übersteht.**

DR Das klingt sehr wahr. Man hat mir gesagt, daß das bemerkenswerteste Erlebnis in der Wüste der Verlust des Größenmaßstabes ist. Ich vermute, in der anscheinend endlosen Wüste, die sich soweit man sehen kann bis an die Enden der sichtbaren Ferne erstreckt, gibt es keine Norm des Messens. Letzten Endes ist man gezwungen, an seinen eigenen Wahrnehmungsfähigkeiten zu zweifeln.

TW **Und auch an seiner eigene Relevanz und Sterblichkeit. Es muß ein furchterregendes Erlebnis sein-endlose Einsamkeit.**

DR Ich merke, Sie wollen zum Ende kommen. Ich war gerade dabei, zugegebenermaßen provokatorisch, hinzuzufügen, daß Messen im Zusammenhang ungewisser Räume vielleicht ein Trost sein könnte, ein Mittel um Gewißheit und Maßstab wiederherzustellen. Der Mensch war nie zuversichtlicher als er der Renaissance, als er der Mittelpunkt des bekannten Weltalls und das Maß aller Dinge wurde. Damit und nachdem ich Ihnen gedankt habe, daß sie so geduldig auf meine Fragen eingegangen ind, bestehe ich darauf, daß Sie das letzte Wort haben.

TW **Voriges Jahr habe ich auf ein Bild geschrieben: 'Bringe keine Wahrheiten! Erzähle keine Lügen!' Dabei bleibe ich immer noch.**

List of Colour Plates
Planchesdecouleur
Farbbilder

pl. 1
The Family, 1985–1990
La Famille
Die Familie
Oil and acrylic on canvas. 48" × 60", (122 × 152.5 cm).
Glasgow Art Gallery and Museum.

pl. 2
Saskla, 1990
Saskia
Saskia
Oil on paper. 18" × 24", (46 × 61 cm).
Private Collection.

pl. 3
Elinor with Red Bowl, 1990
Elinor avec Bassine Rouge
Elinor mit Roter Schüssel
Oil on paper. 12" × 30", (30.5 × 76.5 cm).
Private Collection.

pl. 4
The Red Tourist, 1990
Le Touriste Rouge
Der Rote Tourist
Oil on board. 53½" × 47½", (136 × 120.5 cm).
Private Collection.

pl. 5
A Museum Incident, 1990
Incident dans un Musée
Museumsvorsall
Oil on board. 47½" × 53½", (120.5 × 136 cm)
Wakefield City Art Gallery.

pl. 6
Red Vessel/White Bowl, 1991
Recipient Rouge/Bassine Blanche
Rotes Gefäss/Weisse Schüssell
Monoprint. 11½" × 16¼", (29 × 41 cm)
Private Collection.

pl. 7
Collage, 1991
Collage
Collage
Collage. 17" × 24", (43 × 61 cm)
Private Collection.

pl. 8
White Bowl, 1990
Bassine Blanche
Weisse Schüssel
Linocut (Edition of 5). 18" × 16", (46 × 40.5 cm)
Private Collection.

pl. 9
The Green Book, 1991
Le Livre Vert
Das Grüue Buch
Linocut (Edition of 5). 18" × 18", (46 × 40.5 cm)
Private Collection.

pl. 10
Portrait of Rosie and Peter Hart, 1991
Portrait de Rosie et Peter Hart
Portrait von Rosie und Peter Hart
Oil on board. 25½" × 29½", (65 × 75 cm)
Private Collection.

pl. 11
Portrait of Keith Holmes and Sheila Fairbrass — Conservators
Portrait de Keith Holmes et Sheila Fairbrass — Conservateurs
Portrait von Keith Holmes und Sheila Fairbrass — Konservatoren
Oil on panel. 72" × 72", (183 × 183 cm)
Private Collection.

pl. 12
Portrait of Alan Bennett, 1993
Portrait d'Alan Bennett
Portrait von Alan Bennett
Oil on panel. 43½" × 48", (110.5 × 122 cm)
The National Portrait Gallery.

pl. 13
Portrait of Alan Bennett, 1992
Portrait d'Alan Bennett
Portrait von Alan Bennett
Oil on panel. 72" × 72", (183 × 183 cm)

pl. 14
Alchemist in Search of The Voice, 1992
Alchemiste Chercant la Voix
Alchemist auf der Suche nach der Stimme
Linocut (Edition of 4). 63" × 42", (136 × 120.5 cm)
Private Collection.

pl. 15
Standing Alone, 1991
Etant seul
Alleinstehend
Oil on board. 53½" × 47½", (136 × 120.5 cm)
Private Collection.

pl. 16
Soldier/Grill, 1992
Soldat/Grille
Soldat/Gitter
Oil on card. 20" × 30", (51 × 76.5 cm)
Private Collection.

pl. 17
Philosopher Soldier, 1992
Soldat Philosophe
Philosophen soldat
Oil on card. 30" × 40", (76.5 × 101.5 cm)
Private Collection.

pl. 18
Fossil Man and Lyre, 1992
Homme Fossile et Lyre
Fossilienmann und Lyra
Oil on panel. 60" × 72", (152.5 × 183 cm)

pl. 19
Tomorrow and Tomorrow and Tomorrow, 1993
Demain et Demain et Demain
Morgen und Morgen und Morgen
Oil on panel. 68" × 72", (173 × 183 cm)
Private Collection.

pl. 20
Into The Ether To Dissolve, 1992
Daus l'Ether Afin de se Dossoudre
In deu Äther um sich Aufzulösen
Oil on paper. 73" × 24", (185.5 × 61 cm)
Private Collection.

pl. 21
The Night Museum, 1992
Le Musée de Nuit
Das Nachtmuseum
Oil on paper. 73" × 24", (185.5 × 61 cm)
Private Collection.

pl. 22
Tattoo Man 1, 1993
Homme Tatoué 1
Tätowierter Mann 1
Oil on paper. 20" × 15", (51 × 38 cm)
Private Collection.

pl. 23
Tattoo Man 2, 1993
Homme Tatoué 2
Tätowierter Mann 2
Oil on paper. 20" × 15", (51 × 38 cm)
Private Collection.

pl. 24
Angel 3, 1993
Ange 3
Engel 3
Oil on paper on board. 43½" × 48", (110.5 × 122 cm)
Private Collection.

pl. 25
Redemption, 1993
Rédempton
Erlösung
Oil on paper on board. 43½" × 48", (110.5 × 122 cm)
Private Collection.

pl. 26
Detail of plate 27
Detail
Ausschnitt

pl. 27
Parable, 1993-94
Parabole
Parabel
Oil on panel with neon. 72" × 134", (183 × 340 cm)

pl. 28
Red Angel, 1993
Ange Rouge
Roter Engel
Oil on panel. 48" × 43½", (122 × 110.5 cm)
Private Collection.

pl. 29
Lucca, 1994
Lucca
Lucca
Oil on paper on board. 45" × 23½", (114.5 × 60 cm)
Private Collection.

pl. 30
Head in Shadow Study, 1994
Tête en étude d'hombre
Kopf in Schattenstudie
Oil on paper. 13" × 15¼", (33 × 38.5 cm)
Private Collection.

pl. 31
Singer, 1994
Chanteur
Sänger
Oil on paper. 13" × 15¼", (33 × 38.5 cm)
Private Collection.

pl. 32
Dreaming of Colours, 1994
En Rêvant de Couleurs
Von Farben Träumend
Oil on panel. 21" × 23½", (53.5 × 59.5 cm)

pl. 33
Diva, 1994
Diva
Diva
Oil on panel. 21" × 23½", (53.5 × 59.5 cm)
Private Collection.

pl. 34
In My Desert There is a Mirror, 1993
Dans Mon Désert il y a un Miroir
In Meiner Wüste ist ein Spiegel
Oil on panel. 72" × 67", (183 × 170 cm)
Private Collection.

pl. 35
As Smoke Rises So Bees Sink
Comme la Fumée Monte les Abeilles Descendent
Wie Ranch Aufsteigt so Sinken die Bienen
Oil on panel. 72" × 67", (183 × 170 cm)
Private Collection.

pl. 36
Detail of plate 37
Detail
Ausschnitt

pl. 37
West Coast Deluge, 1994
West Coast Deluge
West Coast Sinnflut
Oil on panel. 72" × 134", (183 × 340 cm)

pl. 38
Looking at El Greco, 1995
En Regardant El Greco
El Greco Betrachtend
Oil on paper on board. 43½" × 48", (110.5 × 122 cm)

pl. 39
Miracle, 1994-5
Miracle
Wunder
Oil on paper on board. 48" × 43", (122 × 109 cm)

pl. 40
Furnace, 1994-5
Fourneau
Ofen
Oil on paper on board and perspex. 48" × 43½", (122 × 110 cm)

pl. 41
Burning Up, 1994-5
Brûlant
Verbrennend
Oil on paper on board and perspex. 48" × 43½", (122 × 110 cm)
Private Collection.

pl. 42
Old Science 4. Old Science 5, 1993
Vielle Science 4. Vielle Science 5
Alte Wissenschaft 4. Alte Wissenschaft 5
Oil on paper on board and perspex. 18" × 14", (46 × 35.5 cm) (each)
Private Collection.

pl. 43
Old Science 2, 1993
Vielle Science 2
Alte Wissenschaft 2
Oil on paper on board and perspex. 14" × 18", (35.5 × 46 cm)
Private Collection.

pl. 44
Man and Measure 1, 1993
Homme et Mesure 1
Mensch und Mass 1
Oil on paper on board and perspex. 48" × 43½" (122 × 110 cm)
Private Collection.

pl. 45
History Painting, 1994
Peinture d'Histoire
Beschichts Gemälde
Oil on paper on board. 48" × 43½", (122 × 110 cm)
Private Collection.

pl. 46
Man and Measure 2, 1994
Homme et Mesure 2
Mensch und Mass 2
Oil on panel and wood. 72" × 80", (183 × 203 cm)
Private Collection.

pl. 47
Man and Measure 3, 1994
Homme et Mesure 3
Mensch und Mass 3
Oil on panel and wood. 72" × 80", (183 × 203 cm)
Private Collection.

pl. 48
Shrine, 1995
Lieu de Pélérinage
Schrein
Mixed media on paper. 27½" × 39", (70 × 99 cm)
Private Collection.

pl. 49
Reflection, 1995
Réflection
Reflektion
Mixed media on paper. 27½" × 39", (70 × 99 cm)
Private Collection.

pl. 50
Angel, 1995
Ange
Engel
Mixed media on paper. 27½" × 39", (70 × 99 cm)
Private Collection.

pl. 51
Doppelgänger, 1995
Doppelgänger
Doppelgänger
Mixed media on paper. 27½" × 39", (70 × 99 cm)

pl. 52
Blind Man, 1995
Homme aveugle
Blinder Mann
Mixed media on paper. 27½" × 39", (70 × 99 cm)

pl. 53
Shadow, 1995
Hombre
Schatten
Mixed media on paper. 27½" × 39", (70 × 99 cm)

pl. 54
Toledo 1, 1995
Toledo 1
Toledo 1
Mixed media on paper. 19½" × 27", (49.5 × 68.5 cm)

pl. 55
Toledo 2, 1995
Toledo 2
Toledo 2
Mixed media on paper. 19½" × 27", (49.5 × 68.5 cm)

pl. 56
Toledo 5, 1995
Toledo 5
Toledo 5
Mixed media on paper. 19½" × 27", (49.5 × 68.5 cm)

pl. 57
Toledo 3, 1995
Toledo 3
Toledo 3
Mixed media on paper. 19½" × 27", (49.5 × 68.5 cm)

pl. 58
Detail of plate 59
Detail
Ausschnitt

pl. 59
Drowning in a Desert, 1994
Se Noyant dans un Désert
In Einer Wüste Ertrinkend
Oil on panel. 72" × 134", (183 × 340 cm)

pl. 60
Cathedral, 1994-5
Cathédrale
Kathedrale
Oil on panel. 72" × 67", (183 × 170 cm)

Plate 1 *(Opposite)*

The Family, 1985–1990
Oil and Acrylic on Canvas
48 × 60 inches
Glasgow Art Gallery and Museum

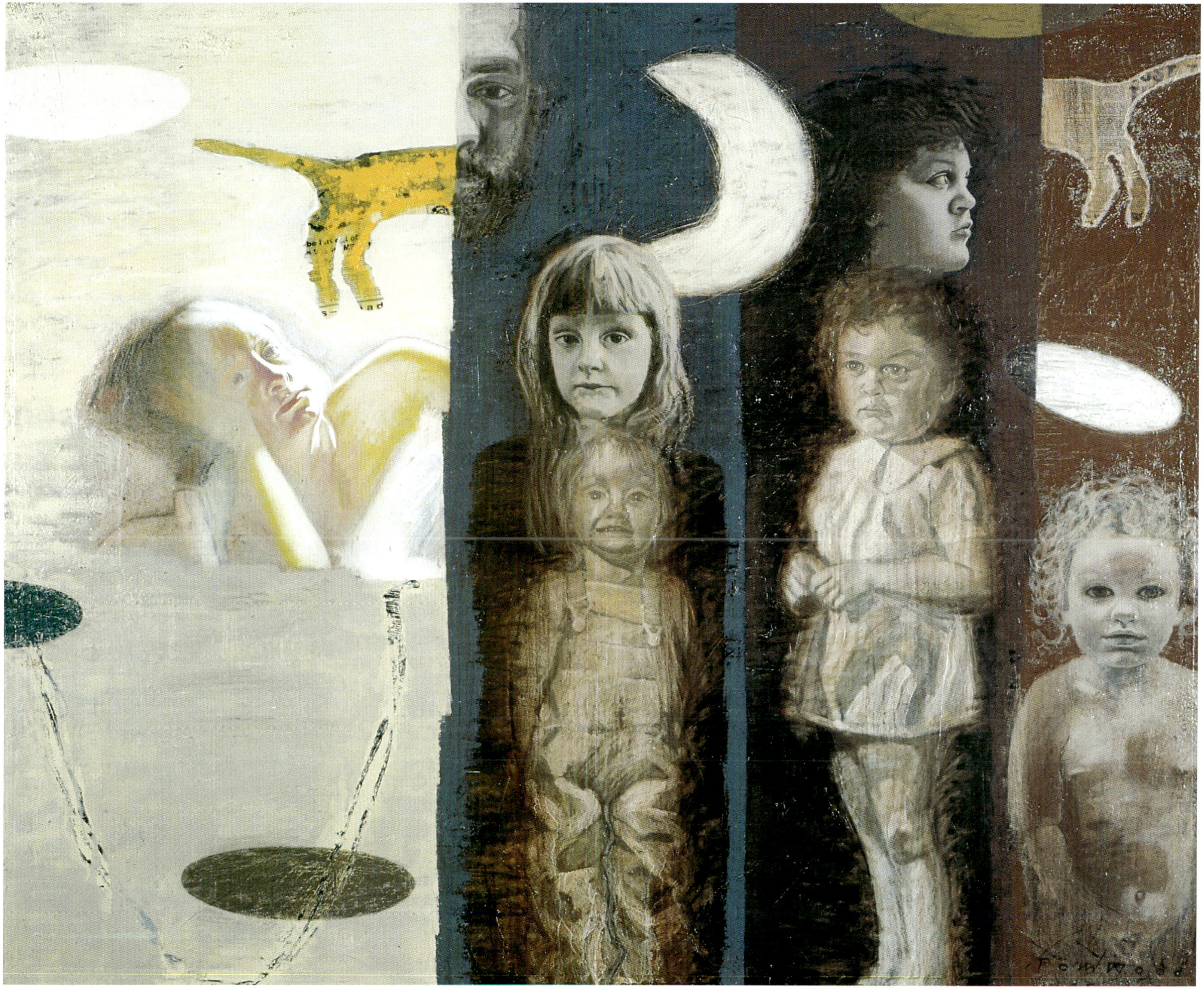
Tom Wood

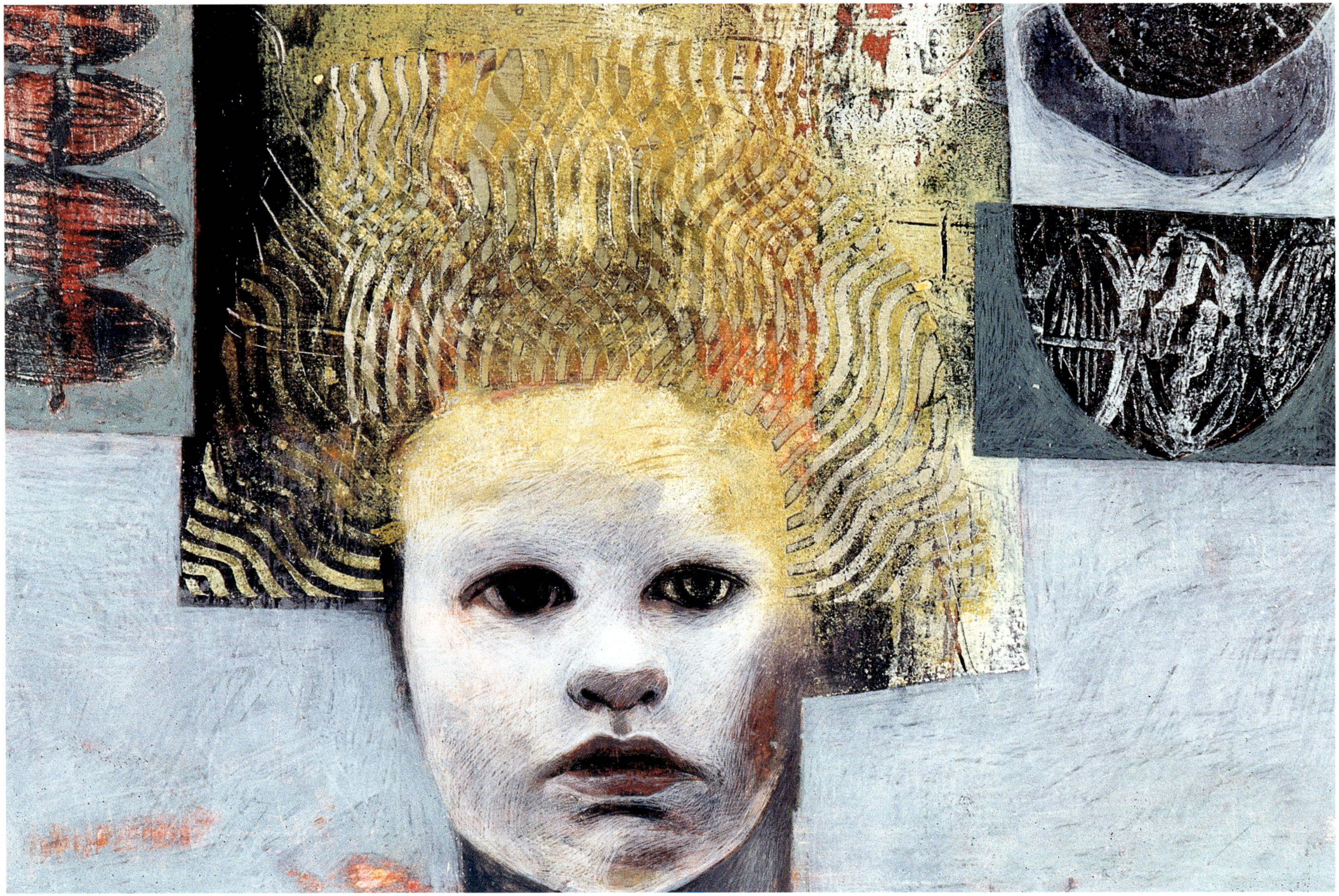

Plate 2

Saskia 1990.
Oil on Paper
18 × 24 inches
Private Collection

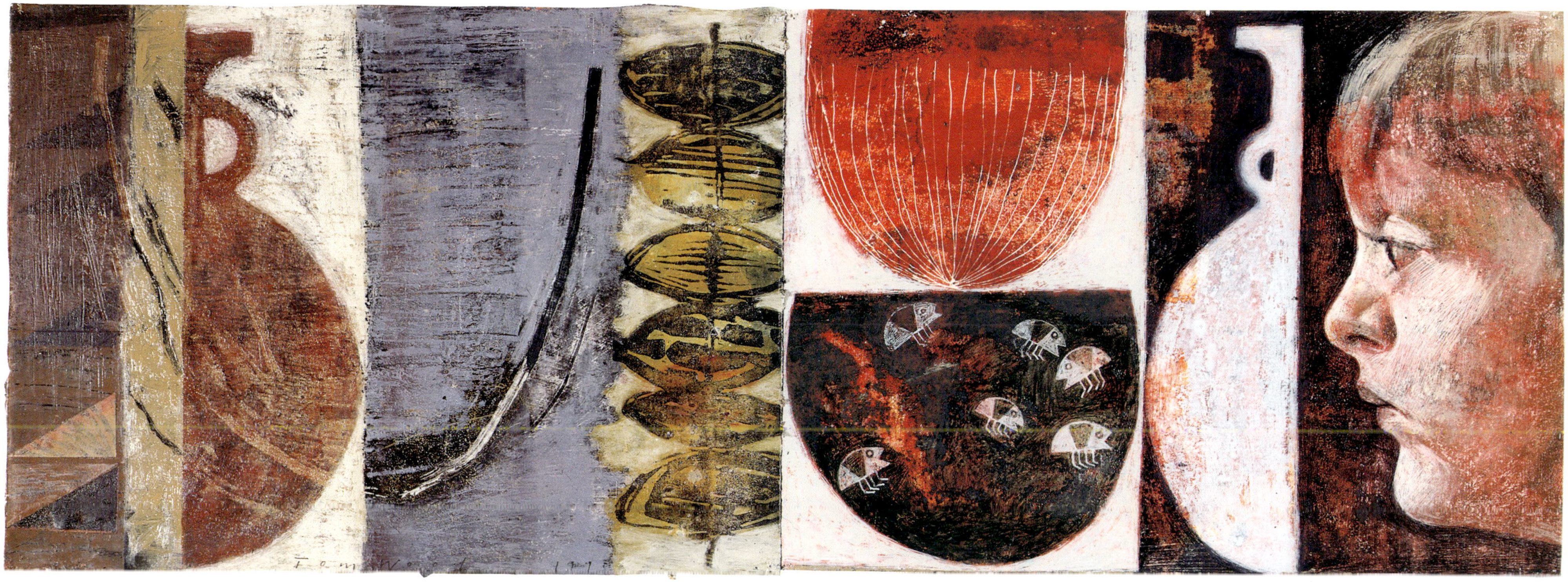

Plate 3

Elinor with Red Bowl 1990.
Oil on Paper
12 × 30 inches
Private Collection

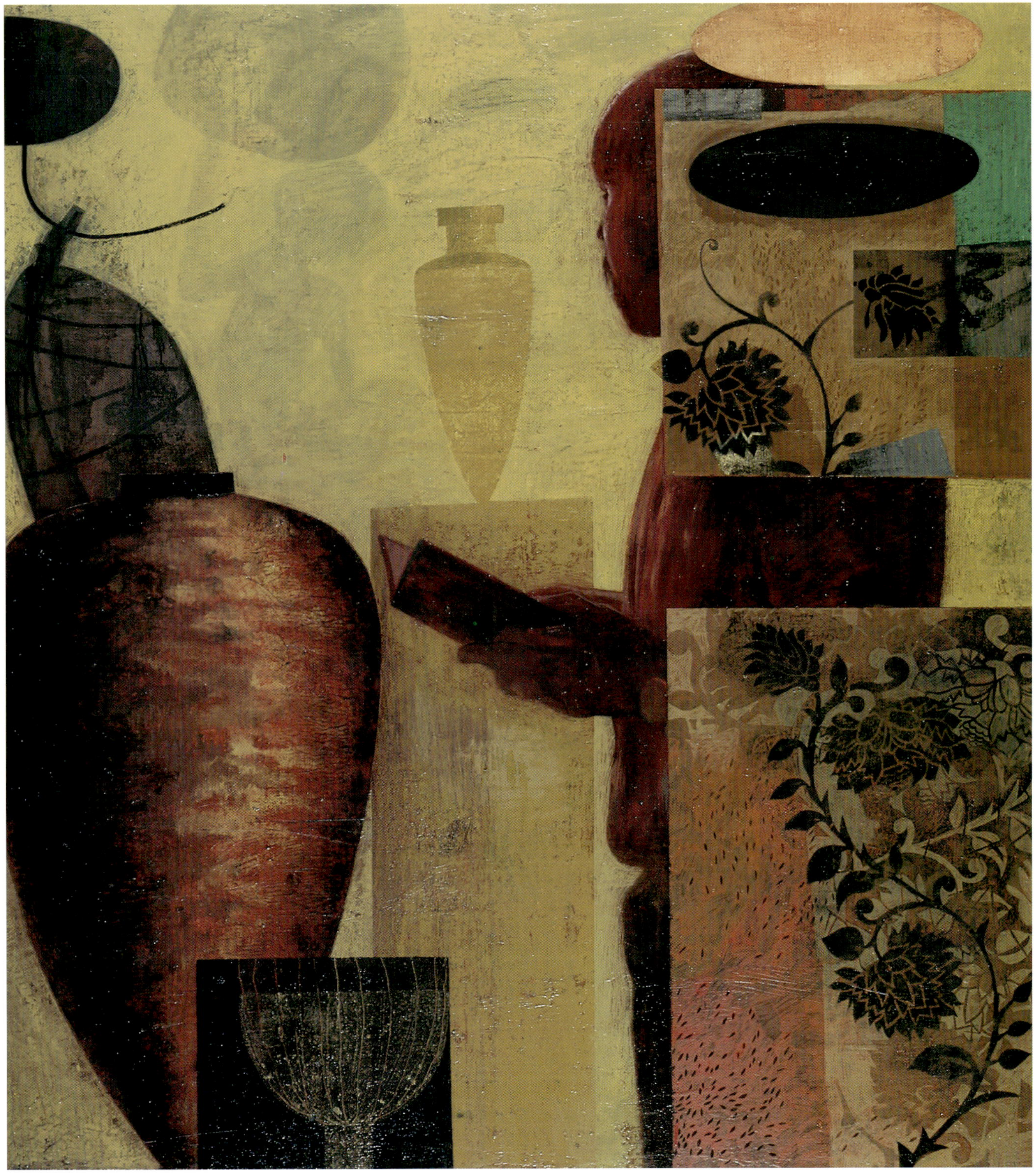

Plate 4

The Red Tourist 1990.
Oil on Board
$53\frac{1}{2} \times 47\frac{1}{2}$ inches
Private Collection

Plate 5 *(Opposite)*

A Museum Incident 1990.
Oil on Board
$47\frac{1}{2} \times 53\frac{1}{2}$ inches
Wakefield City Art Gallery

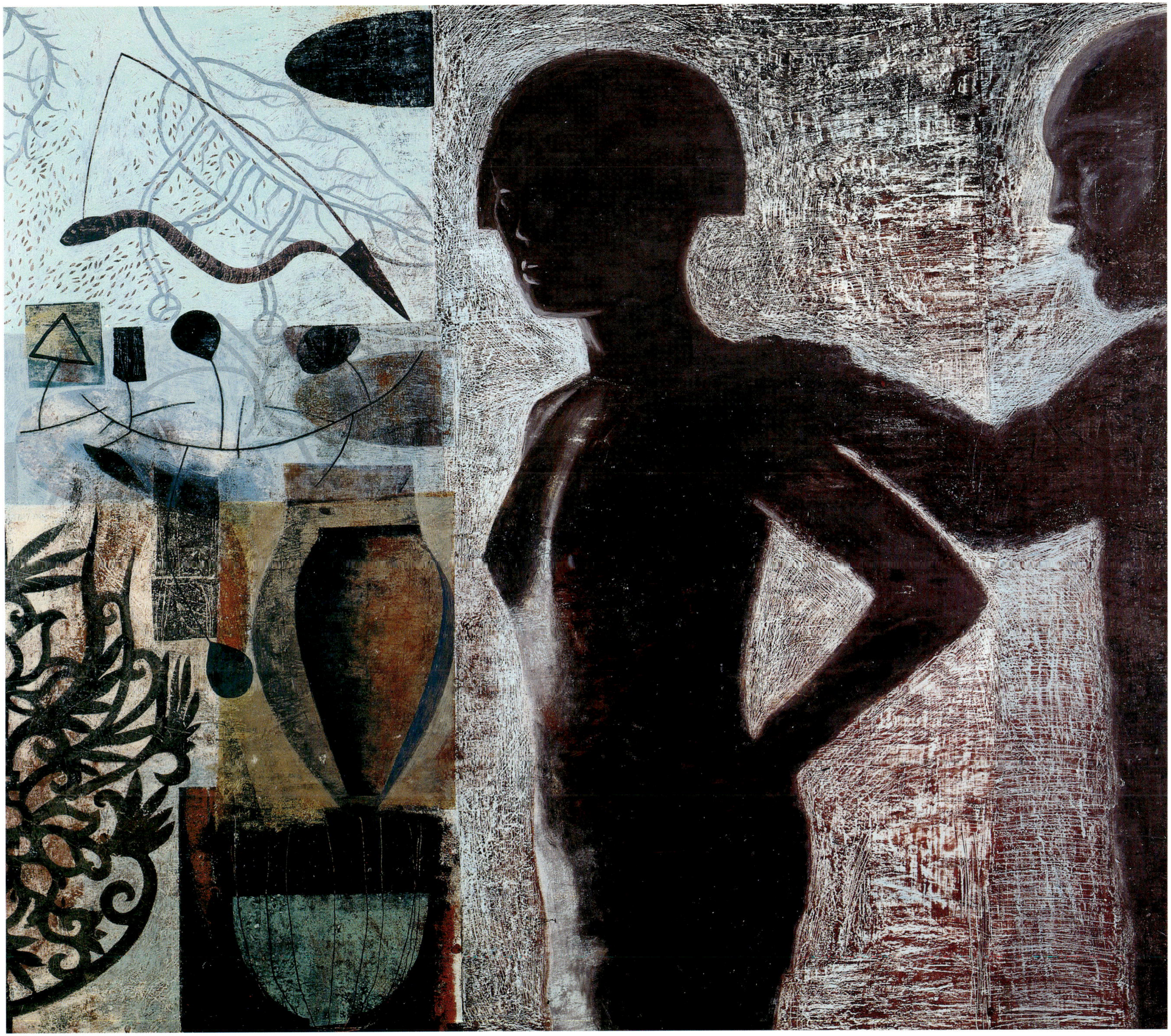

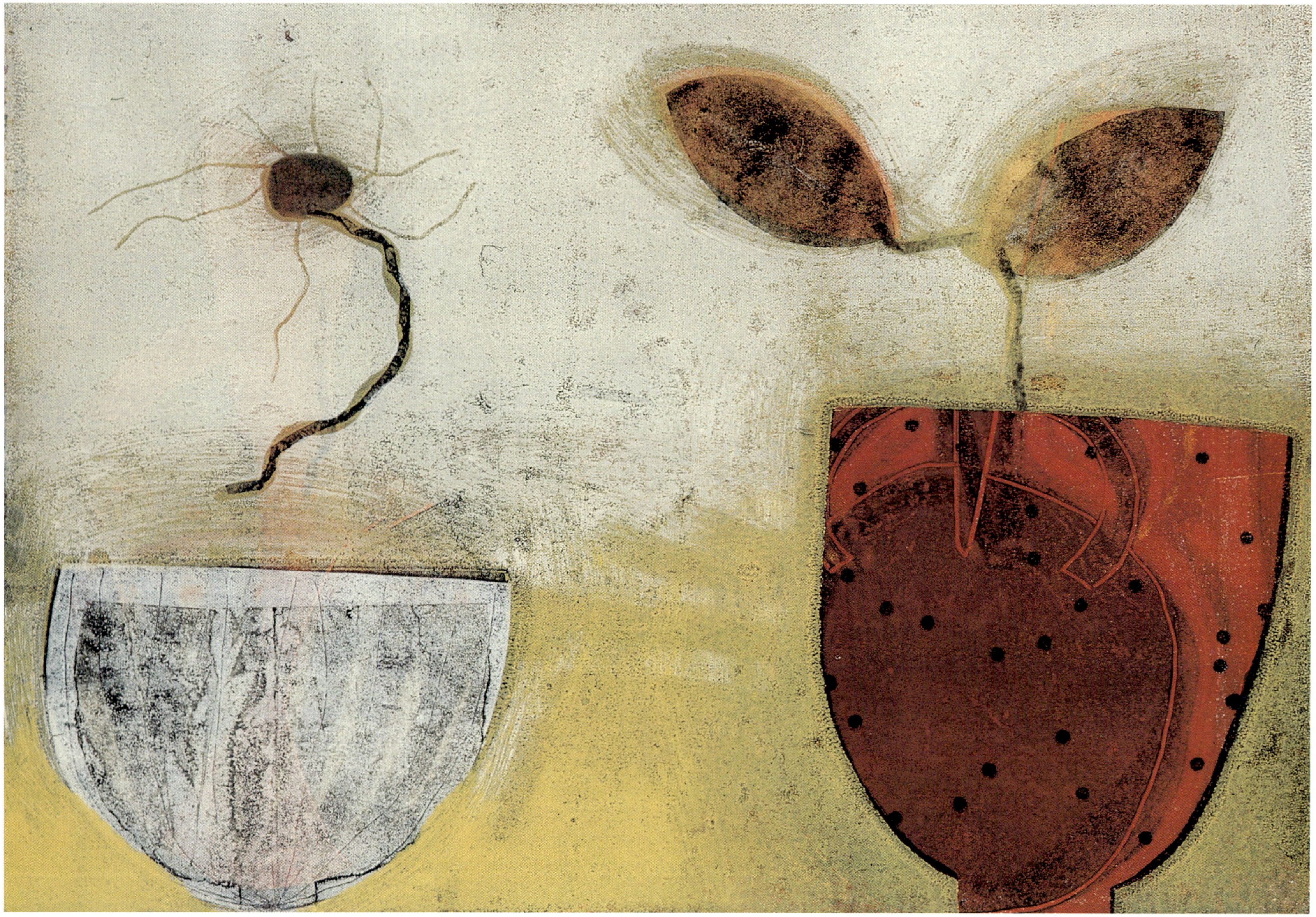

Plate 6

Red Vessel/White Bowl 1991
Monoprint
$11\frac{1}{2} \times 16\frac{1}{2}$ inches
Private Collection

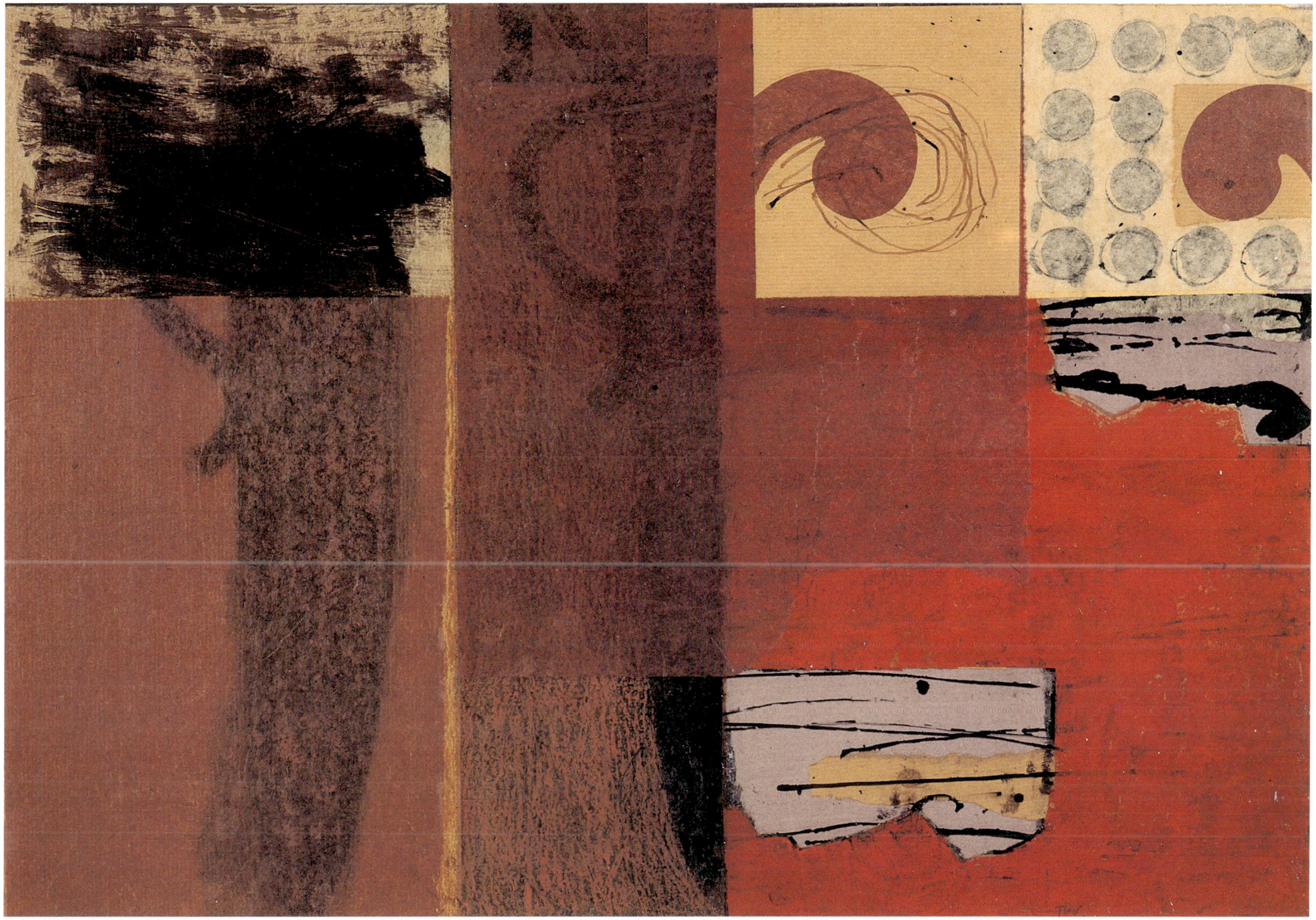

Plate 7

Collage 1991
Collage
17 × 24 inches
Private Collection

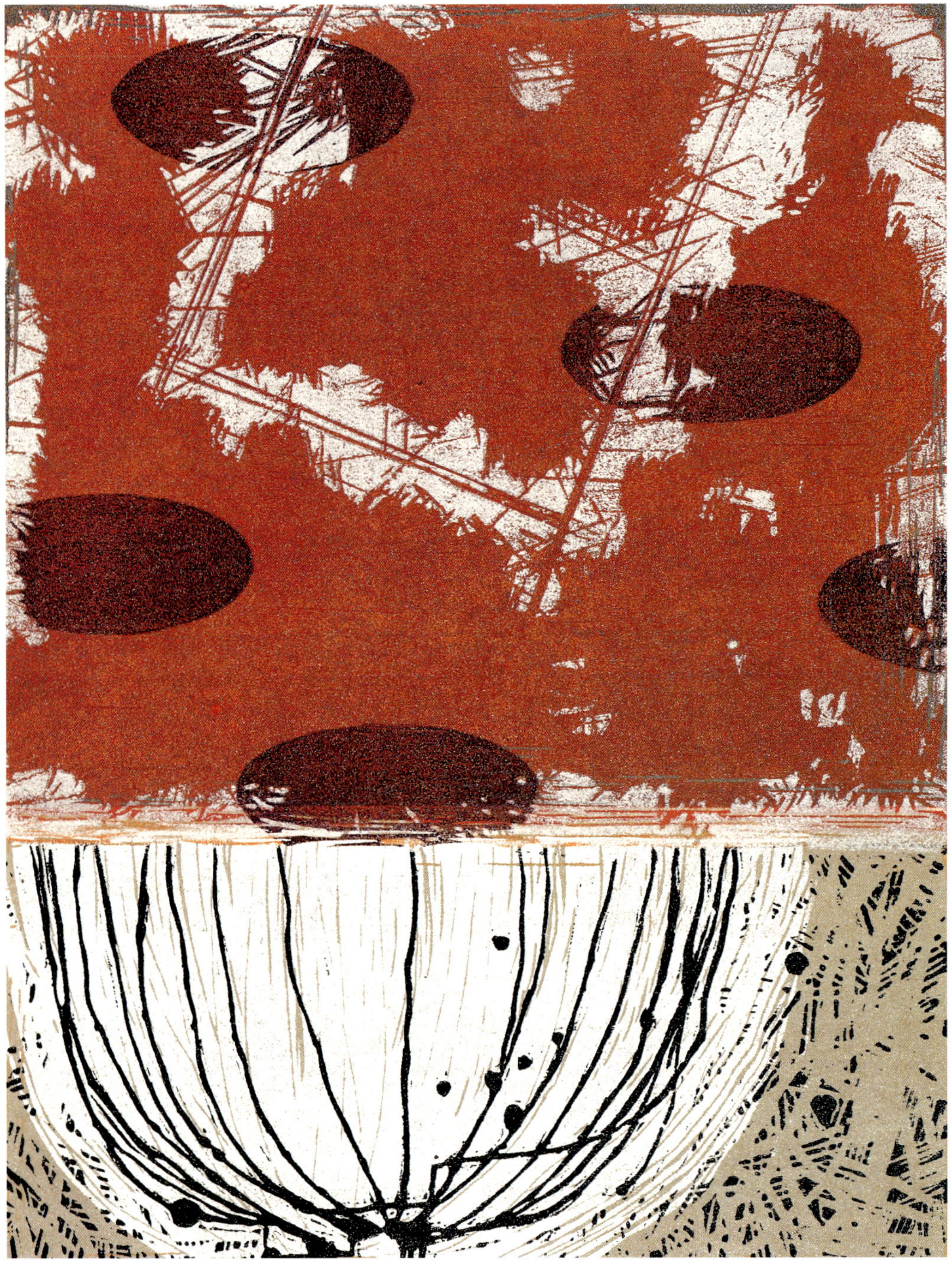

Plate 8

White Bowl 1990.
Linocut (Edition of 5)
18 × 16 inches
Private Collection

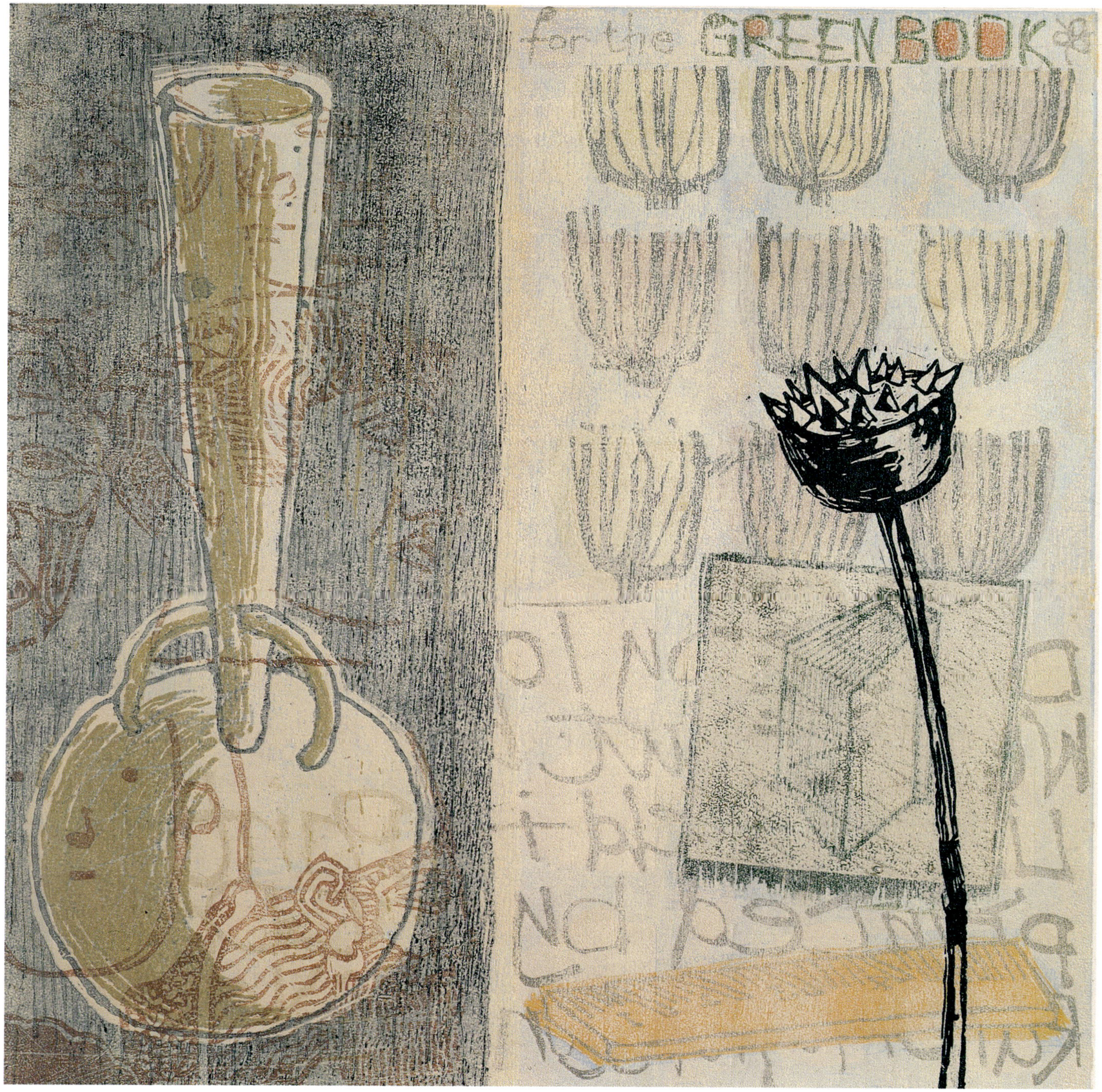

Plate 9

The Green Book 1991.
Linocut (Edition of 5)
18 × 18 inches
Private Collection

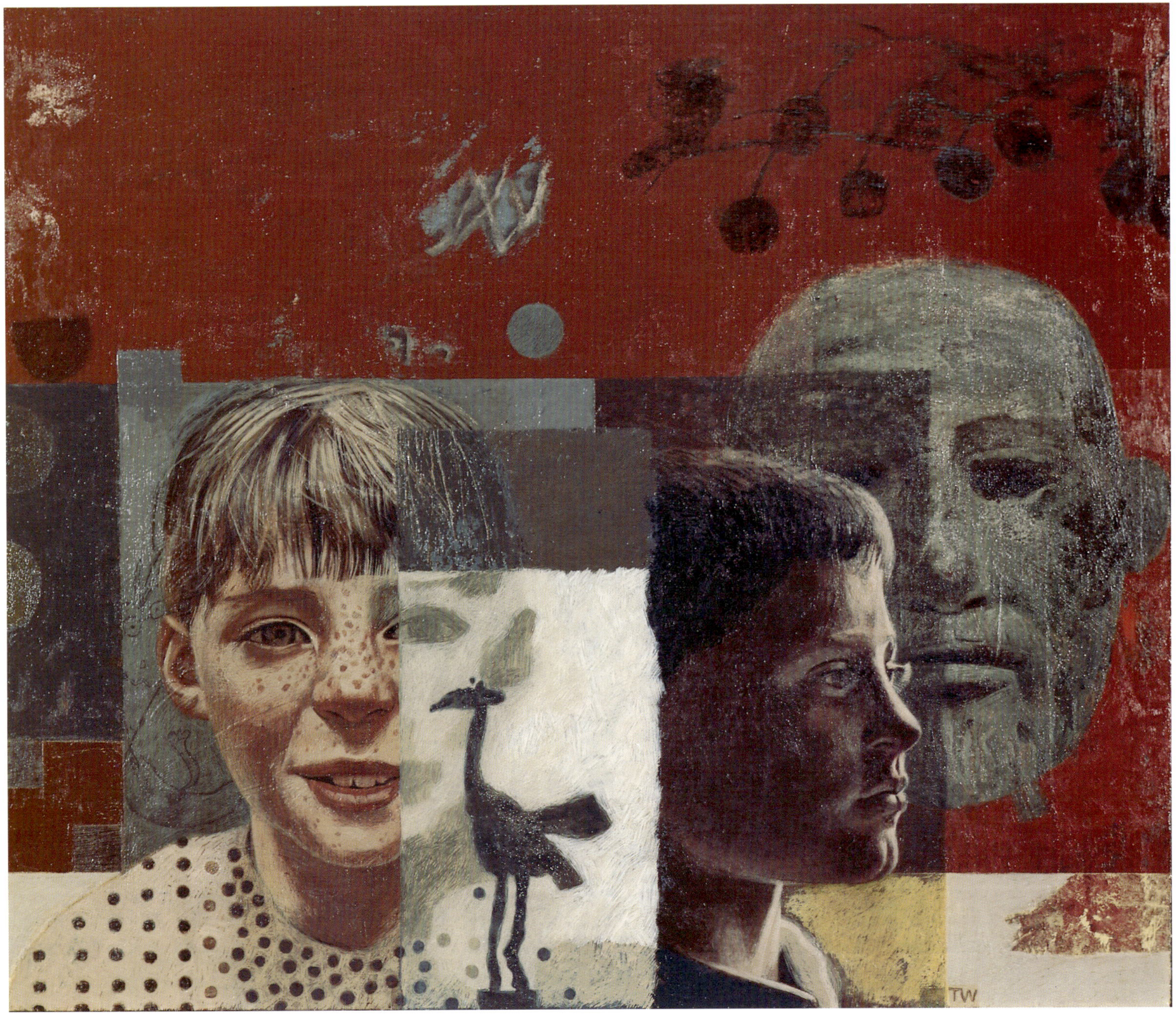

Plate 10

Portrait of Rosie & Peter Hart 1991.
Oil on Board
$25\frac{1}{2} \times 29\frac{1}{2}$ inches
Private Collection

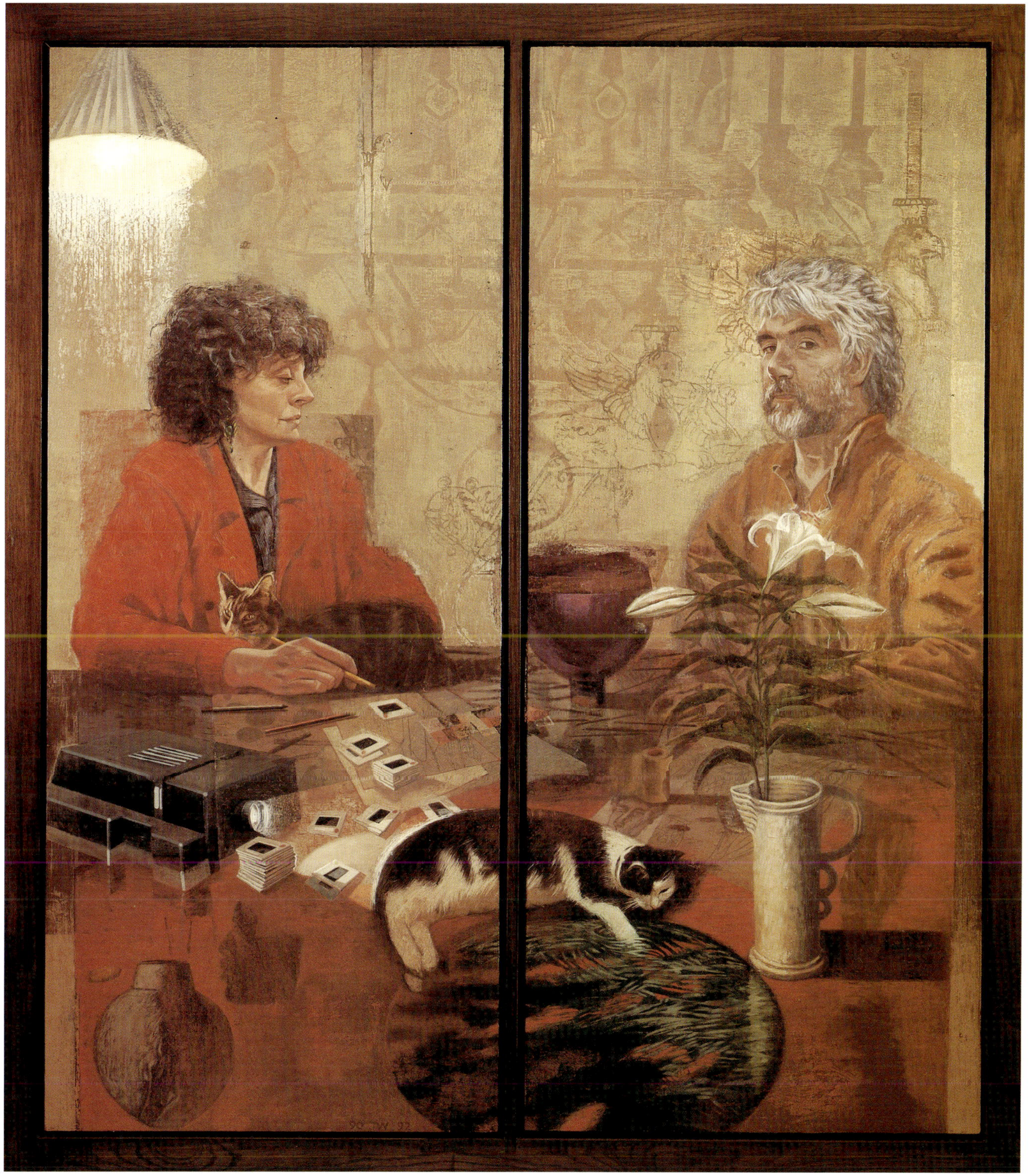

Plate 11

Portrait of Keith Holmes & Sheila Fairbrass Conservators 1993.
Oil on Panel
72 × 72 inches
Private Collection

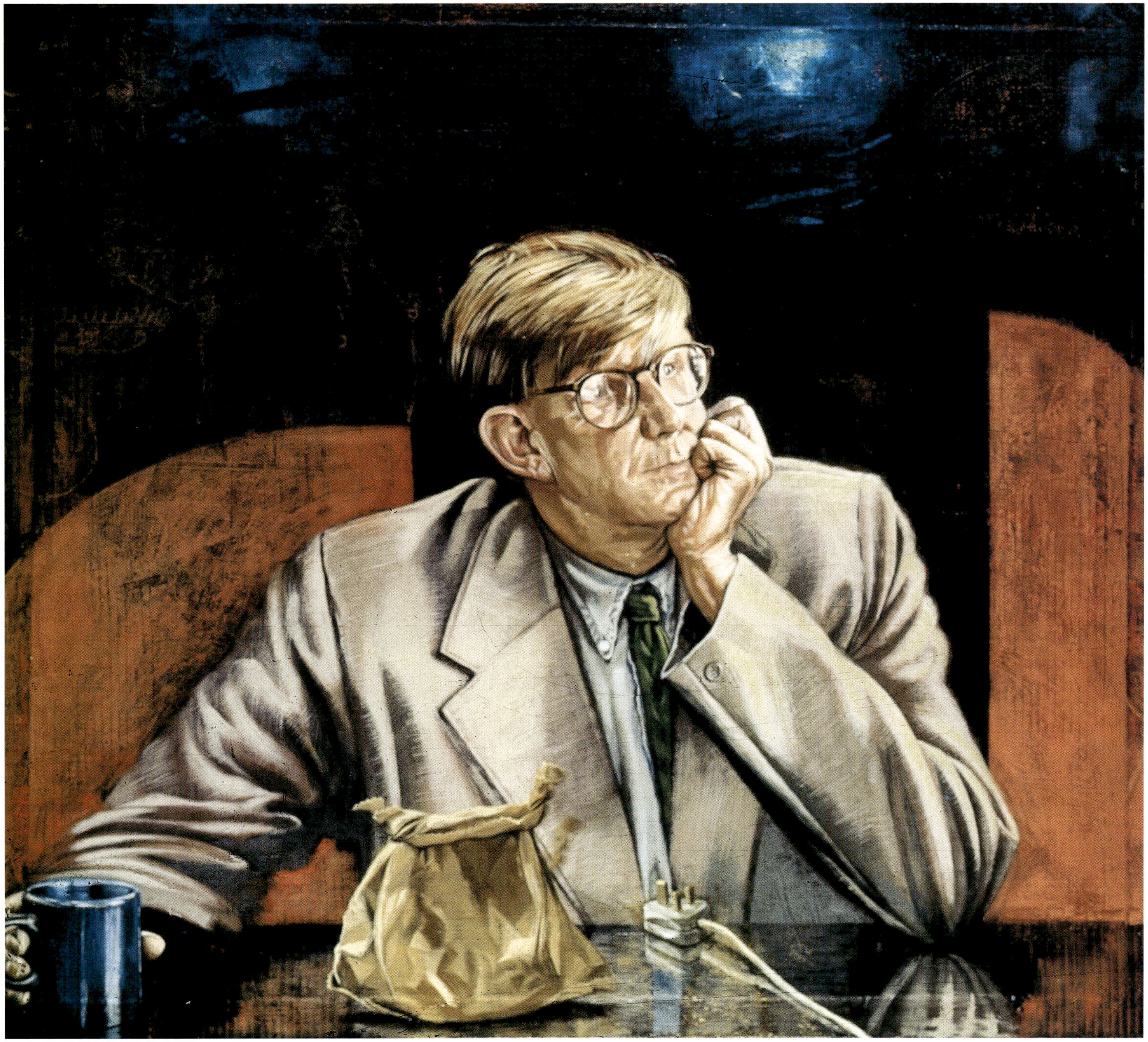

Plate 12

Portrait of Alan Bennett 1993.
Oil on Panel
43½ × 48 inches
The National Portrait Gallery

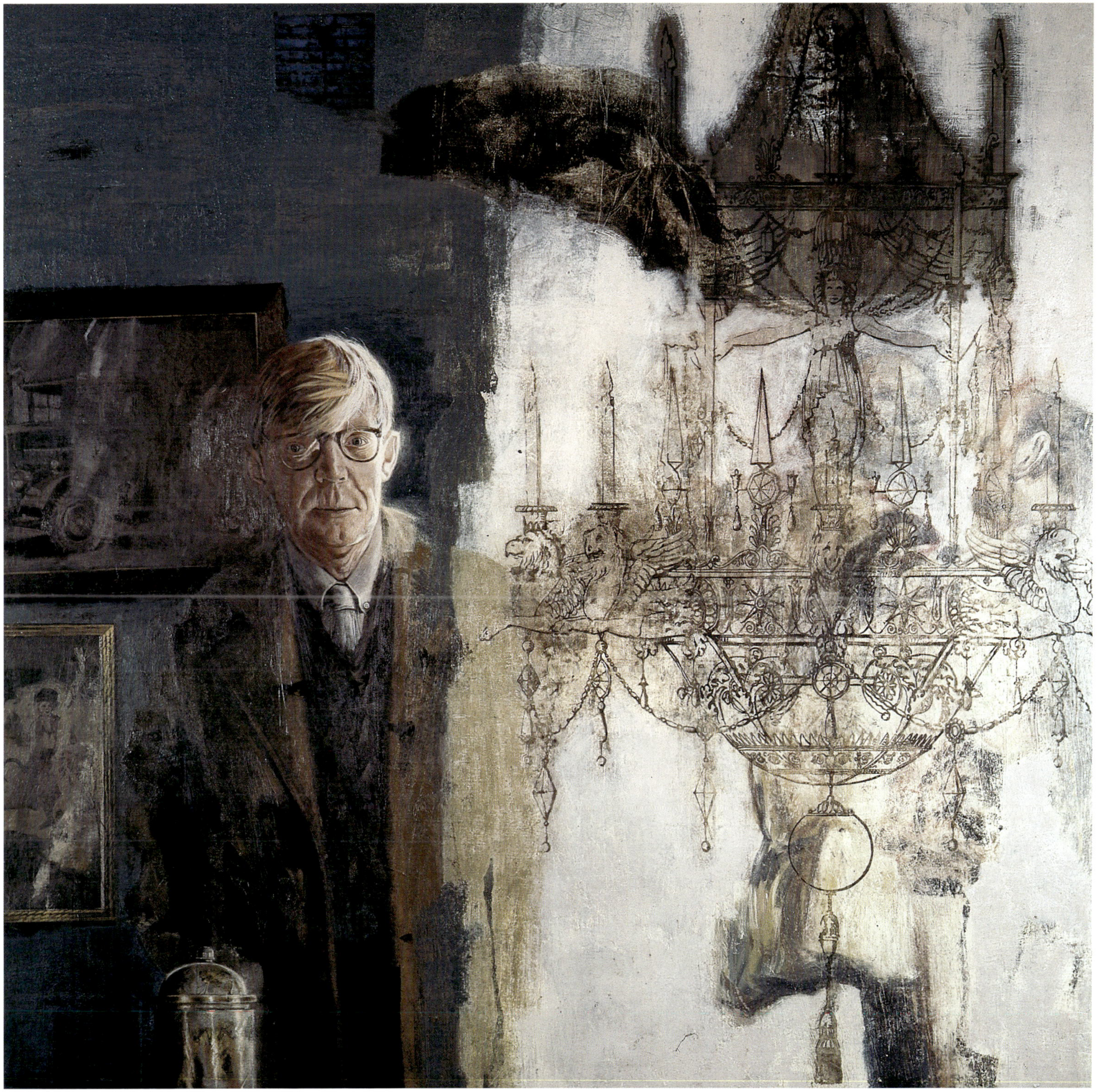

Plate 13

Portrait of Alan Bennett 1992.
Oil on Panel
72 × 72 inches

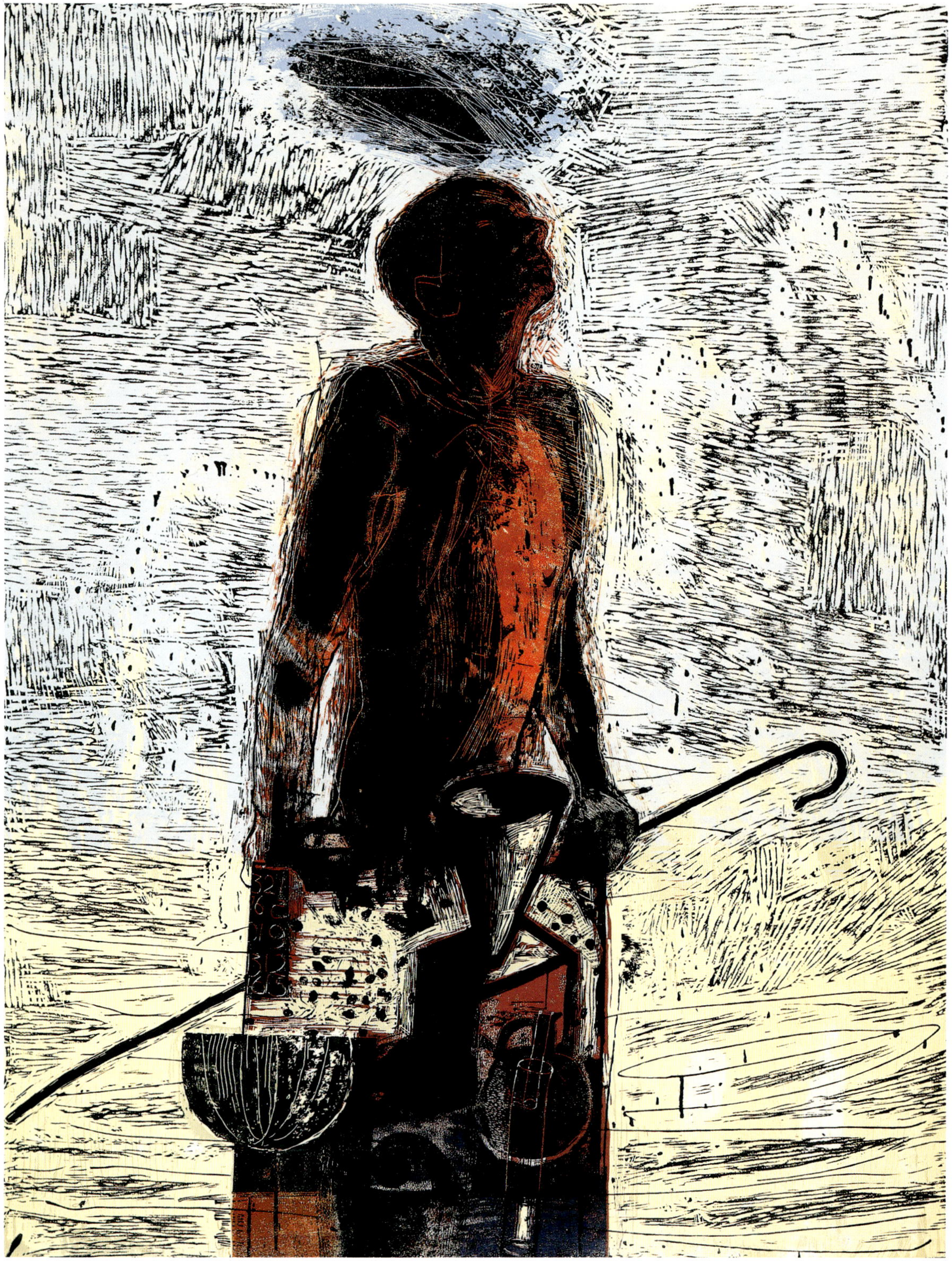

Plate 14

Alchemist in Search of The Voice 1992.
Linocut (Edition of 4)
63 × 42 inches
Private Collection

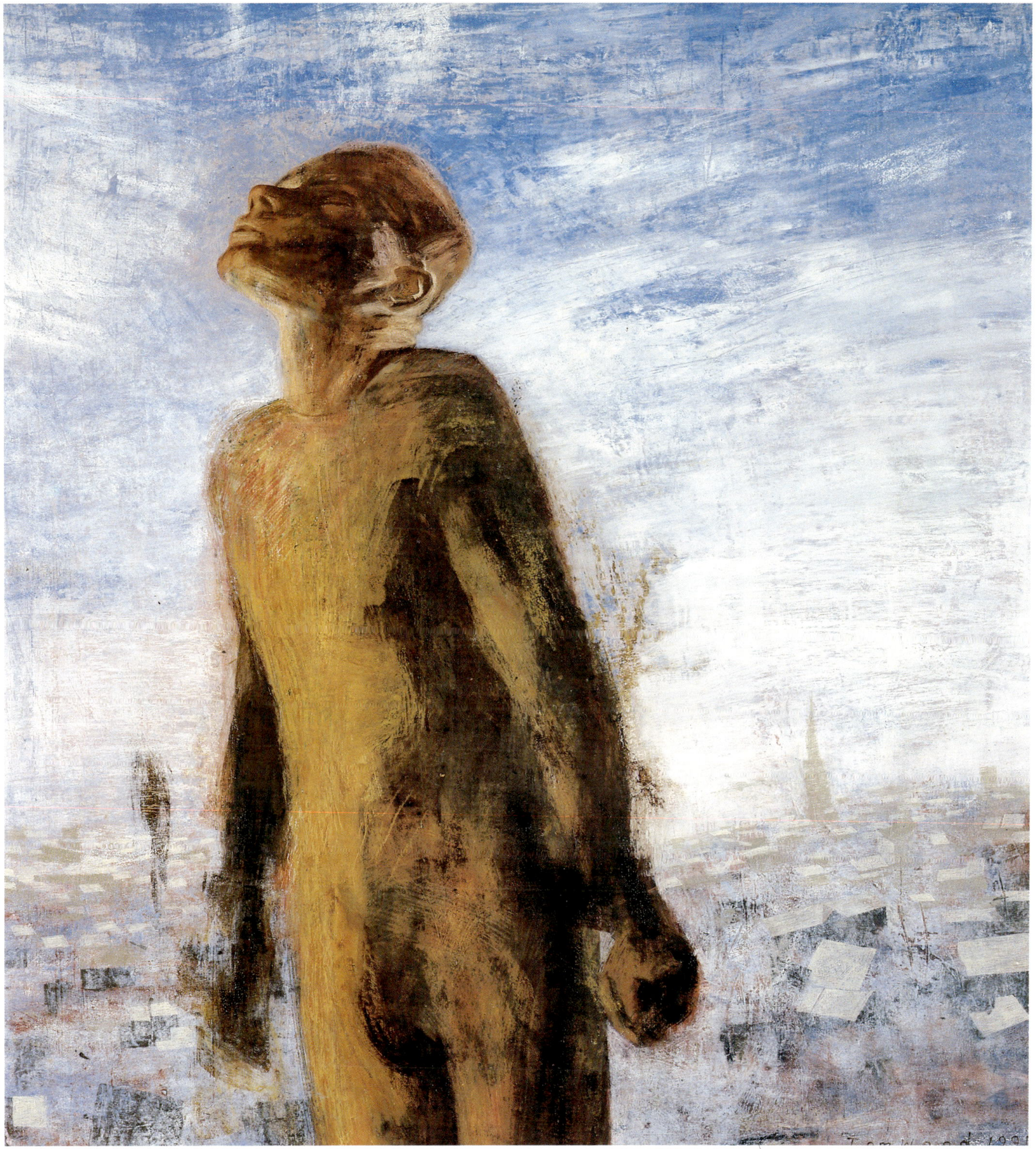

Plate 15

Standing Alone 1991.
Oil on Board
$53\frac{1}{2} \times 47\frac{1}{2}$ inches
Private Collection

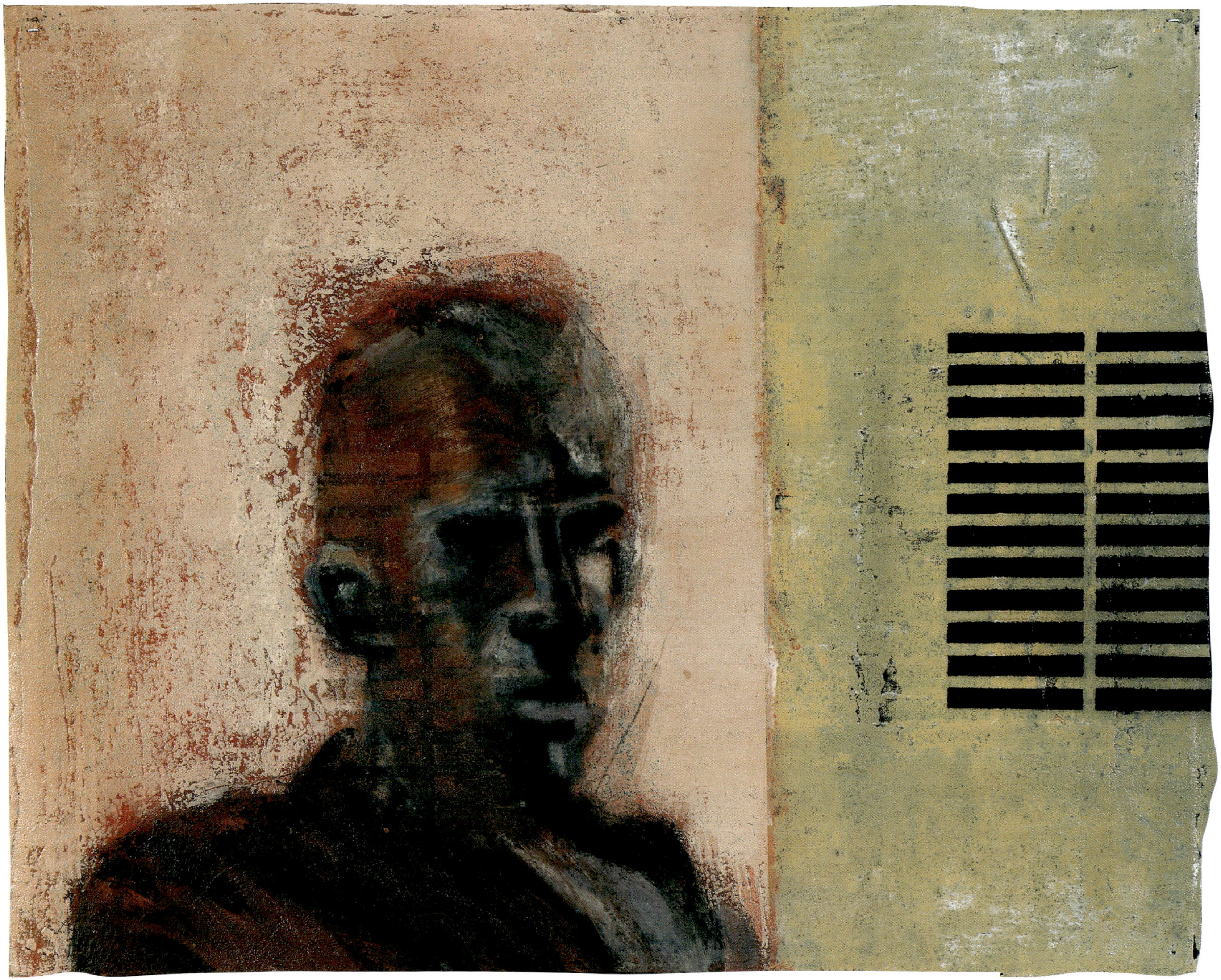

Plate 16

Soldier/Grill 1992.
Oil on Card
20 × 30 inches
Private Collection

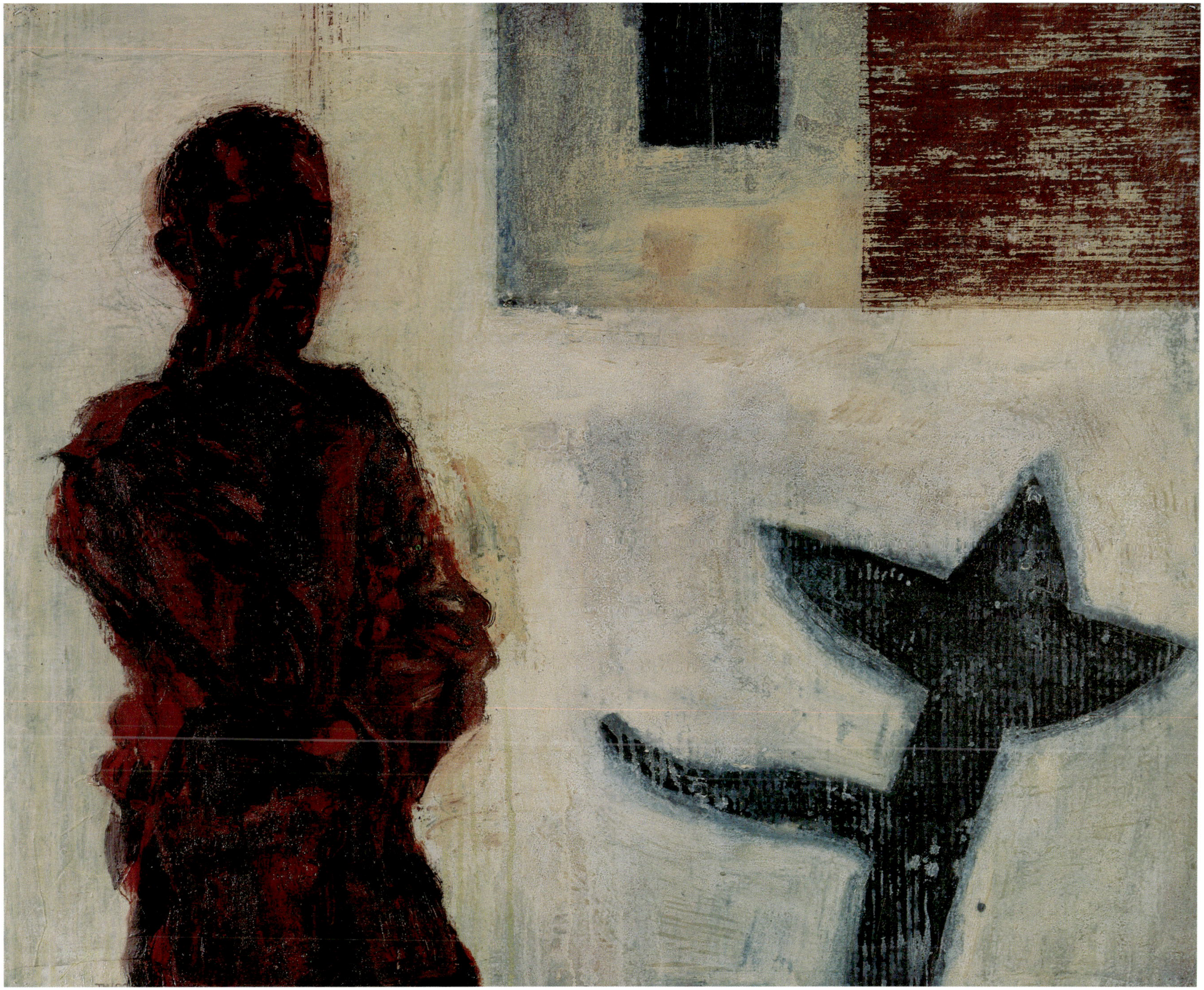

Plate 17

Philosopher Soldier
1992.
Oil on Card
30 × 40 inches
Private Collection

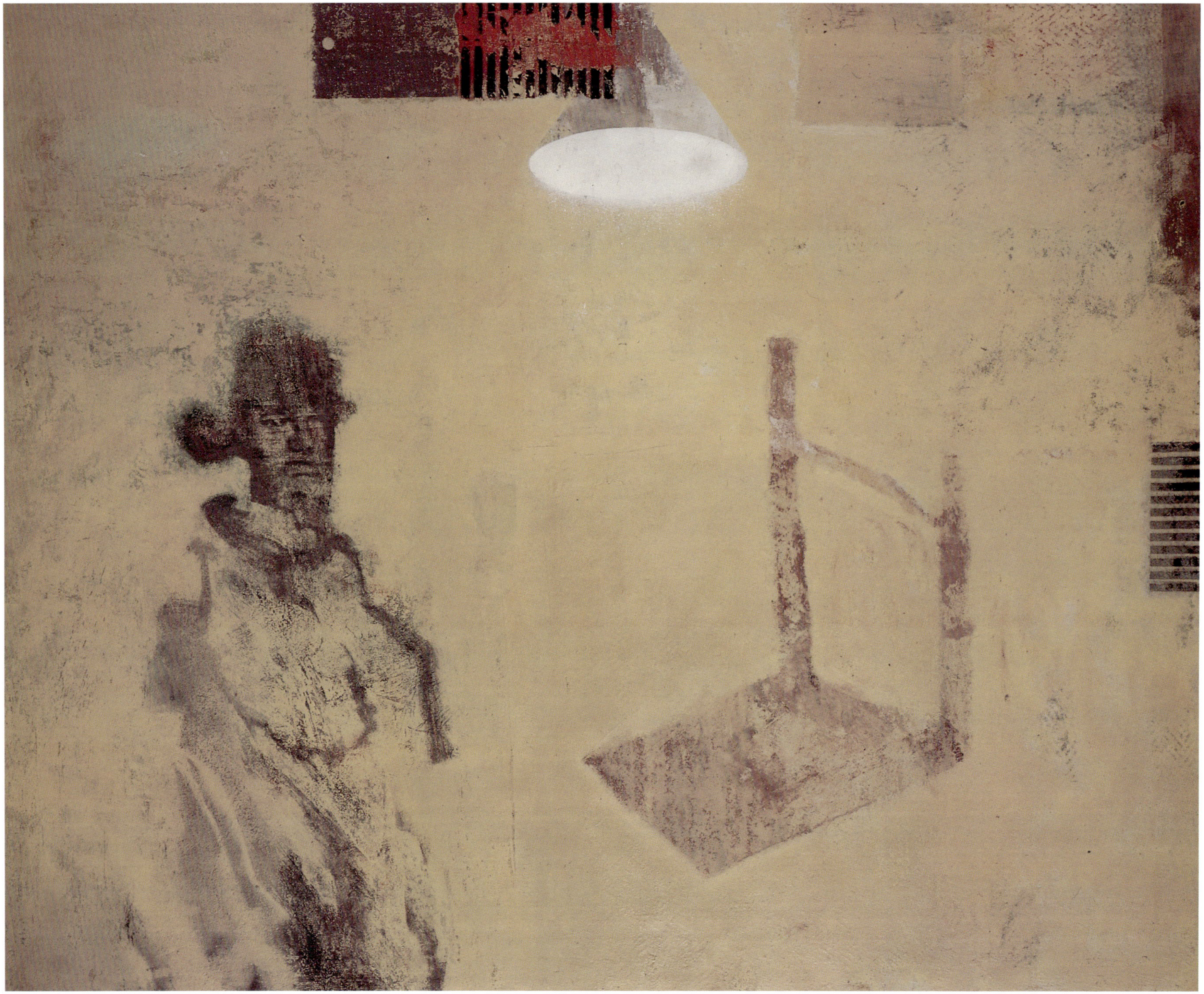

Plate 18

Fossil Man and Lyre 1992.
Oil on Panel
62 × 72 inches

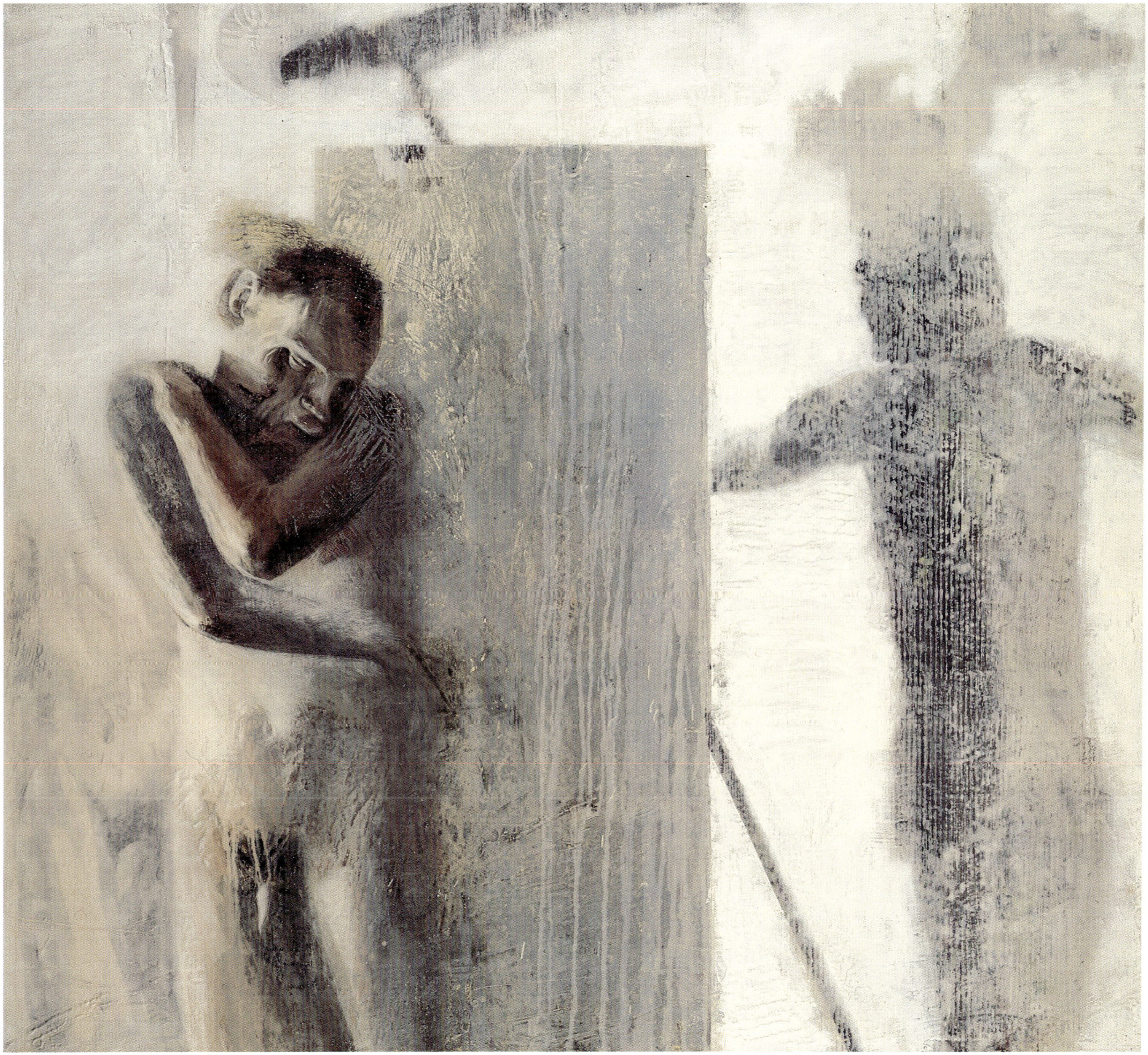

Plate 19

Tomorrow and Tomorrow and Tomorrow 1993.
Oil on Panel
68 × 72 inches
Private Collection

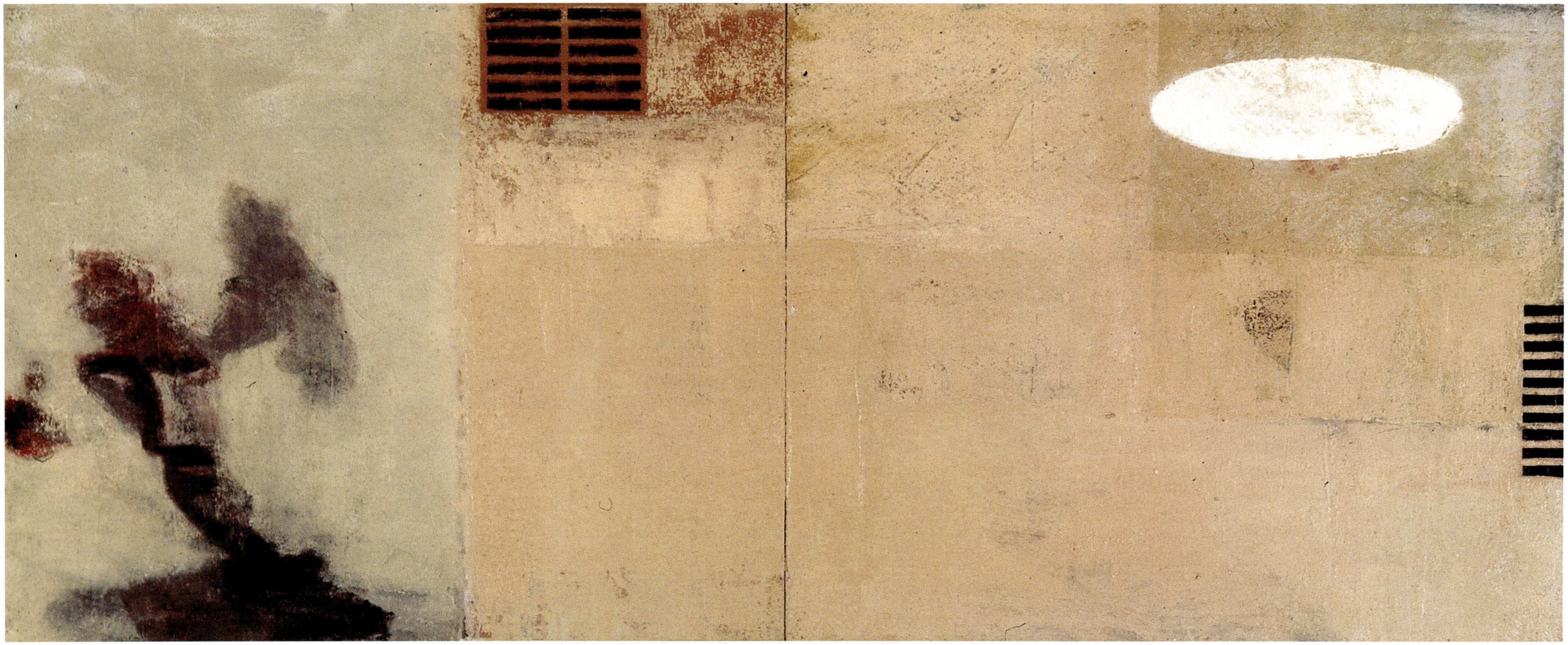

Plate 20

Into the Ether To Dissolve 1992.
Oil on Paper
73 × 24 inches
Private Collection

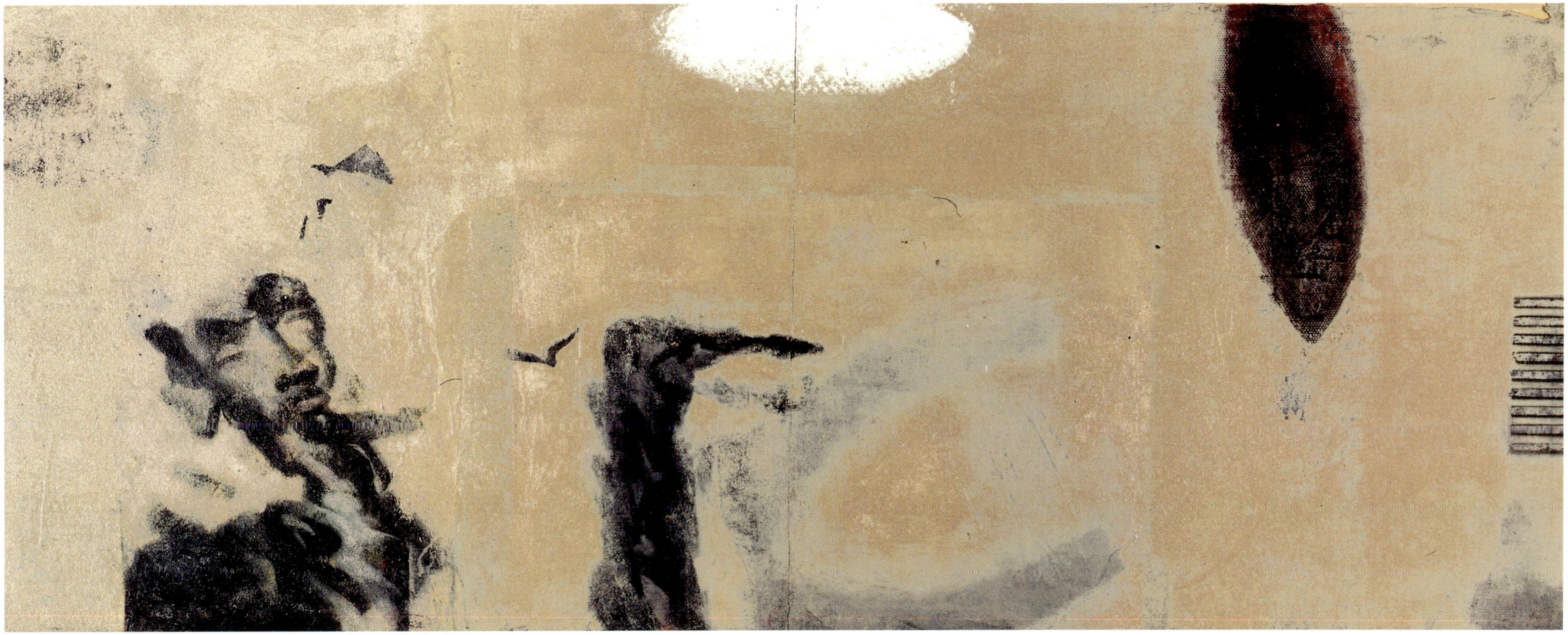

Plate 21

The Night Museum 1992.
Oil on Paper
73 × 34 inches
Private Collection

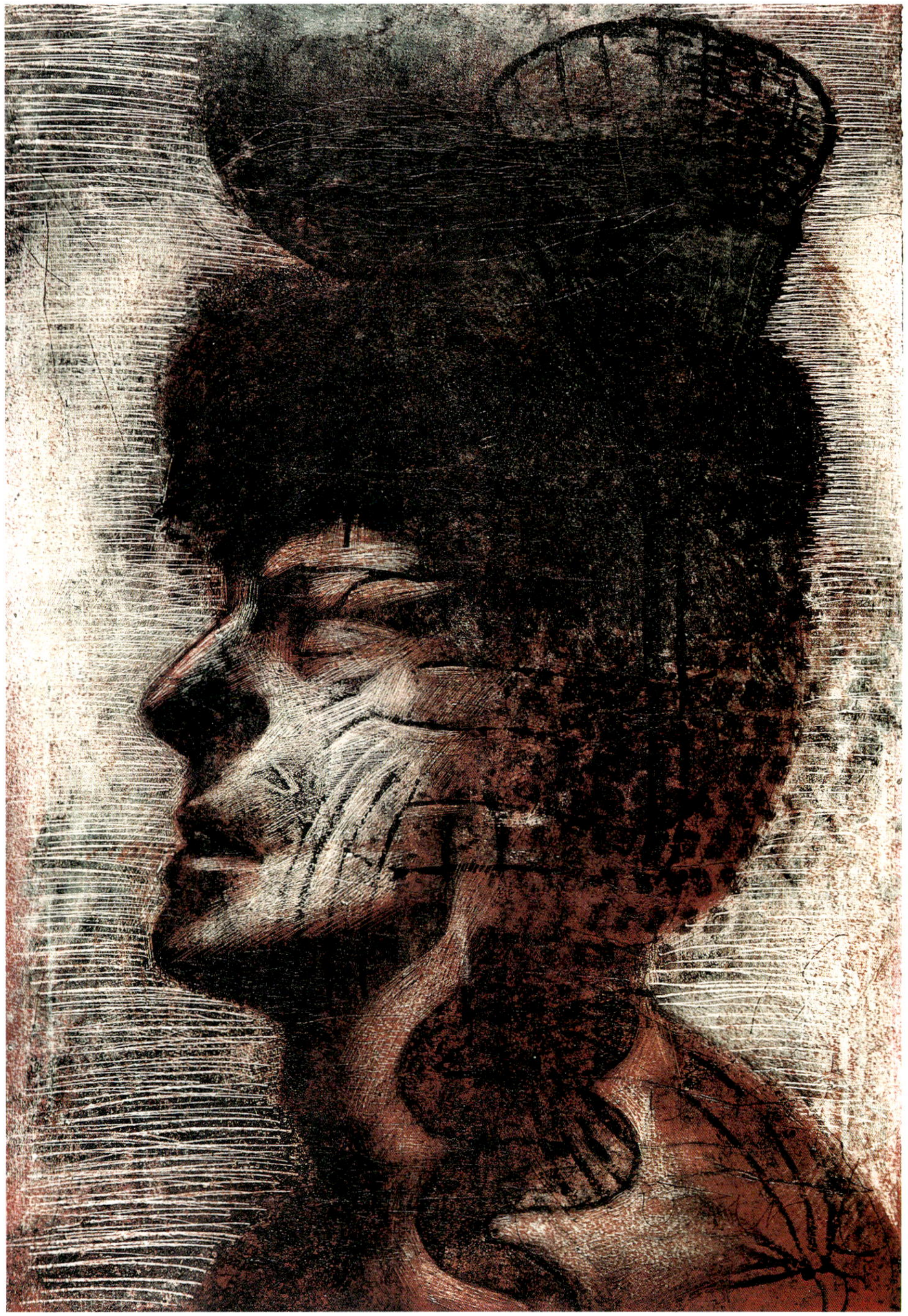

Plate 22

Tattoo Man 1 1993.
Oil on Paper
20 × 15 inches
Private Collection

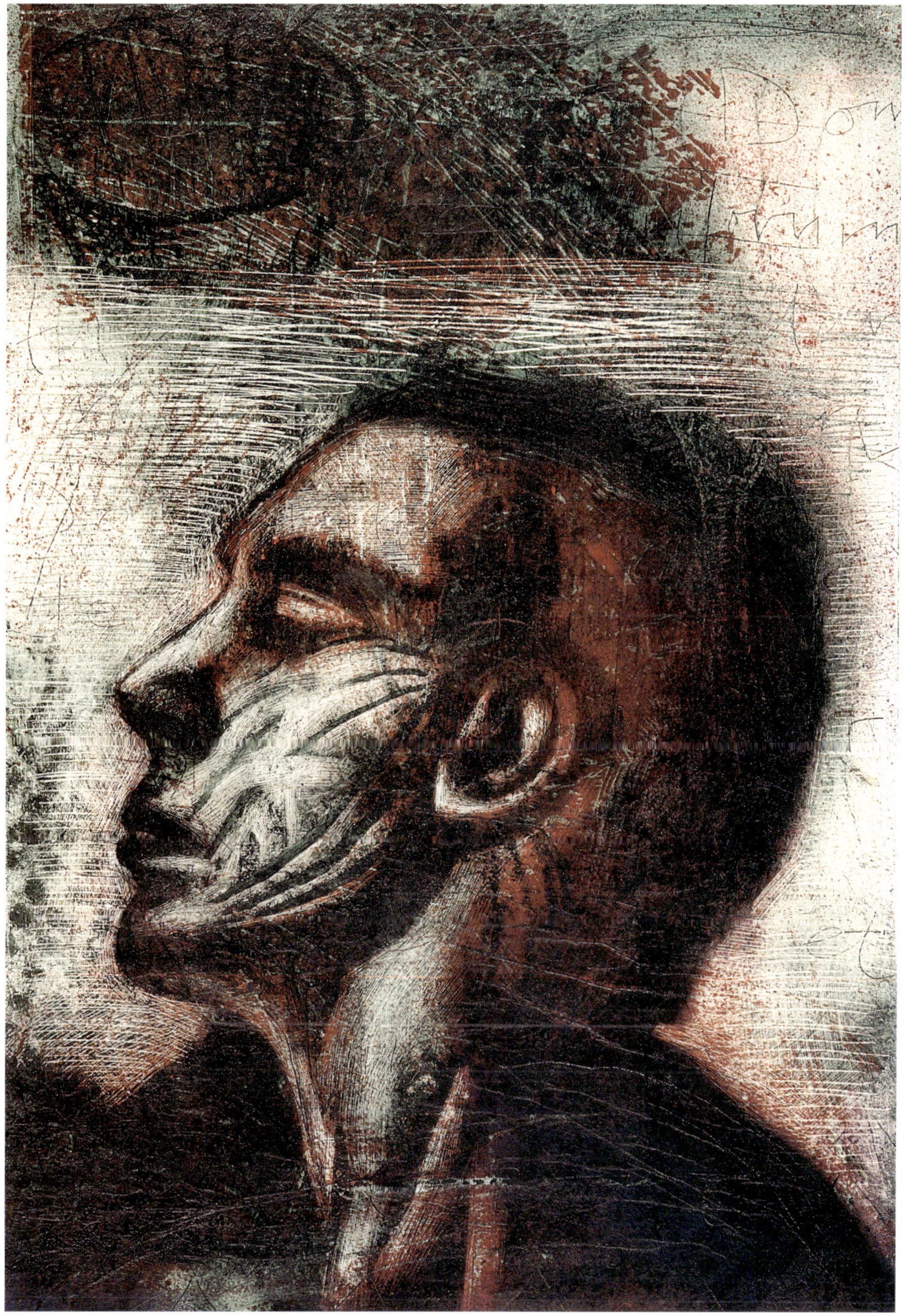

Plate 23

Tattoo Man 2 1993.
Oil on Paper
20 × 15 inches
Private Collection

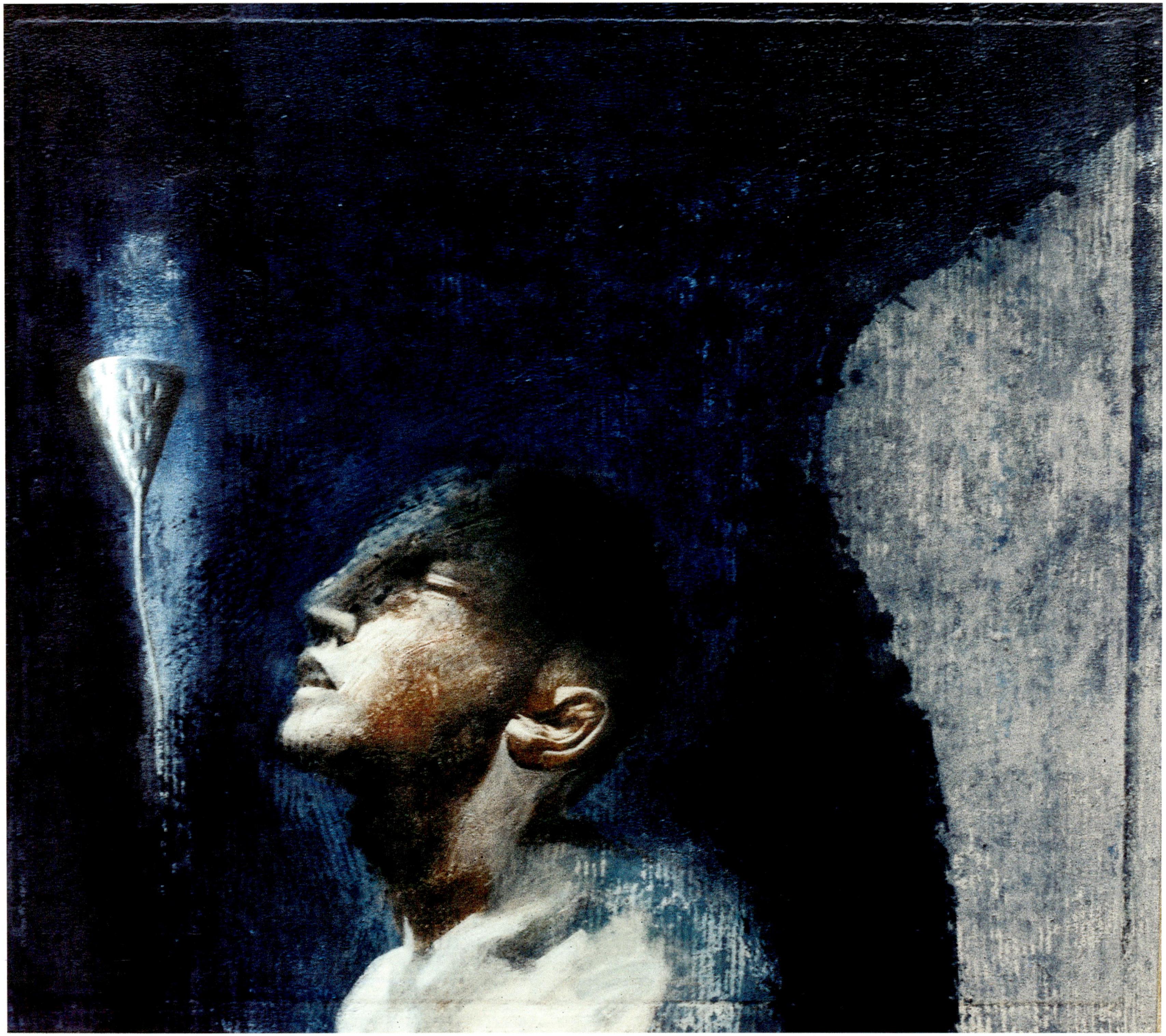

Plate 24

Angel III 1993.
Oil on Paper on Board
$43\frac{1}{2} \times 48$ inches
Private Collection

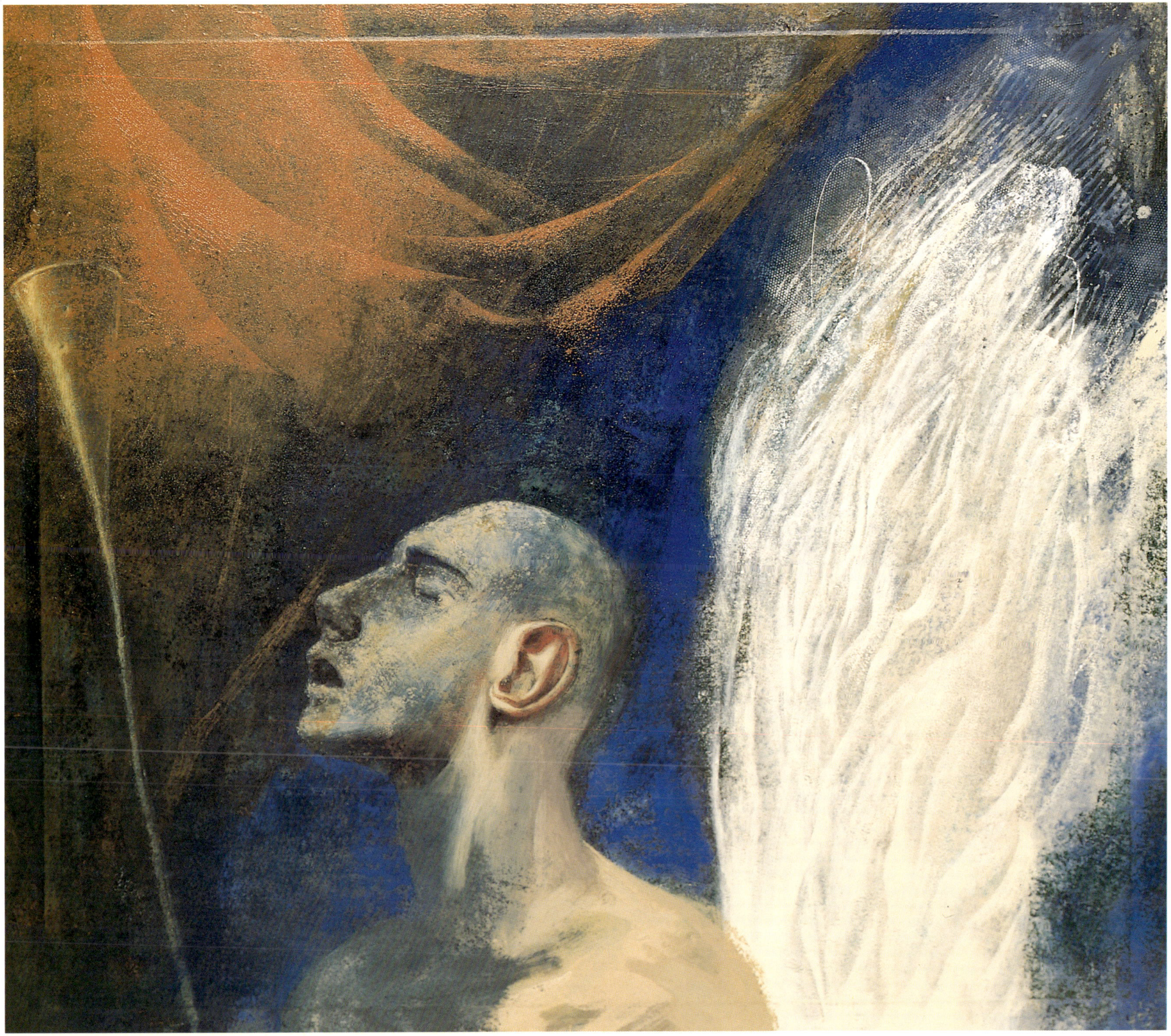

Plate 25

Redemption 1993.
Oil on Paper on Board
$43\frac{1}{2} \times 48$ inches
Private Collection

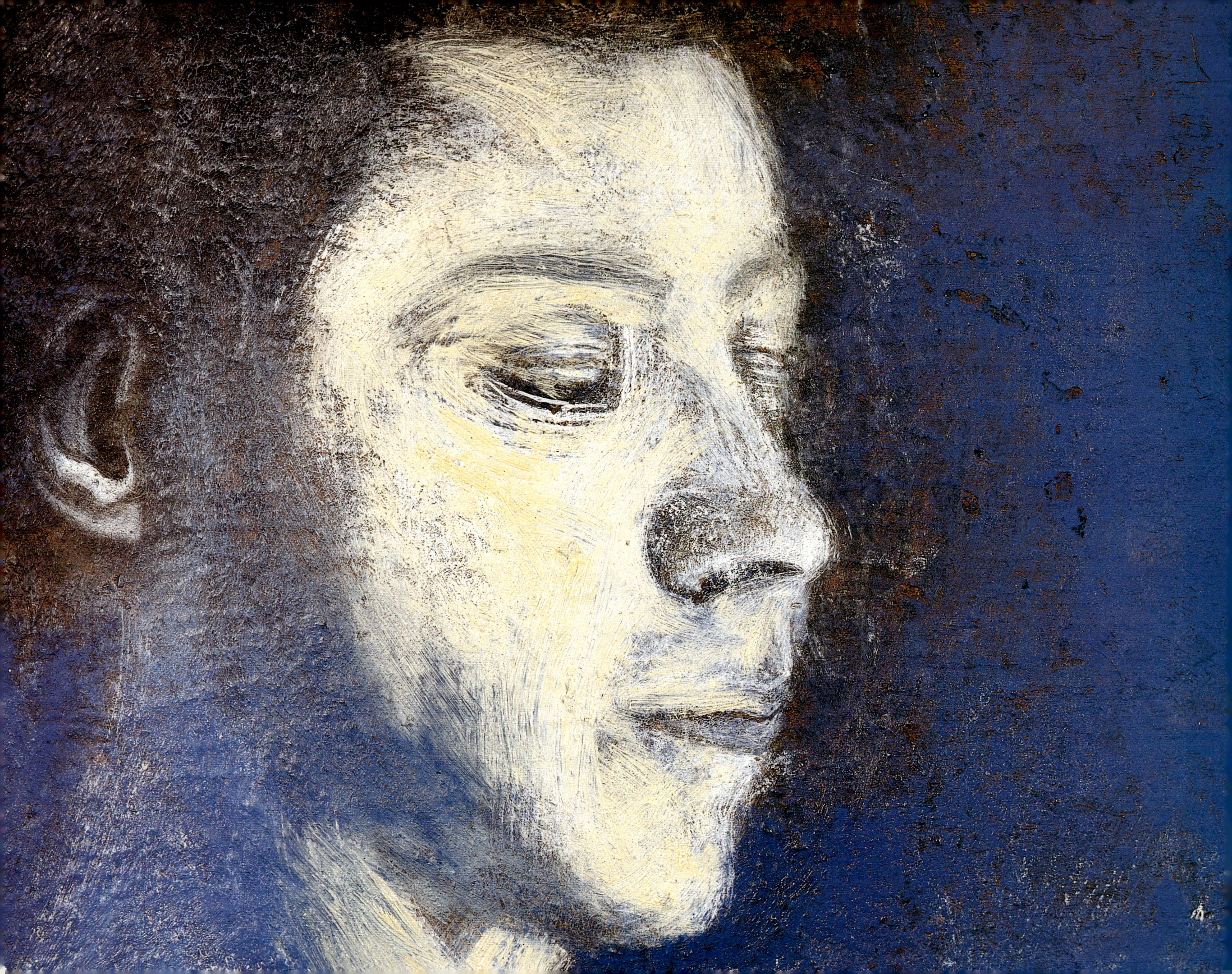

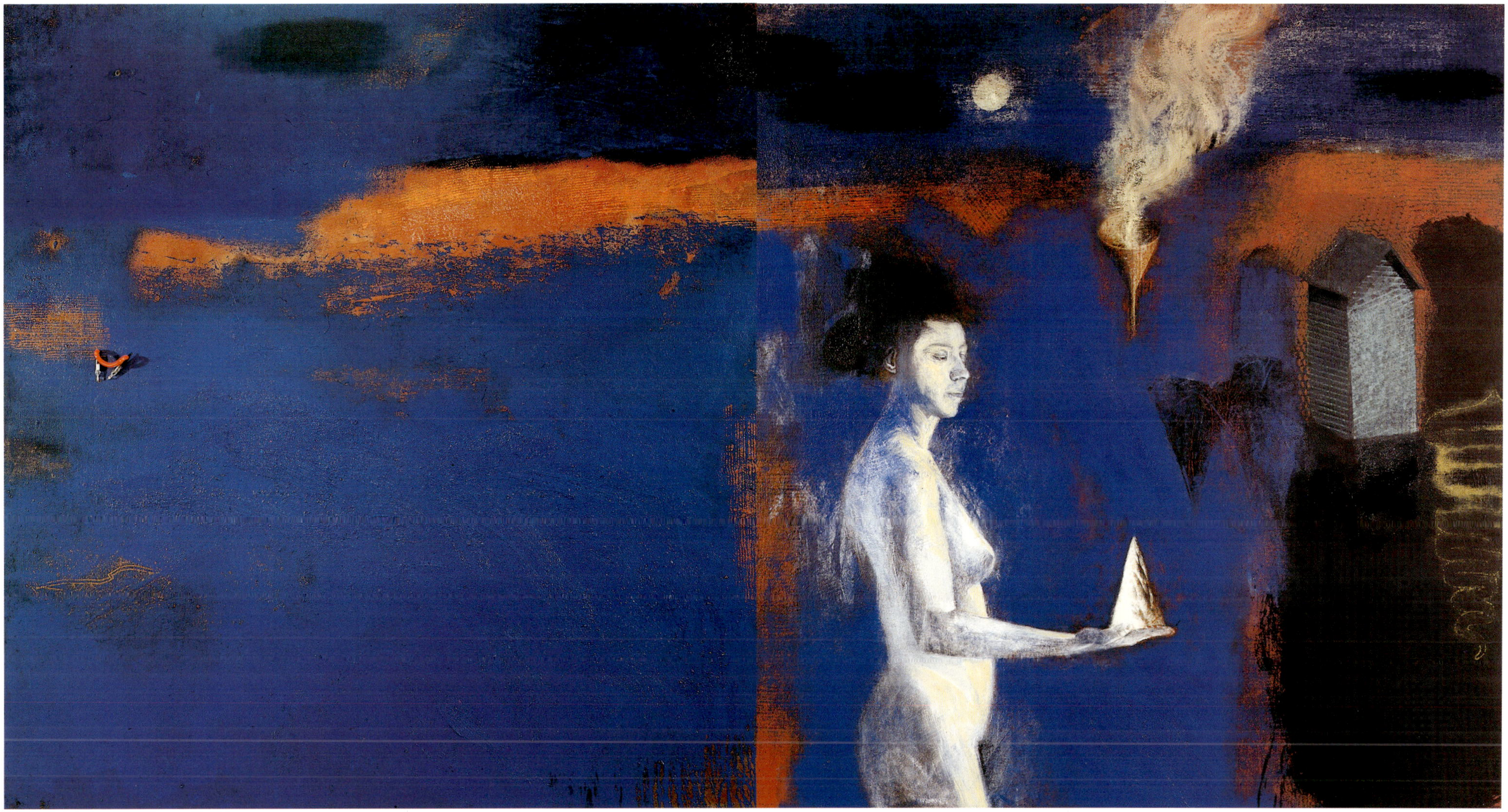

◀ Detail

Plate 27

Parable 1993–94.
Oil on Panel with Neon
72 × 134 inches

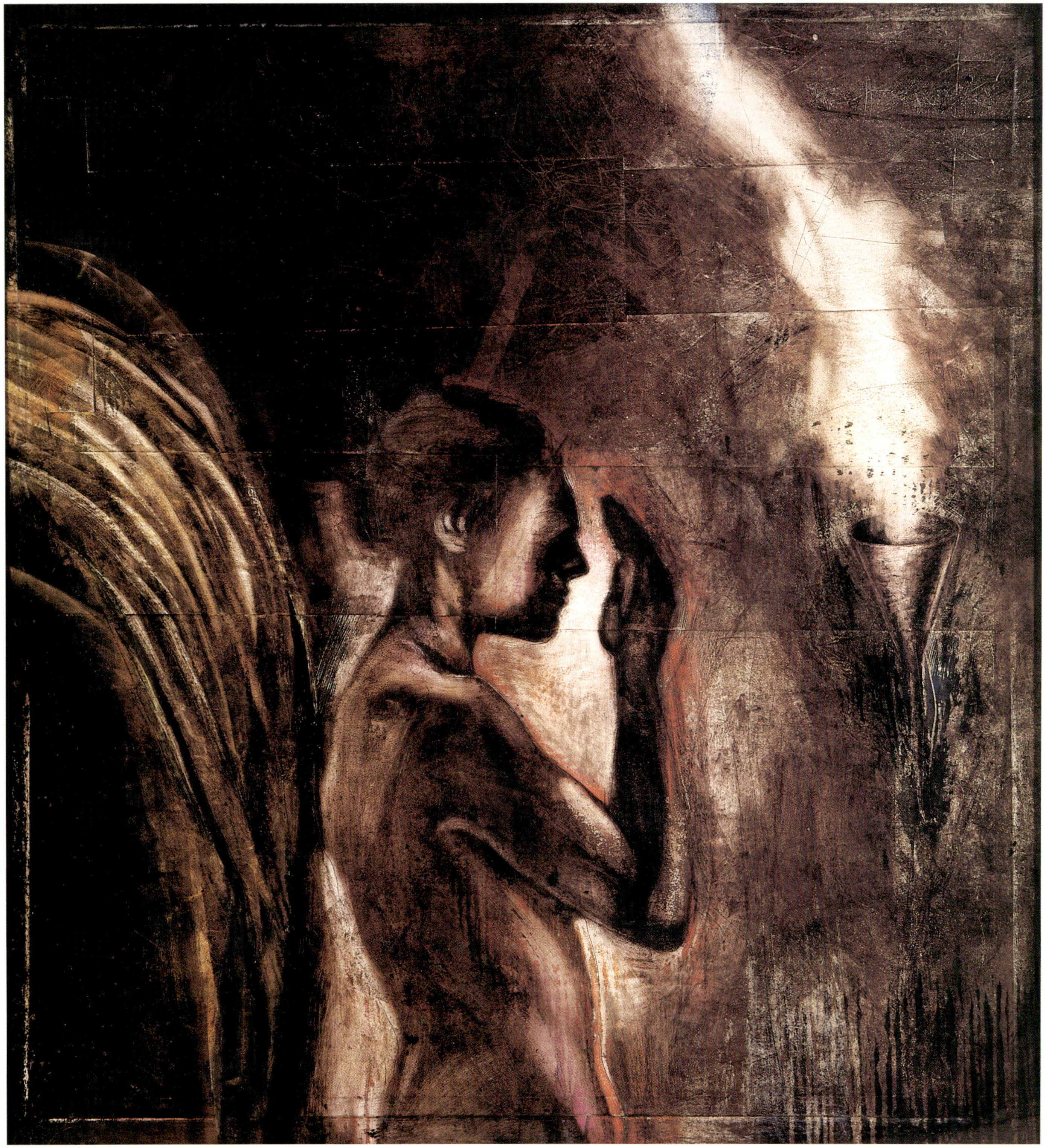

Plate 28

Red Angel 1993.
Oil on Paper on Board
48 × 43½ inches
Private Collection

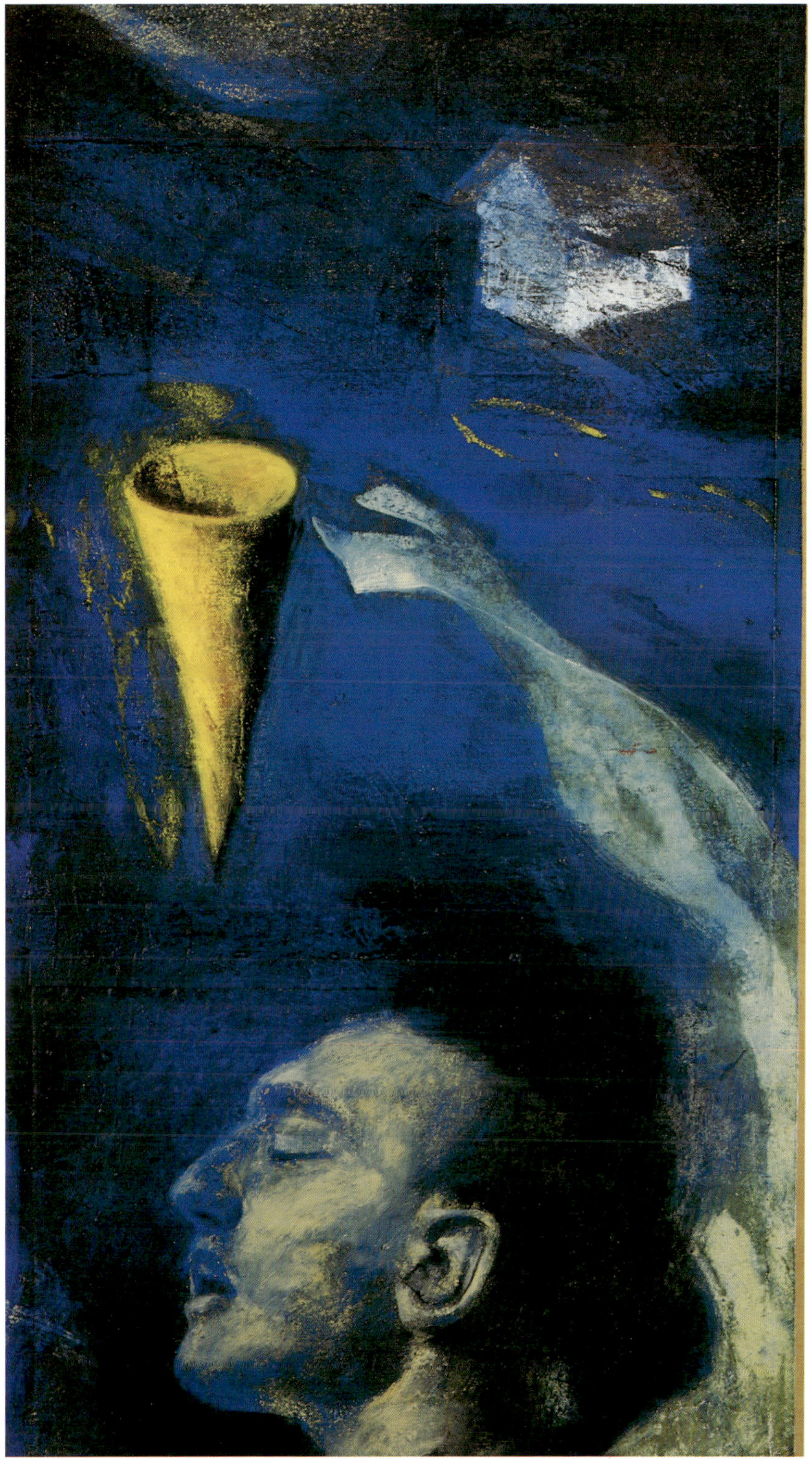

Plate 29

Lucca 1994.
Oil on Panel
45 × 23½ inches
Private Collection

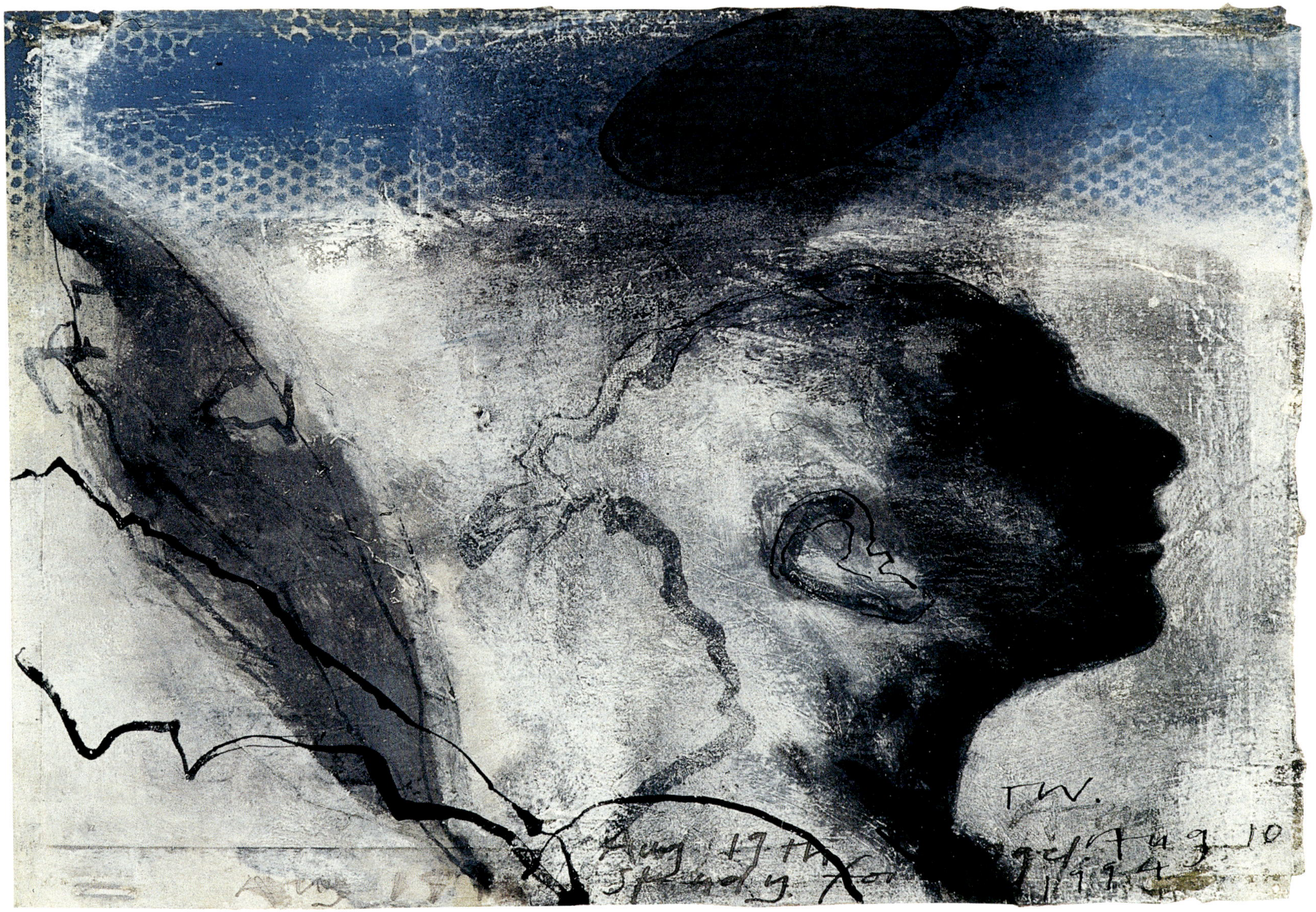

Plate 30

Head in Shadow Study 1994.
Oil on Paper
13 × 15¼ inches
Private Collection

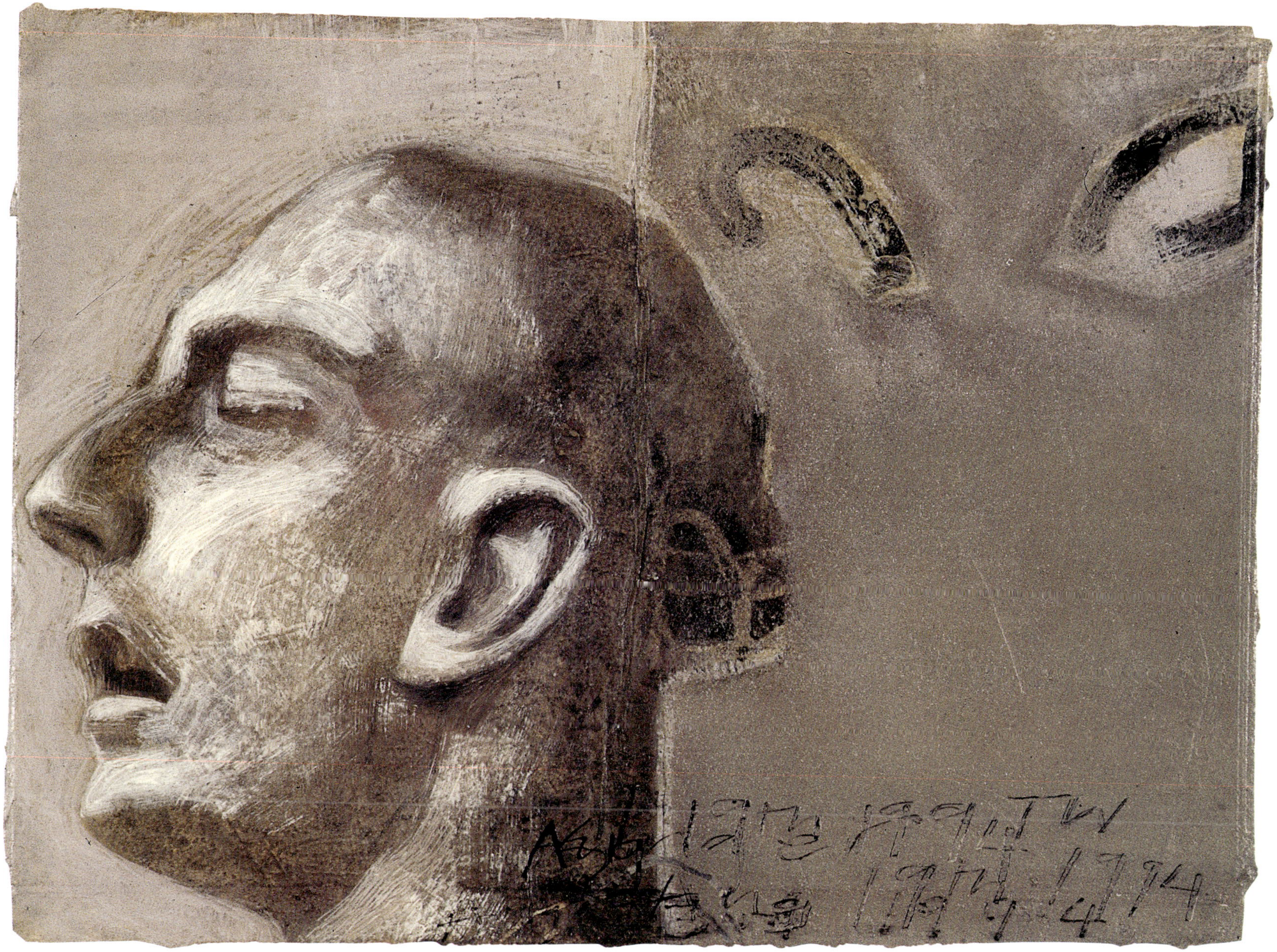

Plate 31

Singer 1994.
Oil on Paper
13 × 15¼ inches
Private Collection

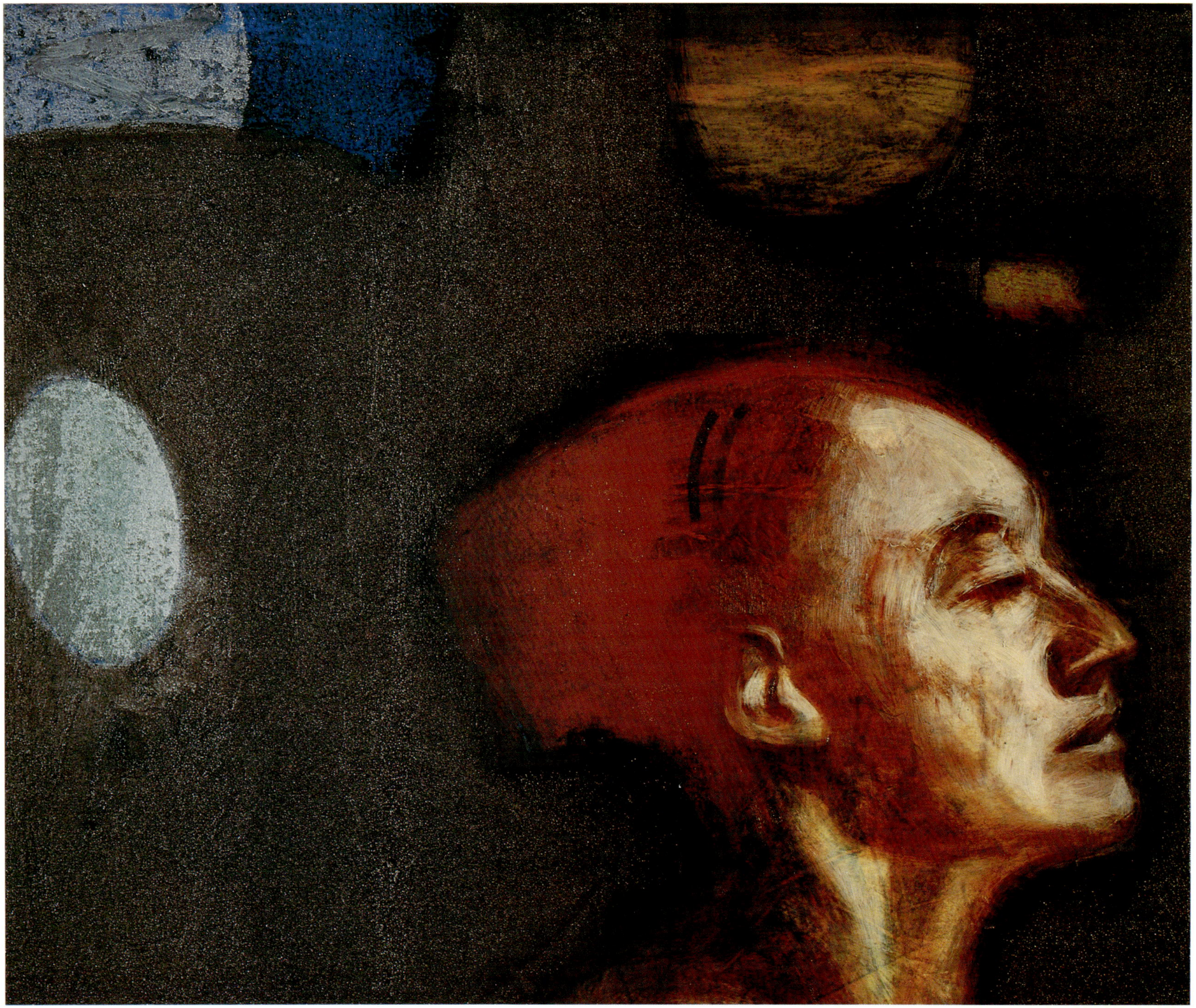

Plate 32

Dreaming of Colours 1994.
Oil on Panel
21 × 23½ inches

Plate 33 *(Opposite)*

Diva 1994.
Oil on Panel
21 × 23½ inches
Private Collection

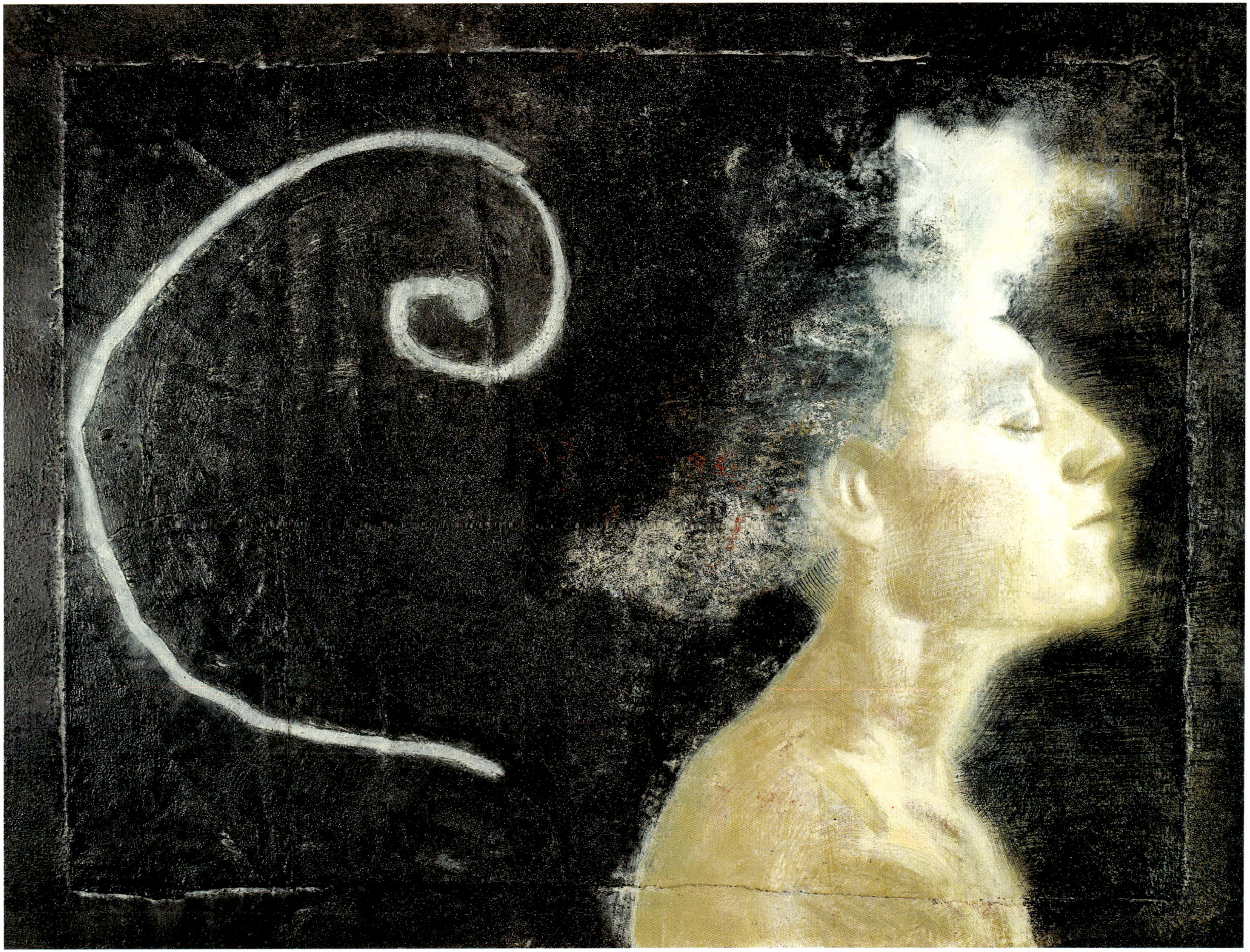

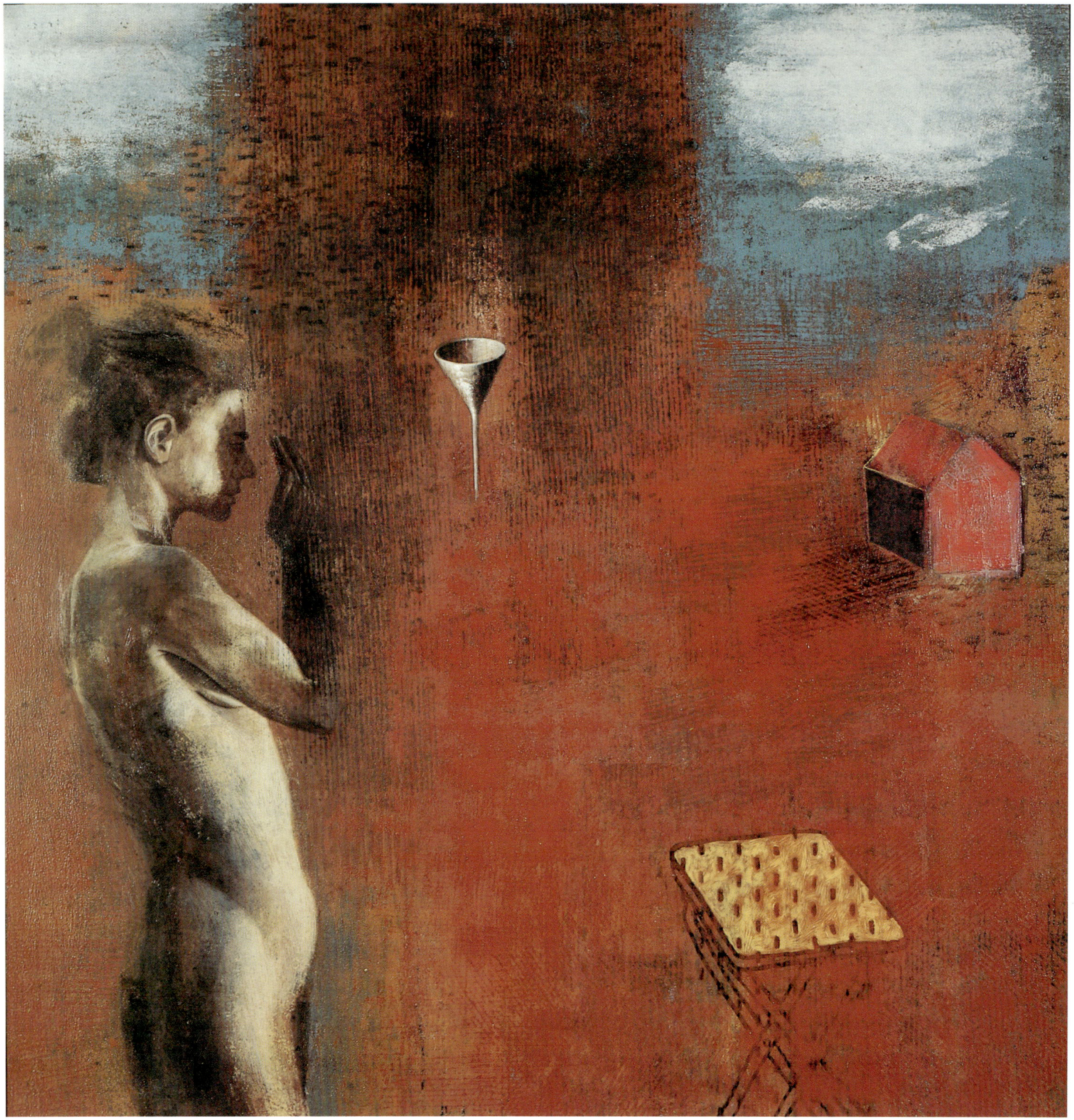

Plate 34

In My Desert There is a Mirror 1993.
Oil on Panel
72 × 67 inches
Private Collection

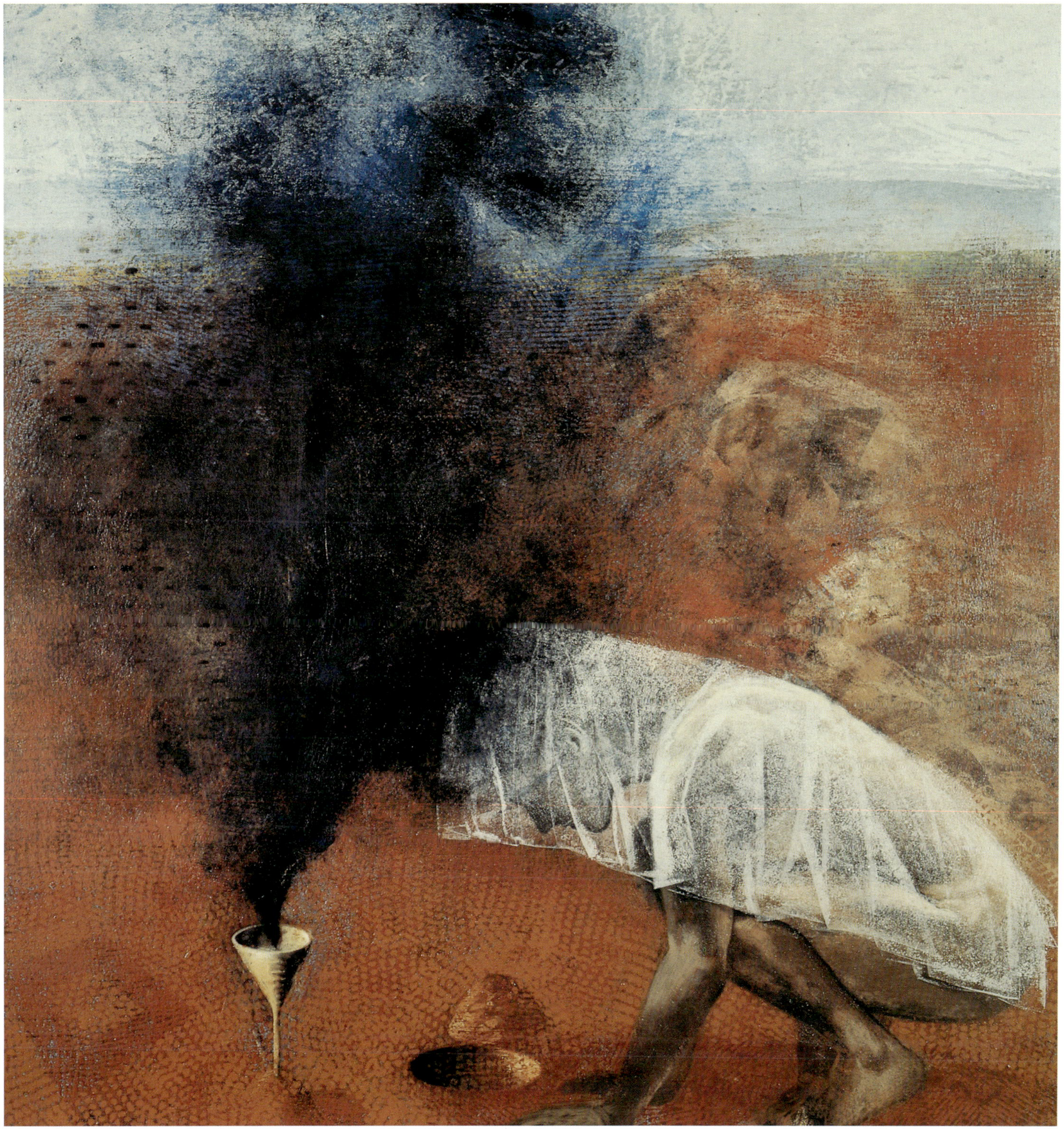

Plate 35

As Smoke Rises so Bees Sink 1993.
Oil on Panel
72 × 67 inches
Private Collection

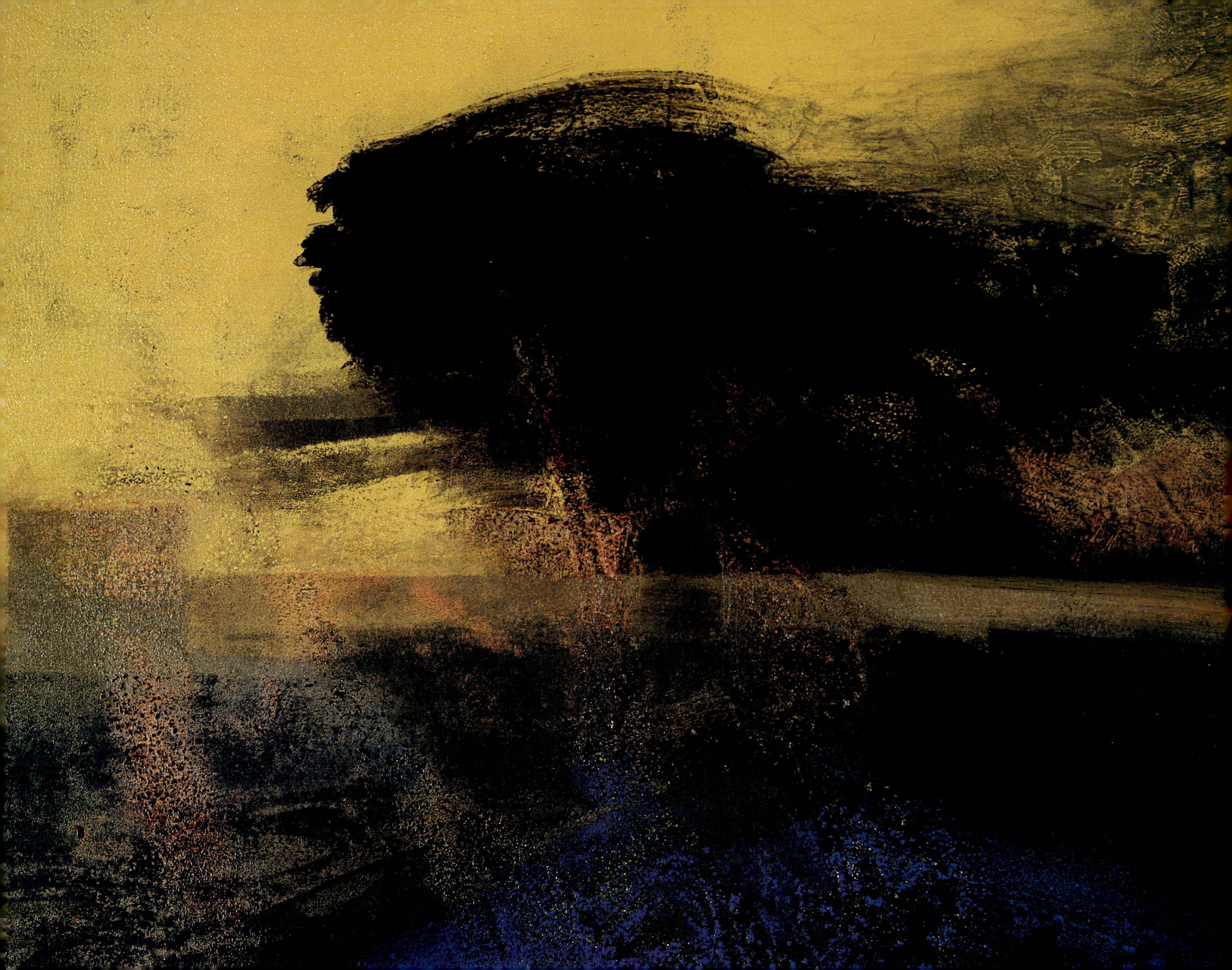

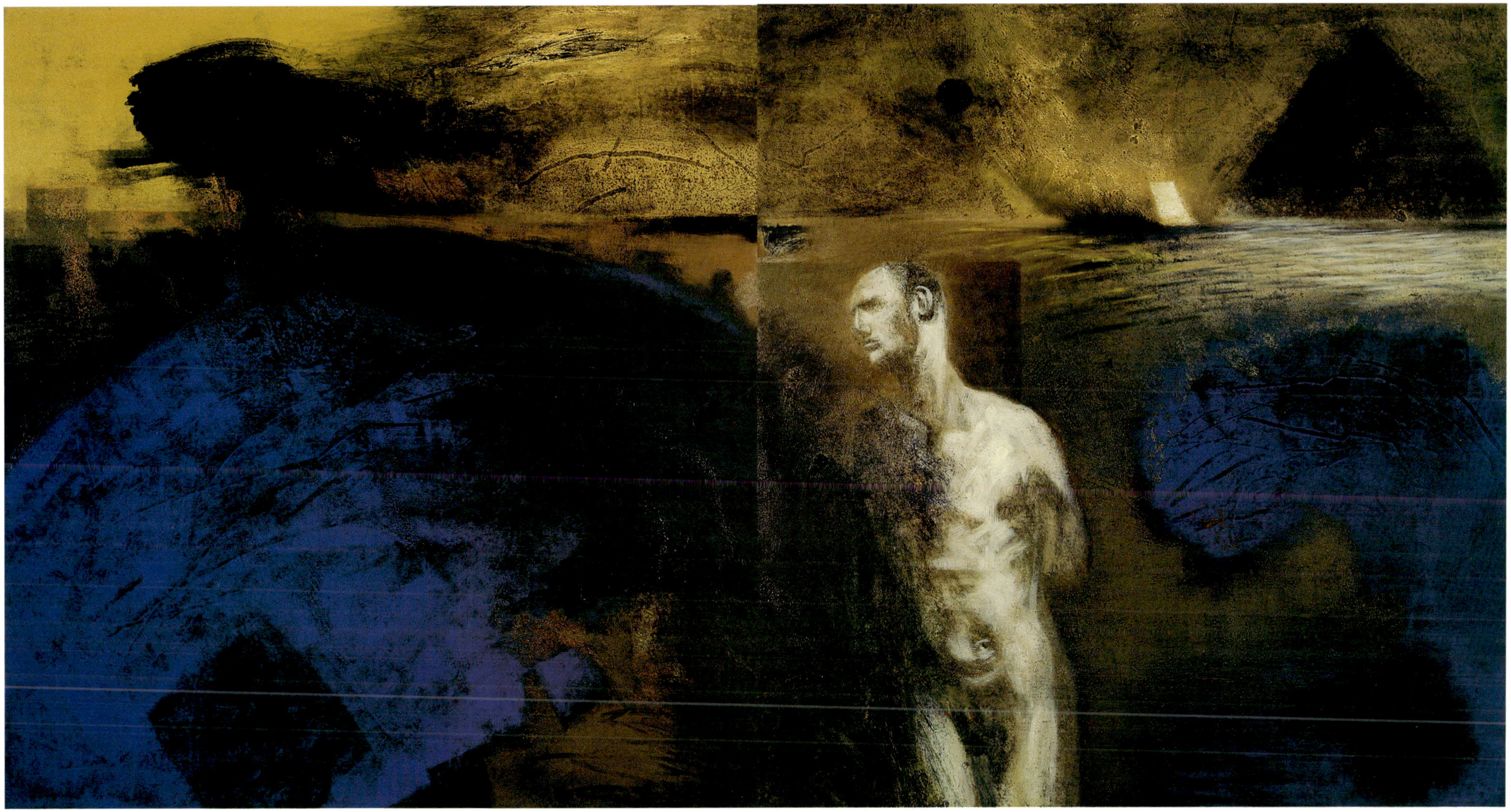

◀ Detail

Plate 37

West Coast Deluge 1994.
Oil on Panel
72 × 134 inches

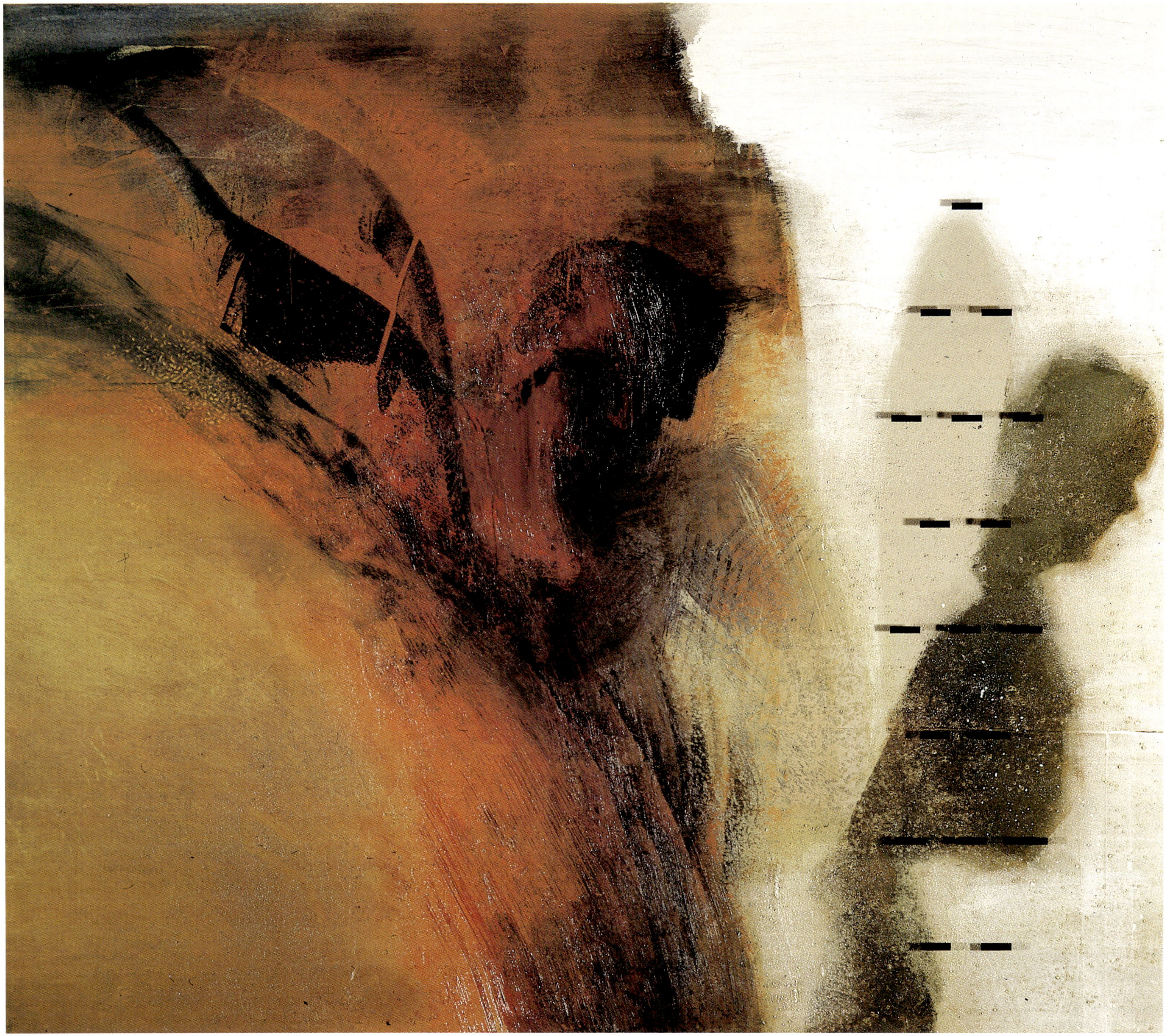

Plate 38

Looking at El Greco 1995.
Oil on Paper on Board and Perspex
$43\frac{1}{2} \times 48$ inches

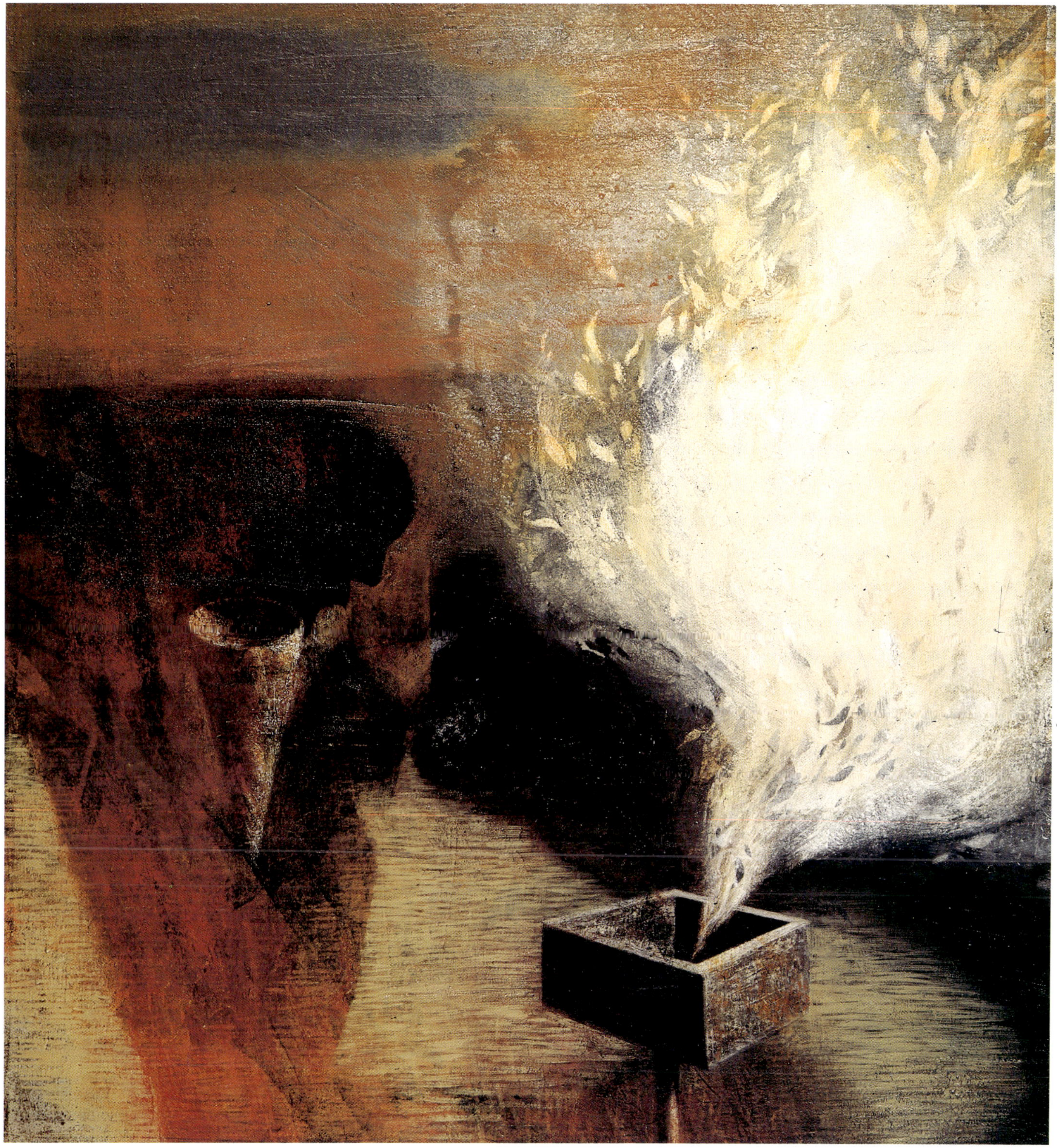

Plate 39

Miracle 1994–95.
Oil on Paper on Board
48 × 43 inches

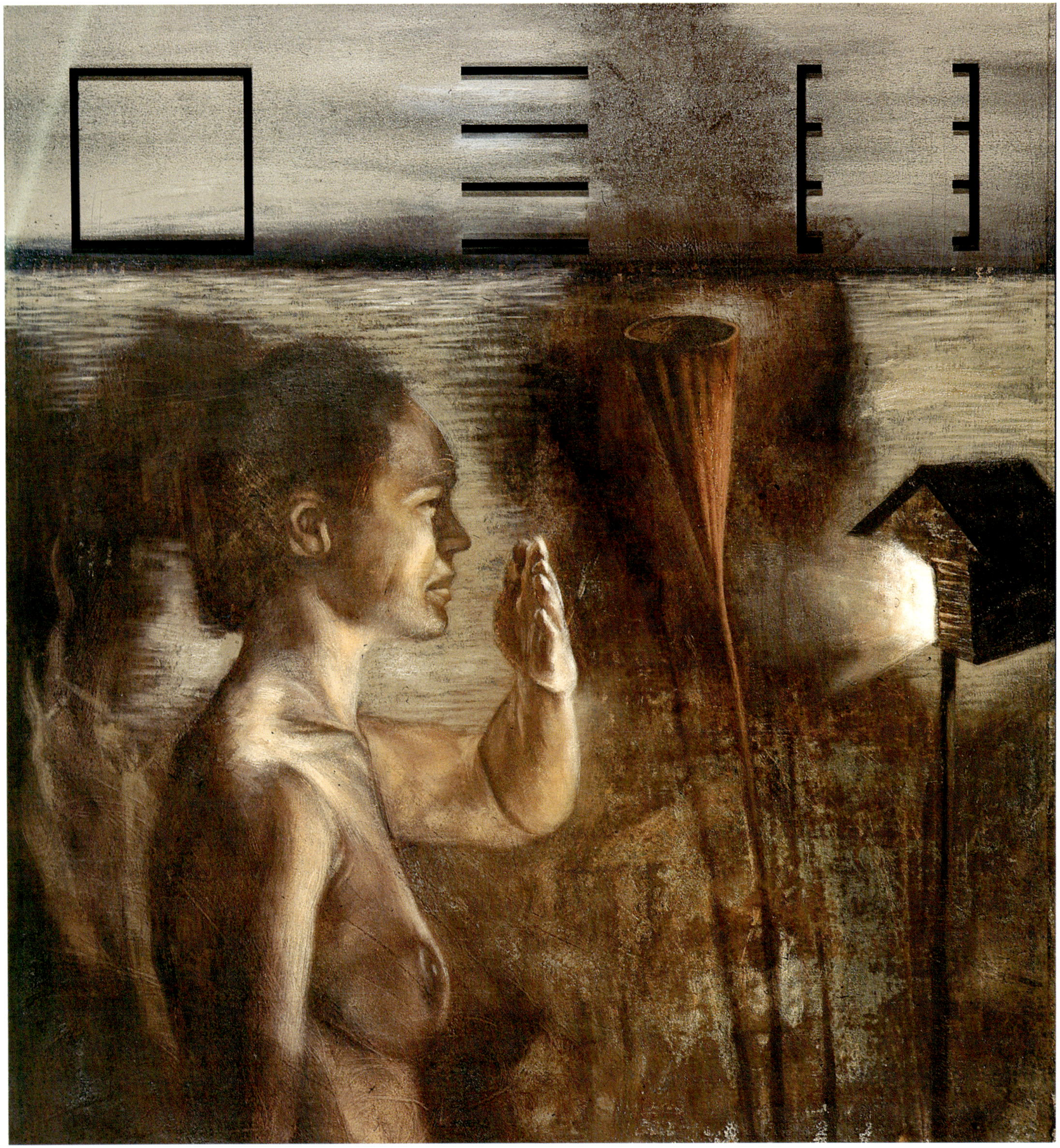

Plate 40

Furnace 1994–95.
Oil on Paper on Board and Perspex
48 × 43½ inches

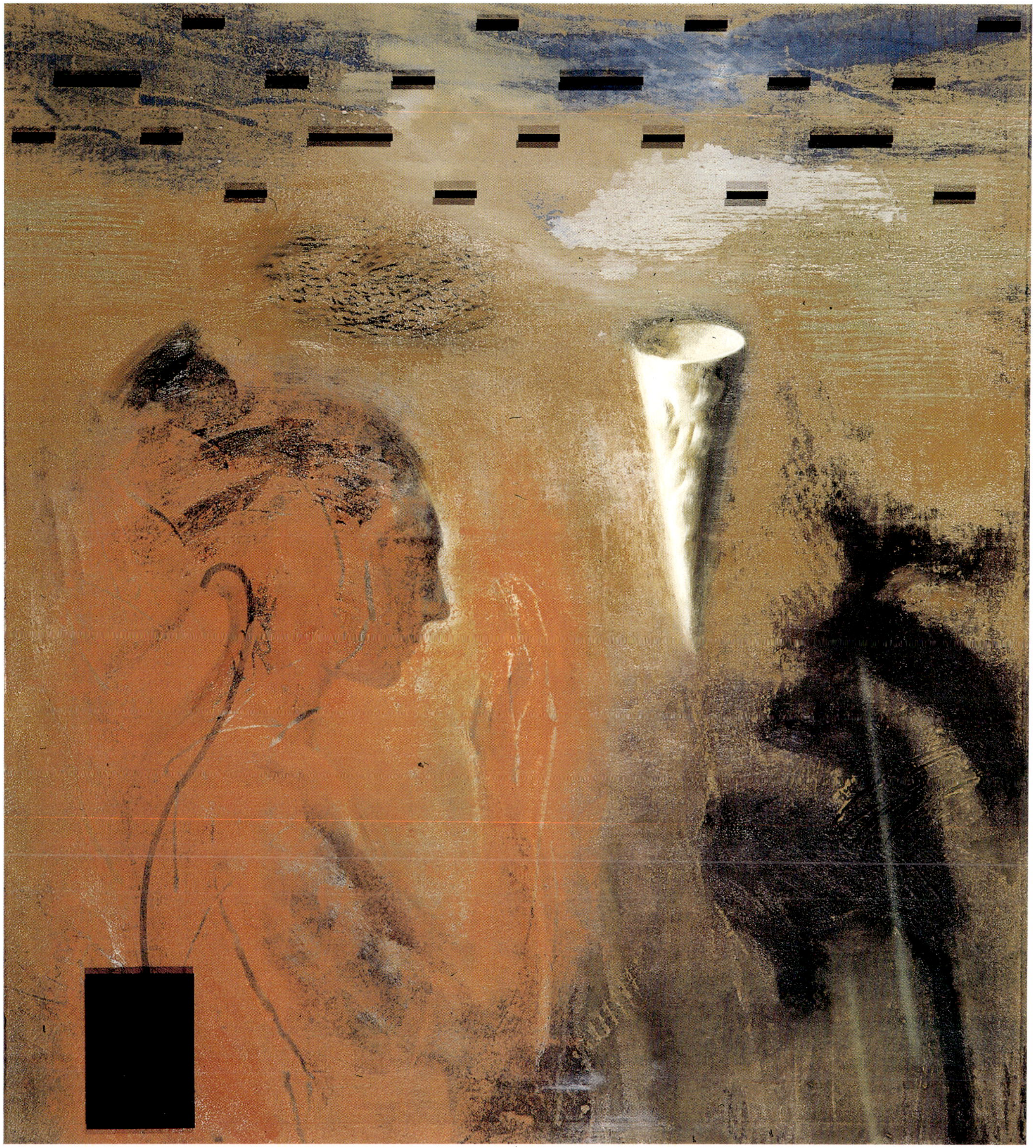

Plate 41

Burning Up 1994–95.
Oil on Paper on Board and Perspex
48 × 43½ inches
Private Collection

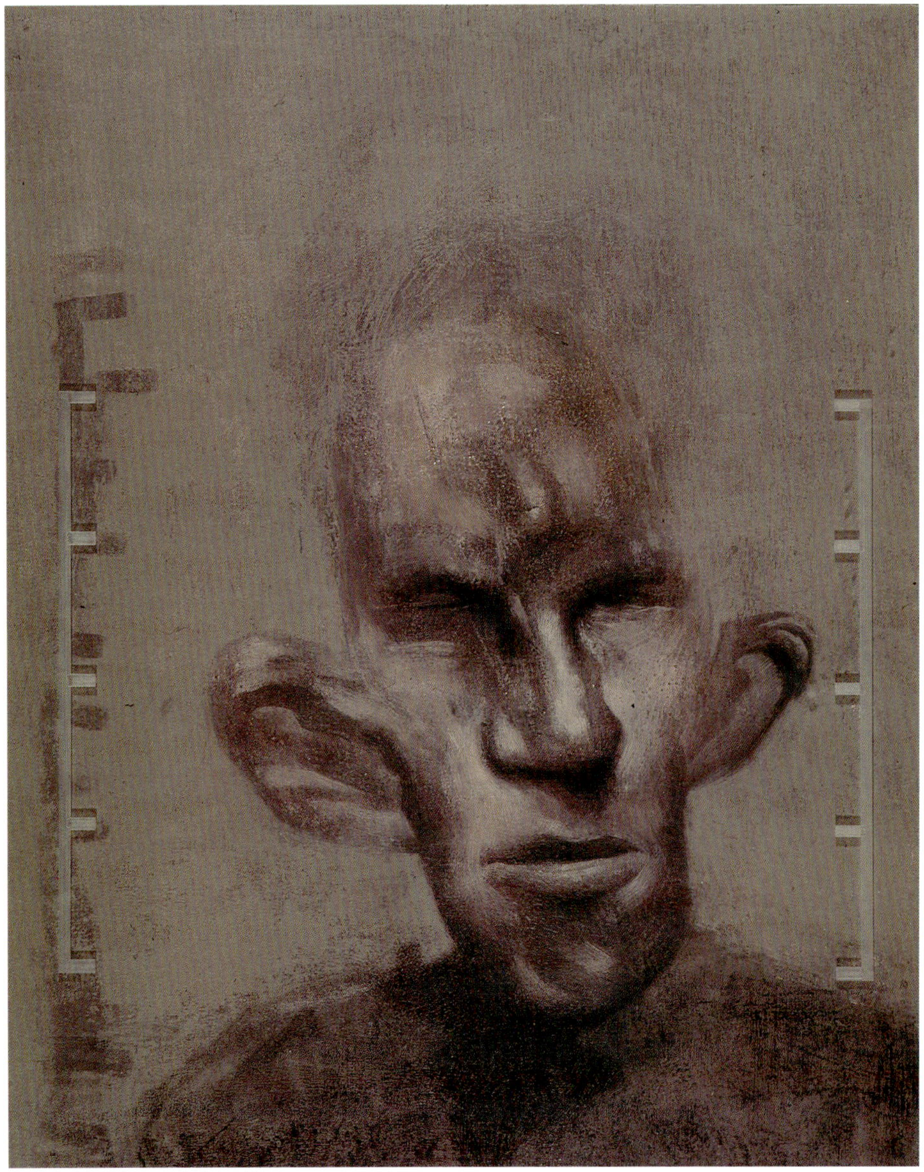

Plate 42

Old Science 4 1993.
Oil on Paper on Board and Perspex
18 × 14 inches
Private Collection

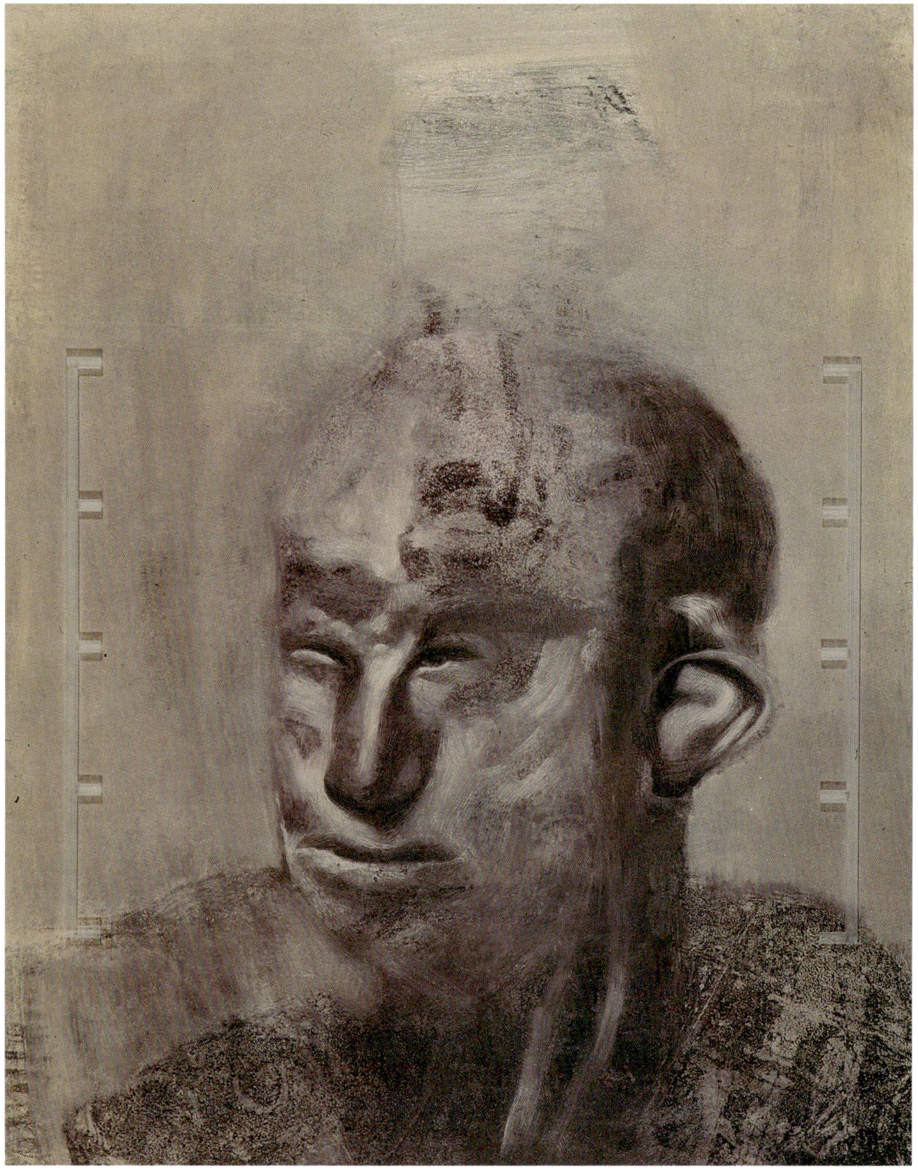

Old Science 5 1993.
Oil on Paper on Board and Perspex
18 × 14 inches
Private Collection

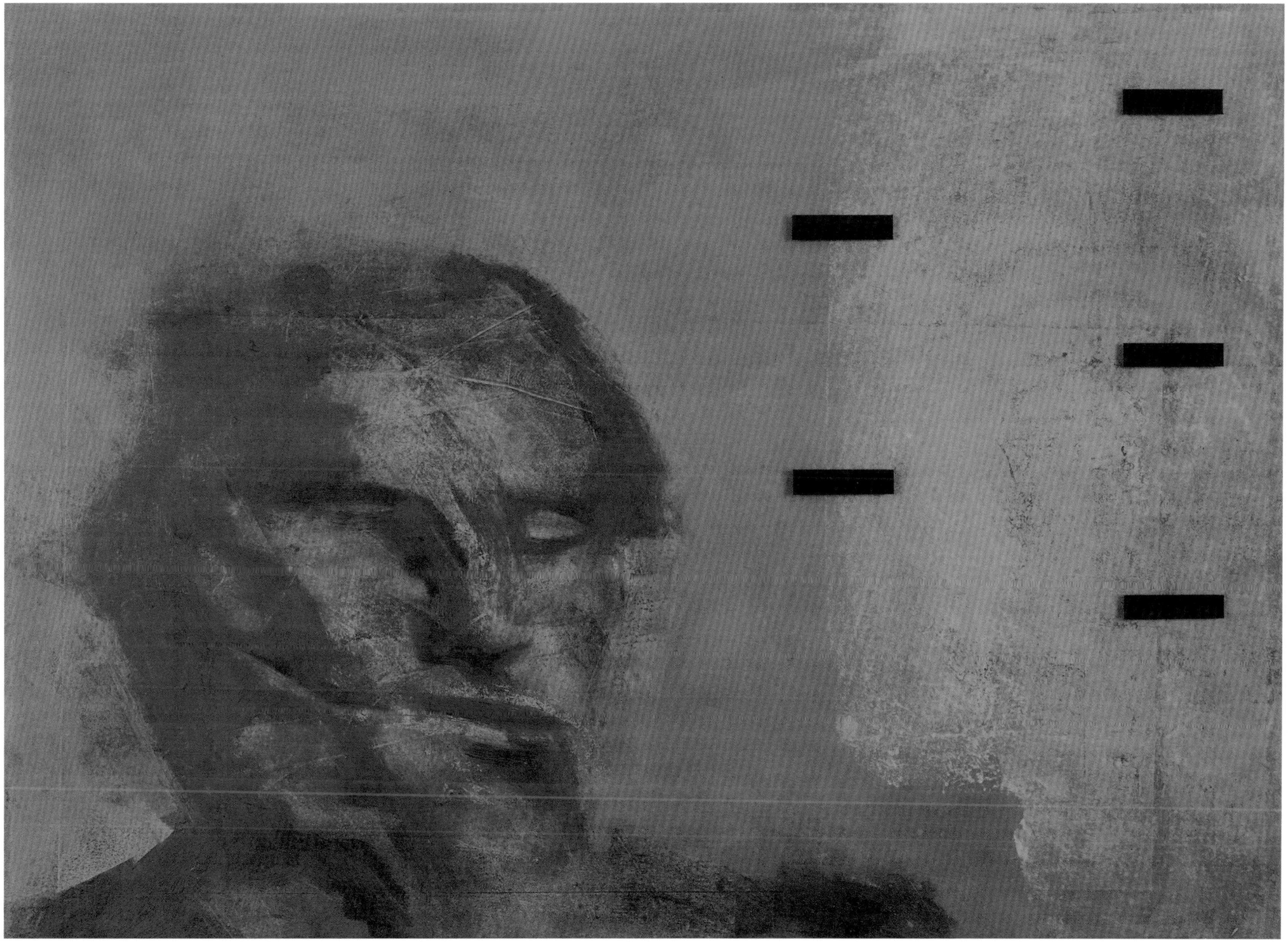

Plate 43

Old Science 2 1993.
Oil on Paper on Board and Perspex
14 × 18 inches
Private Collection

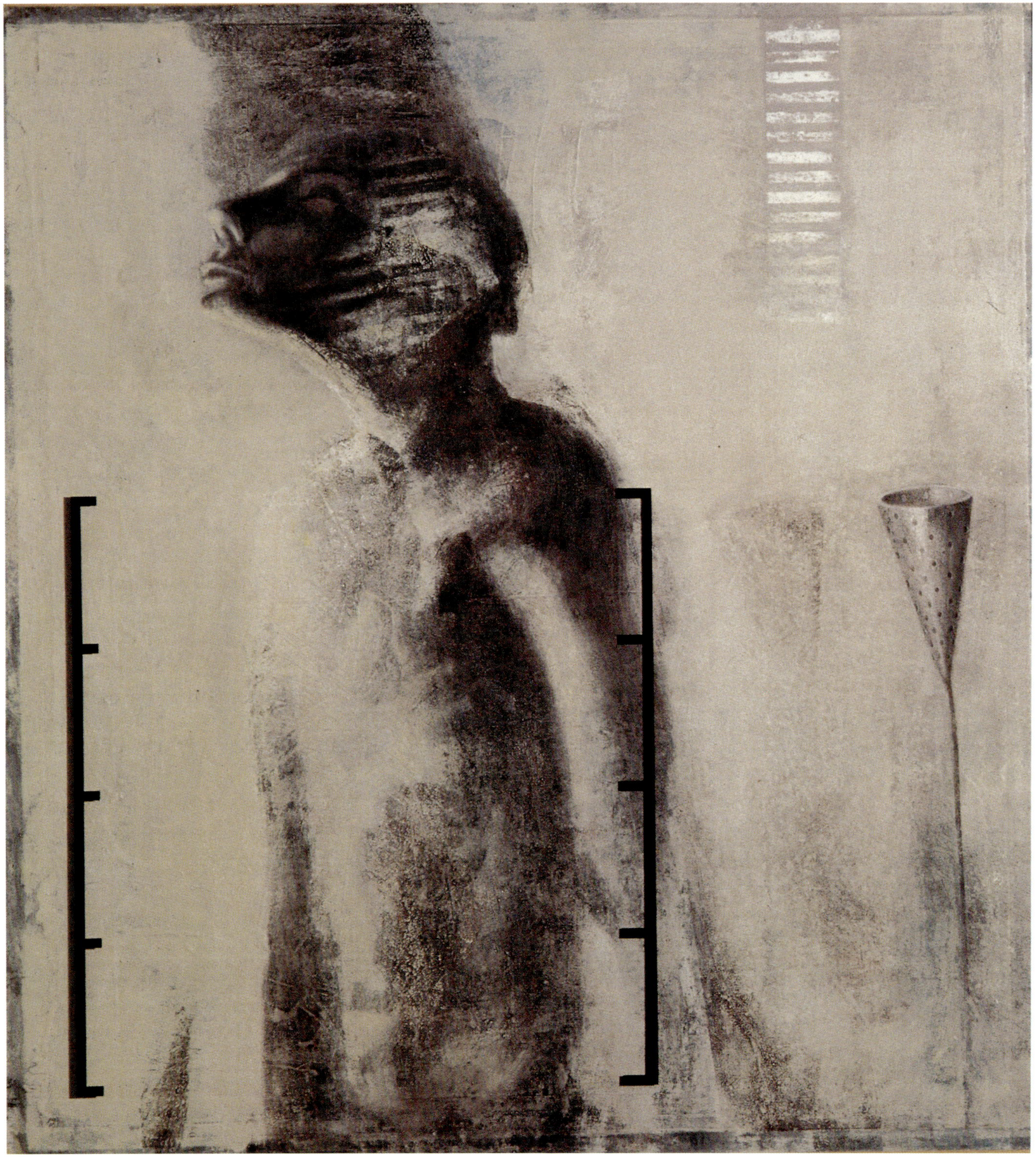

Plate 44

Man and Measure 1 1993.
Oil on Paper on Board and Perspex
48 × 43½ inches
Private Collection

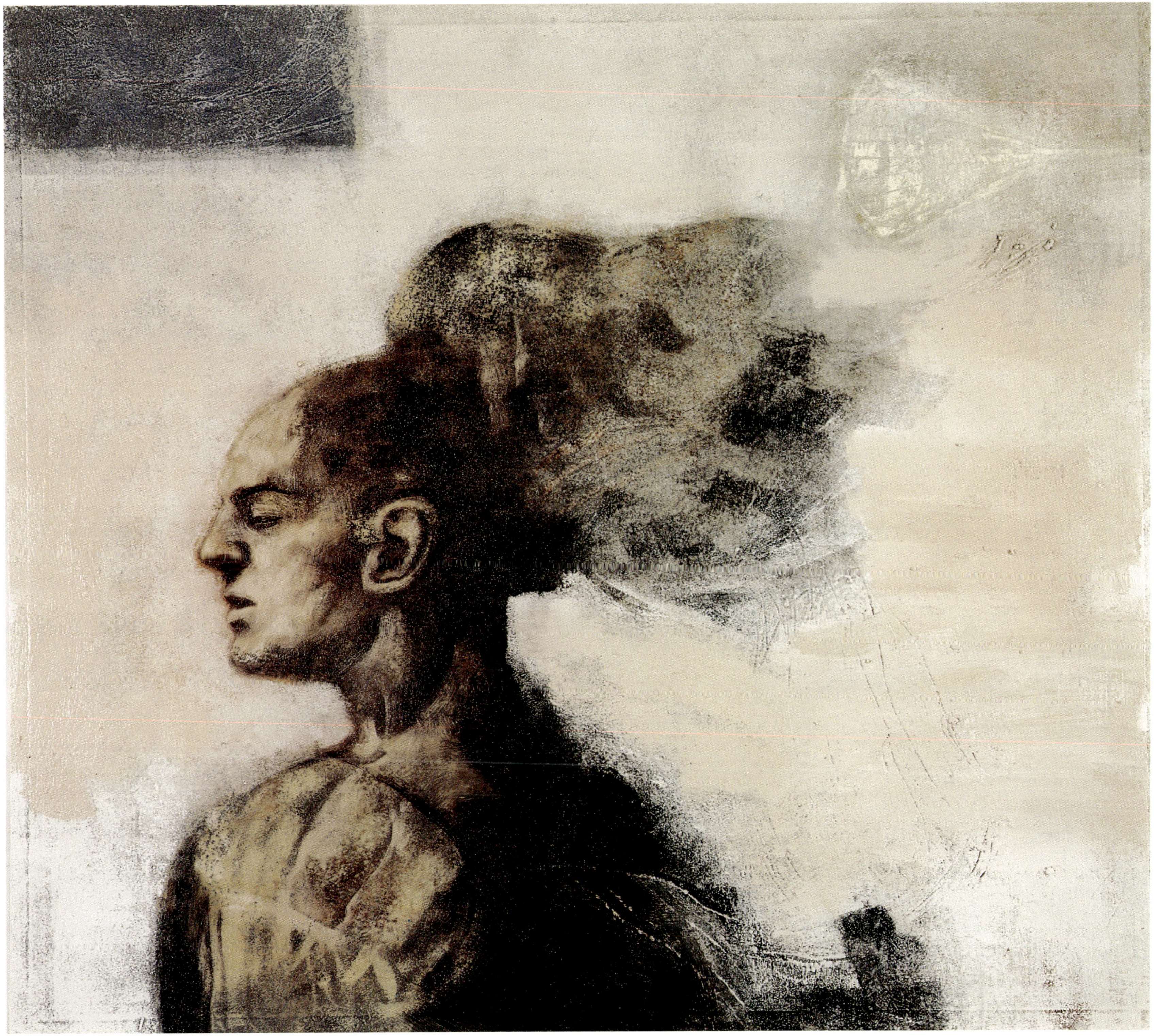

Plate 45

History Painting 1994.
Oil on Paper on Board
48 × 43½ inches
Private Collection

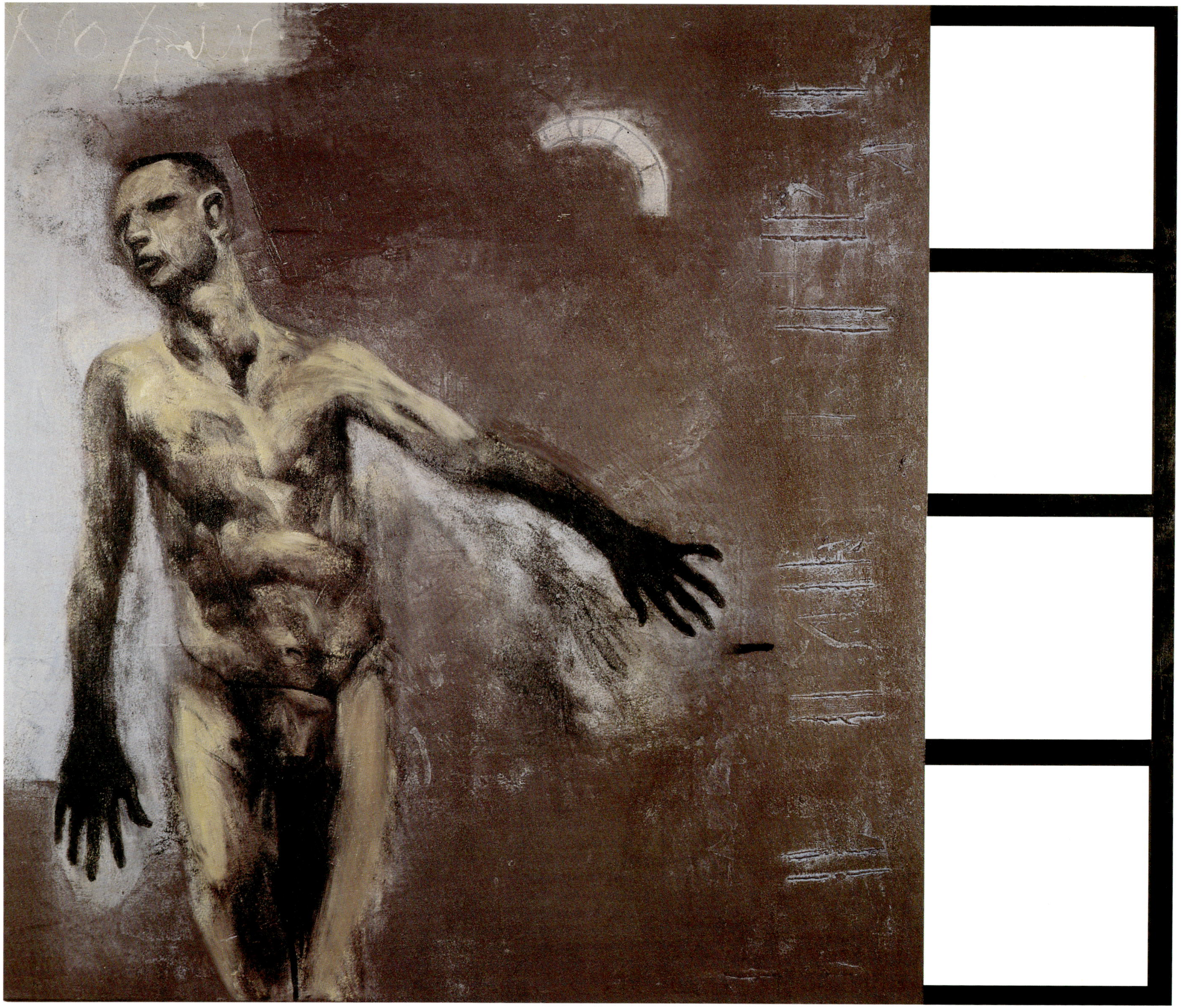

Plate 46

Man & Measure 2 19
Oil on Panel and Wood
72 × 80 inches
Private Collection

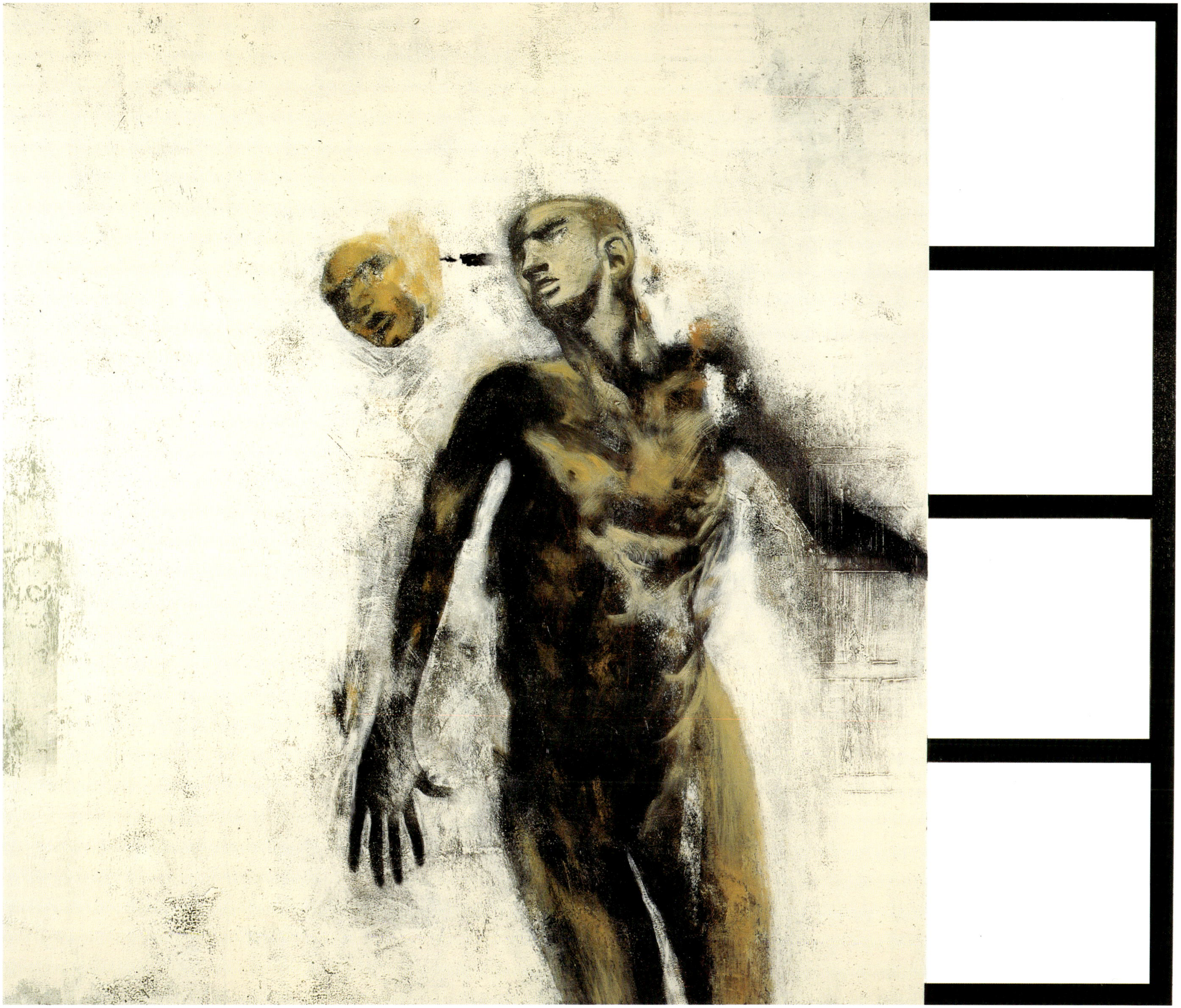

Plate 47

Man & Measure 3 1994.
Oil on Panel and Wood
72 × 80 inches
Private Collection

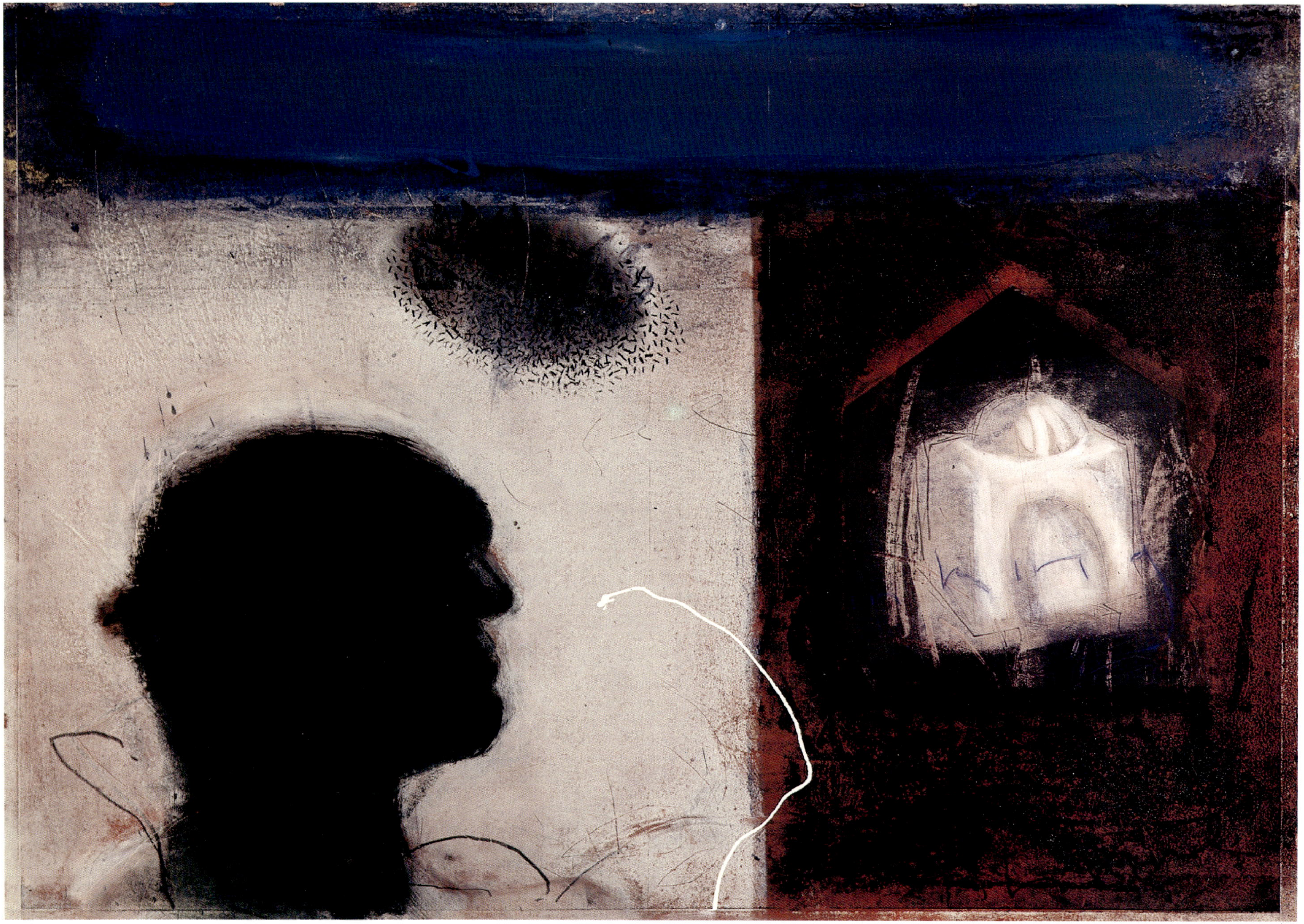

Plate 48

Shrine 1995.
Mixed Media on Paper
27½ × 39 inches
Private Collection

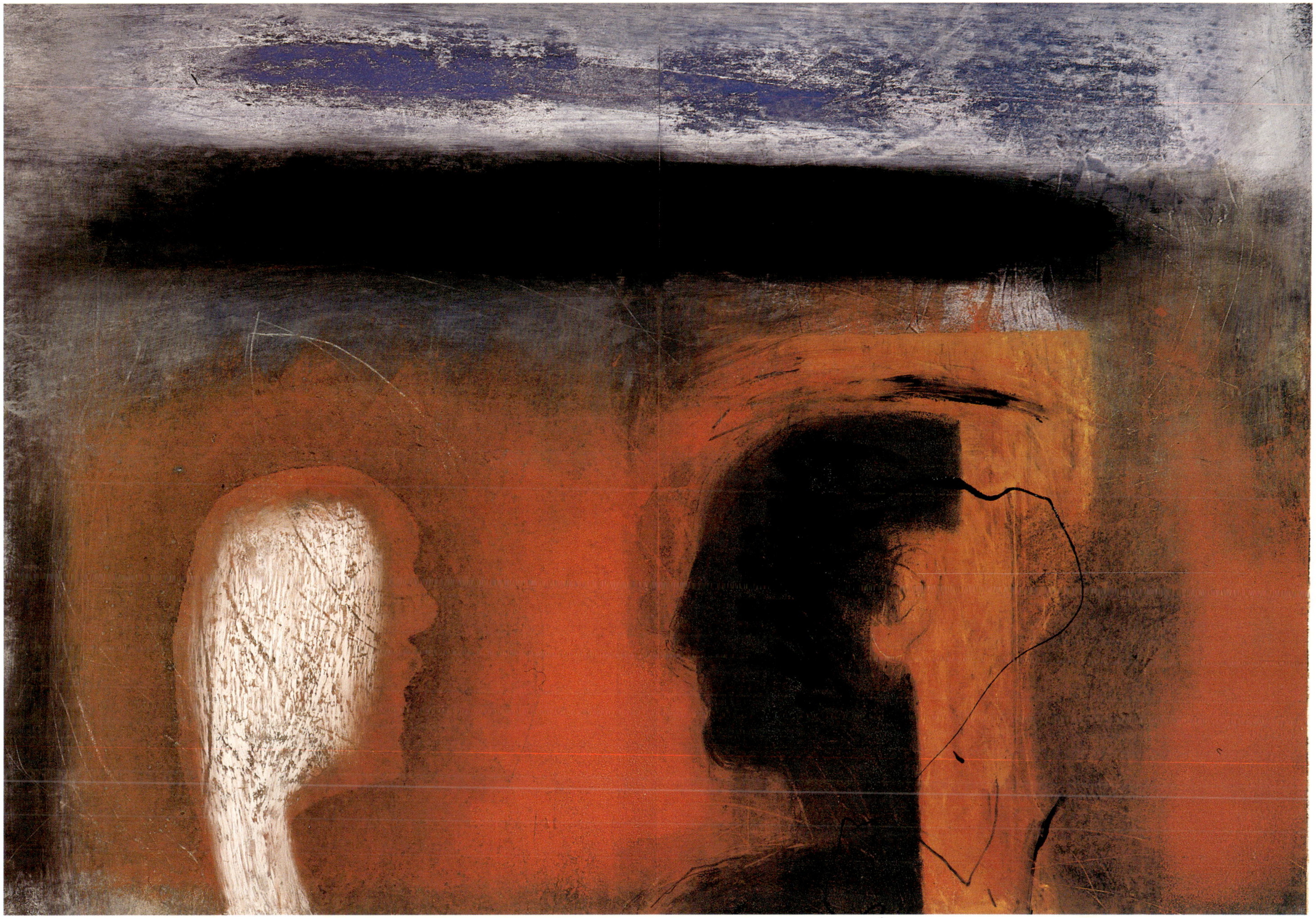

Plate 49

Reflection 1995.
Mixed Media on Paper
27½ × 39 inches
Private Collection

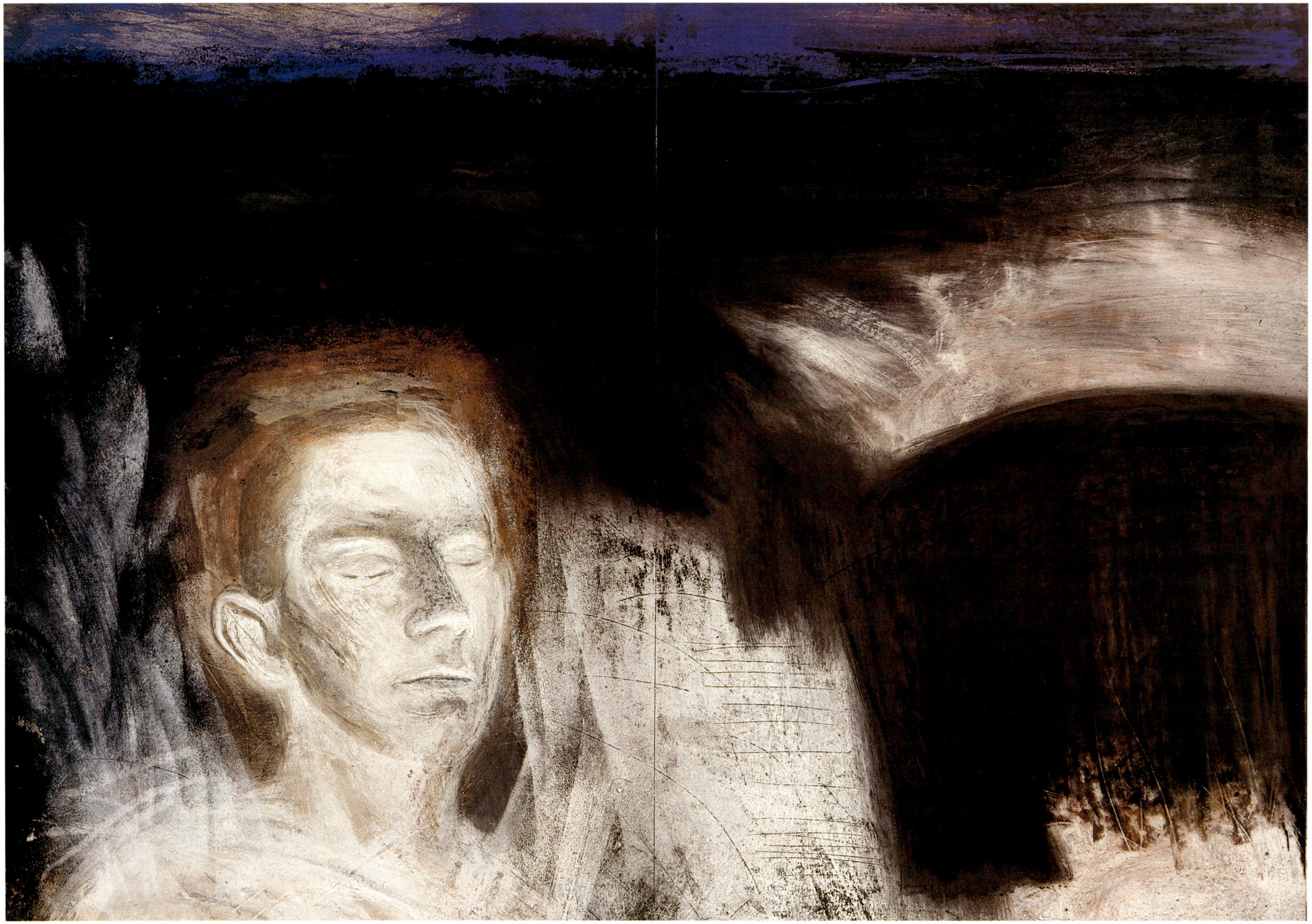

Plate 50

Angel 1995.
Mixed Media on Paper
27½ × 39 inches
Private Collection

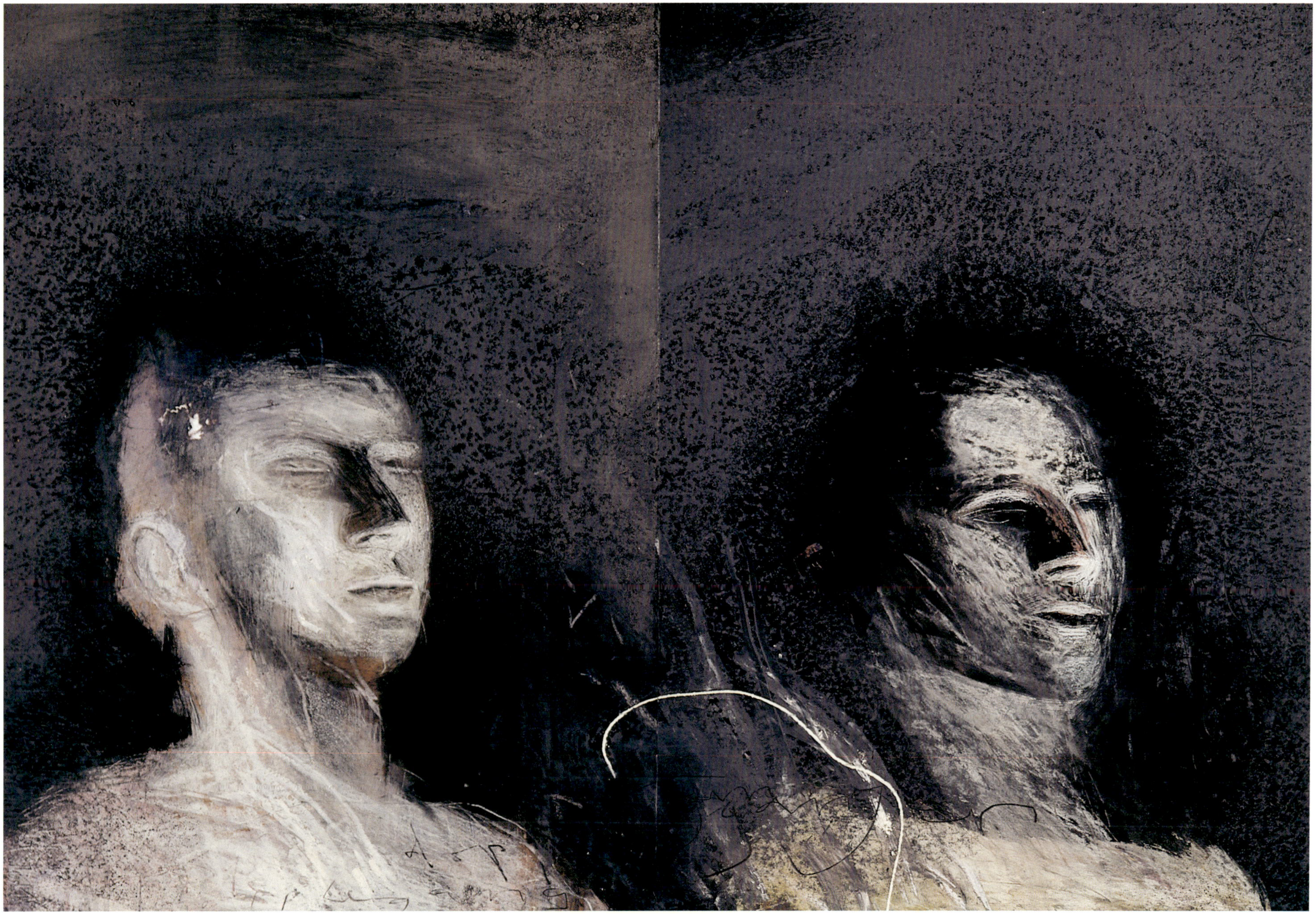

Plate 51

Doppelgänger 1995.
Mixed Media on Paper
27½ × 39 inches

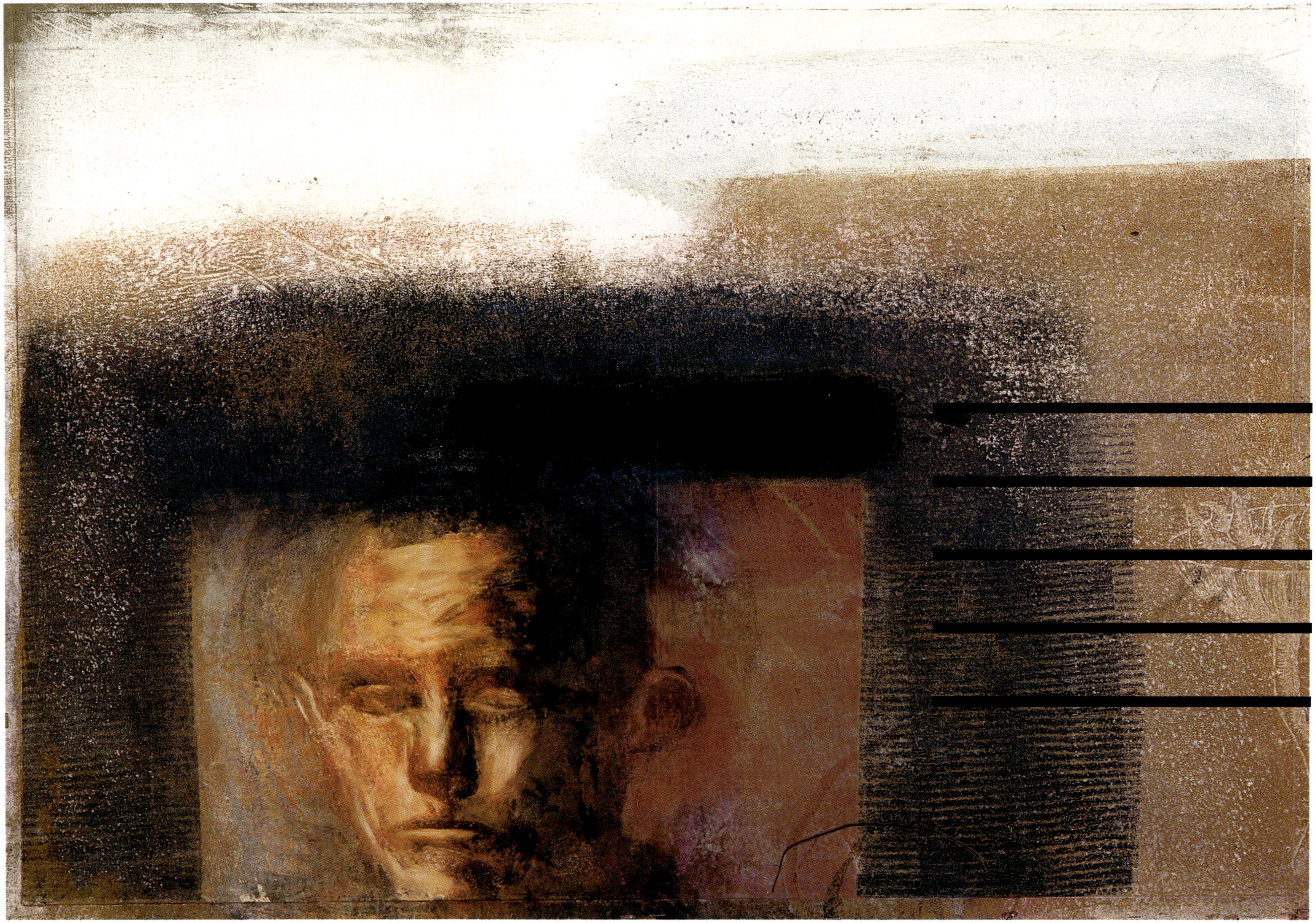

Plate 52

Blind Man 1995.
Mixed Media on Paper and Perspex
27½ × 39 inches

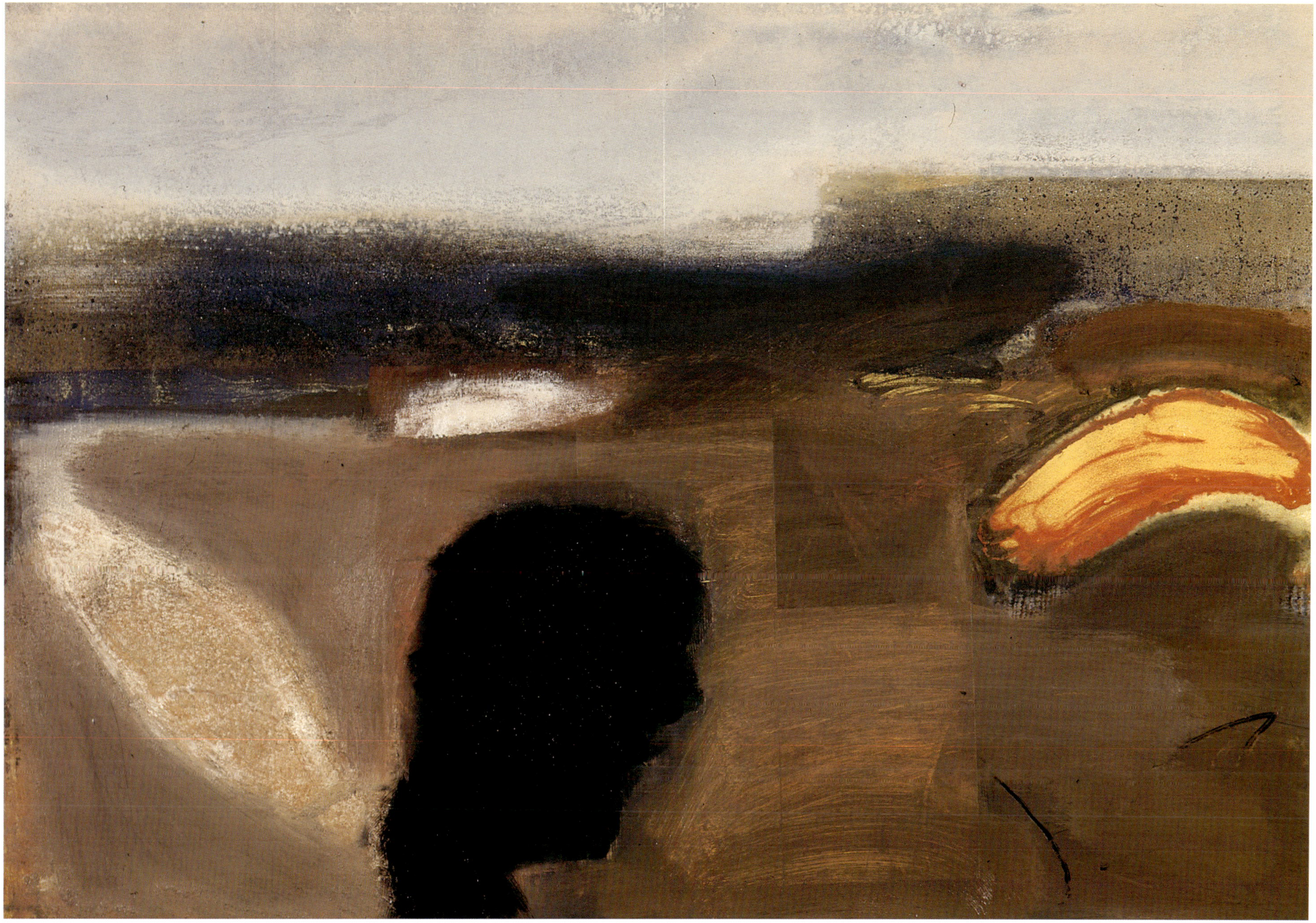

Plate 53

Shadow 1995.
Mixed Media on Paper
$27\frac{1}{2} \times 39$ inches

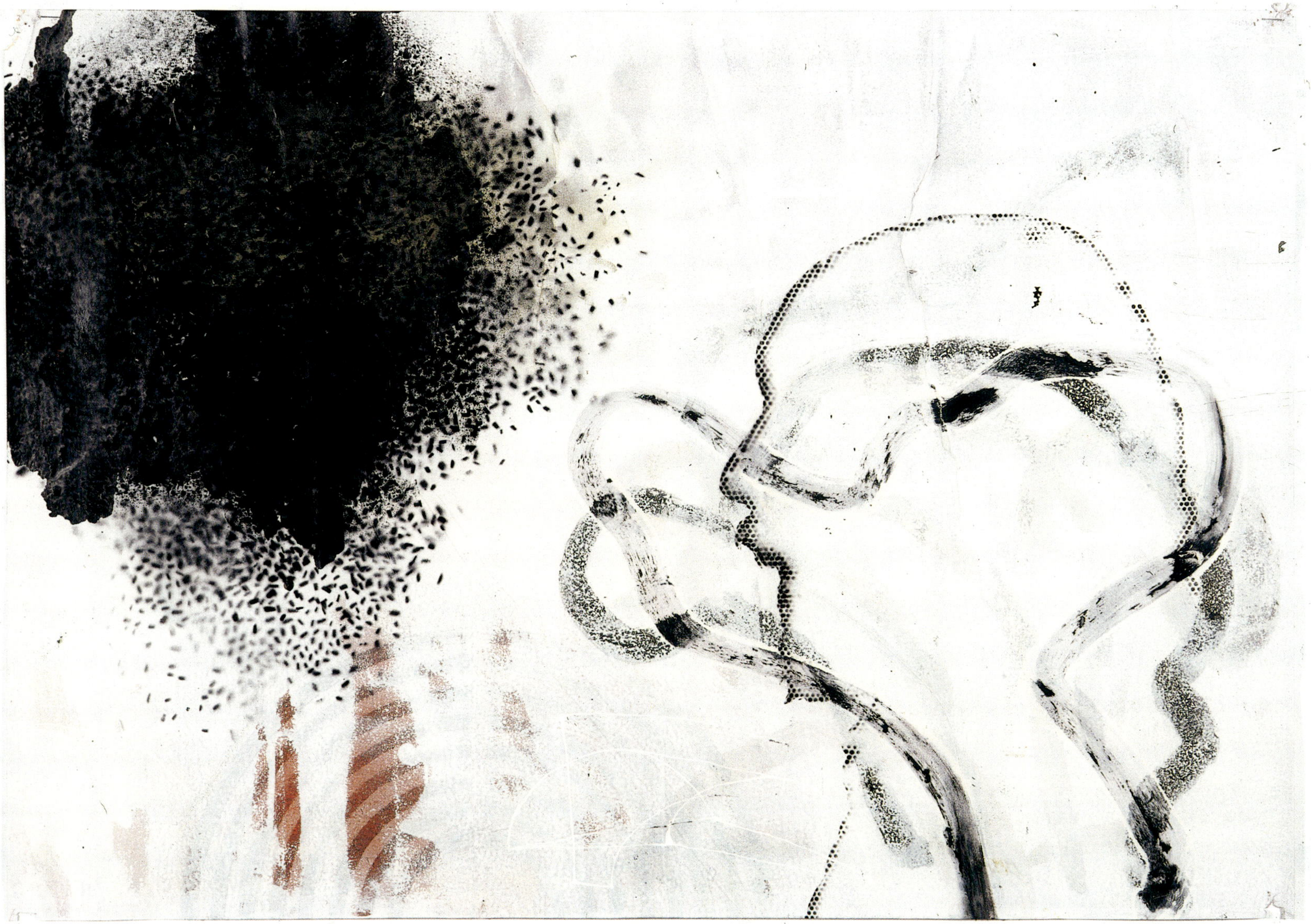

Plate 54

Toledo 1 1995.
Mixed Media on Paper
19½ × 27 inches

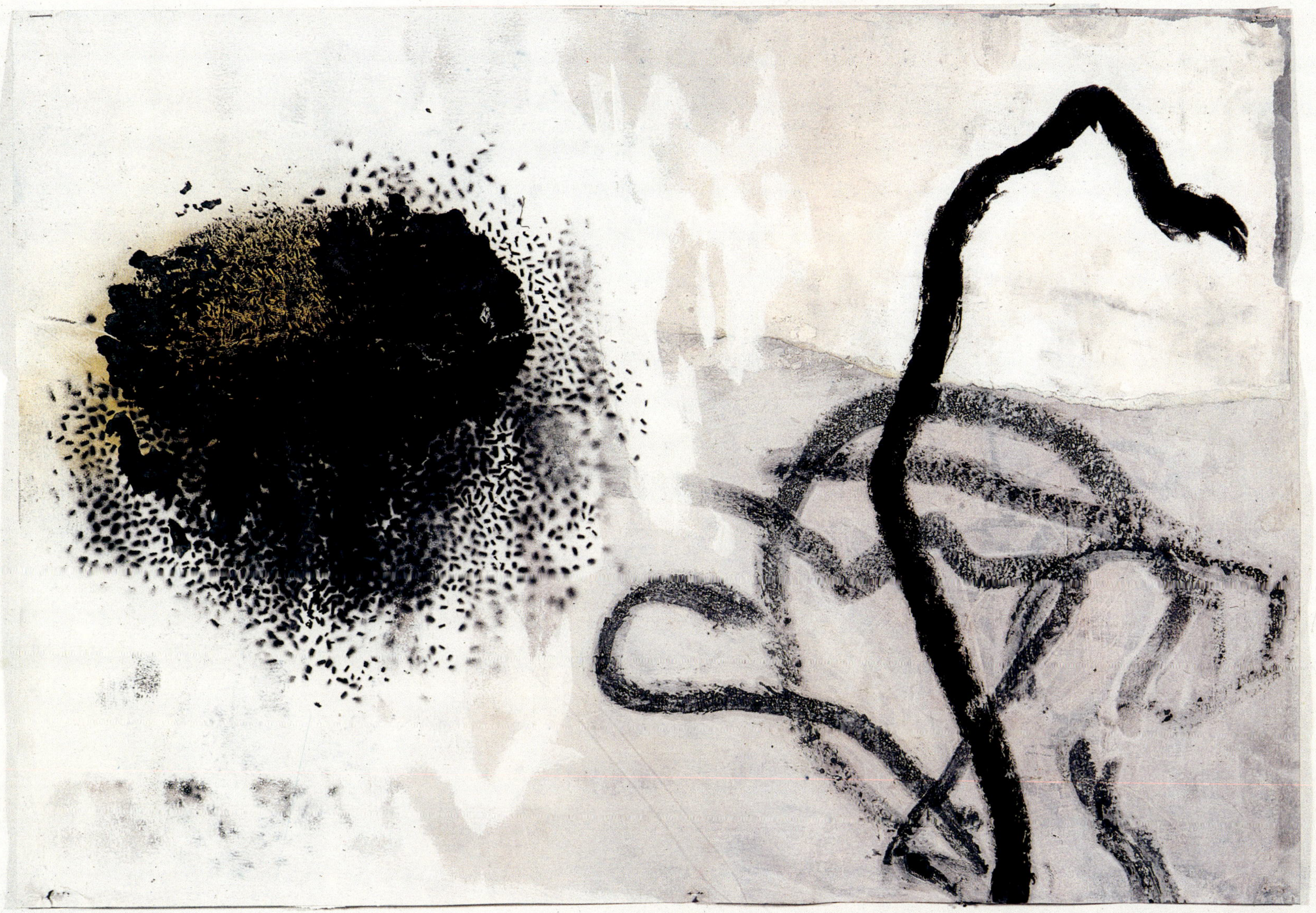

Plate 55

Toledo 2 1995.
Mixed Media on Paper
19½ × 27 inches

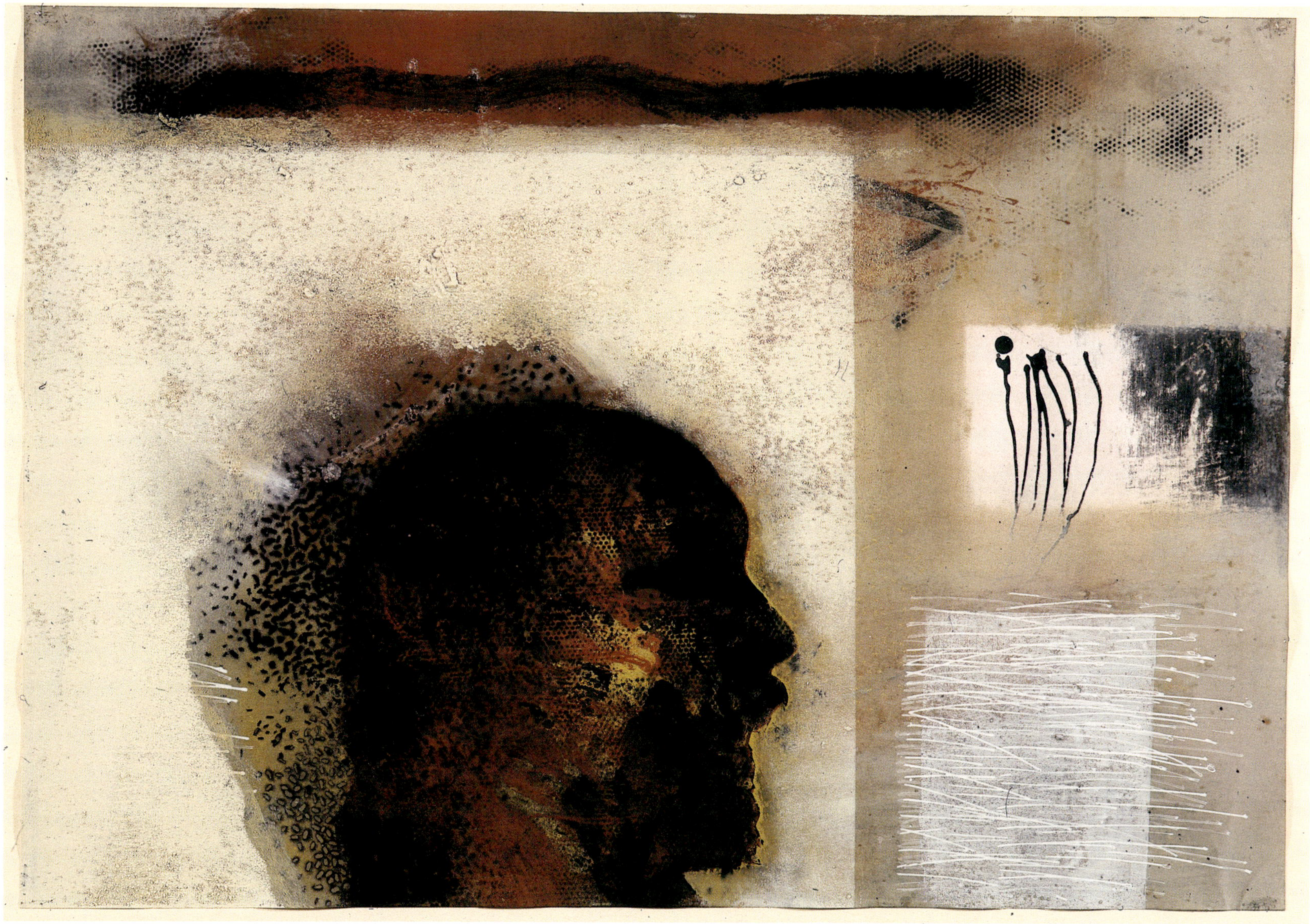

Plate 56

Toledo 5 1995.
Mixed Media on Paper
19½ × 27 inches

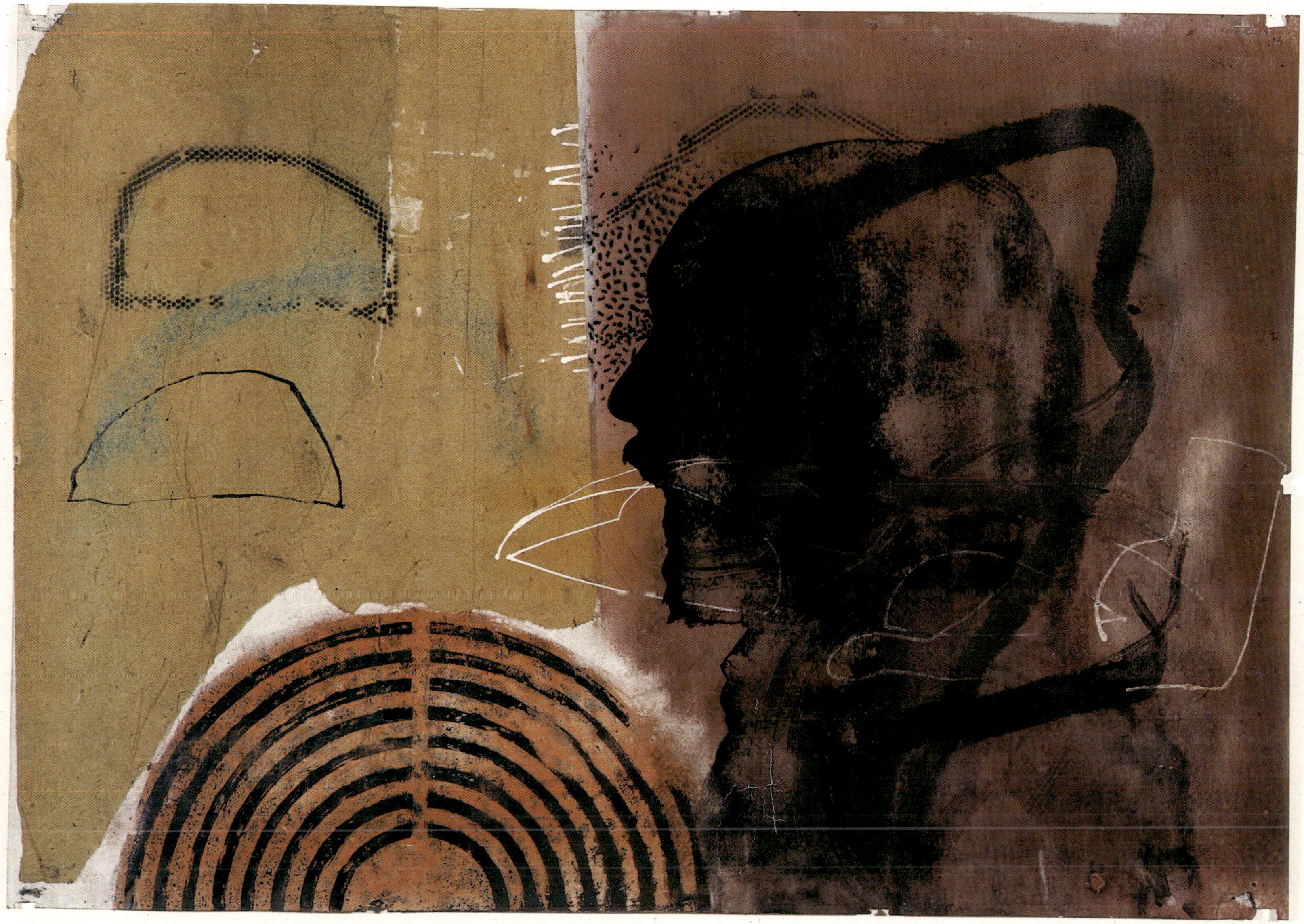

Plate 57

Toledo 3 1995.
Mixed Media on Paper
$19\frac{1}{2} \times 27$ inches

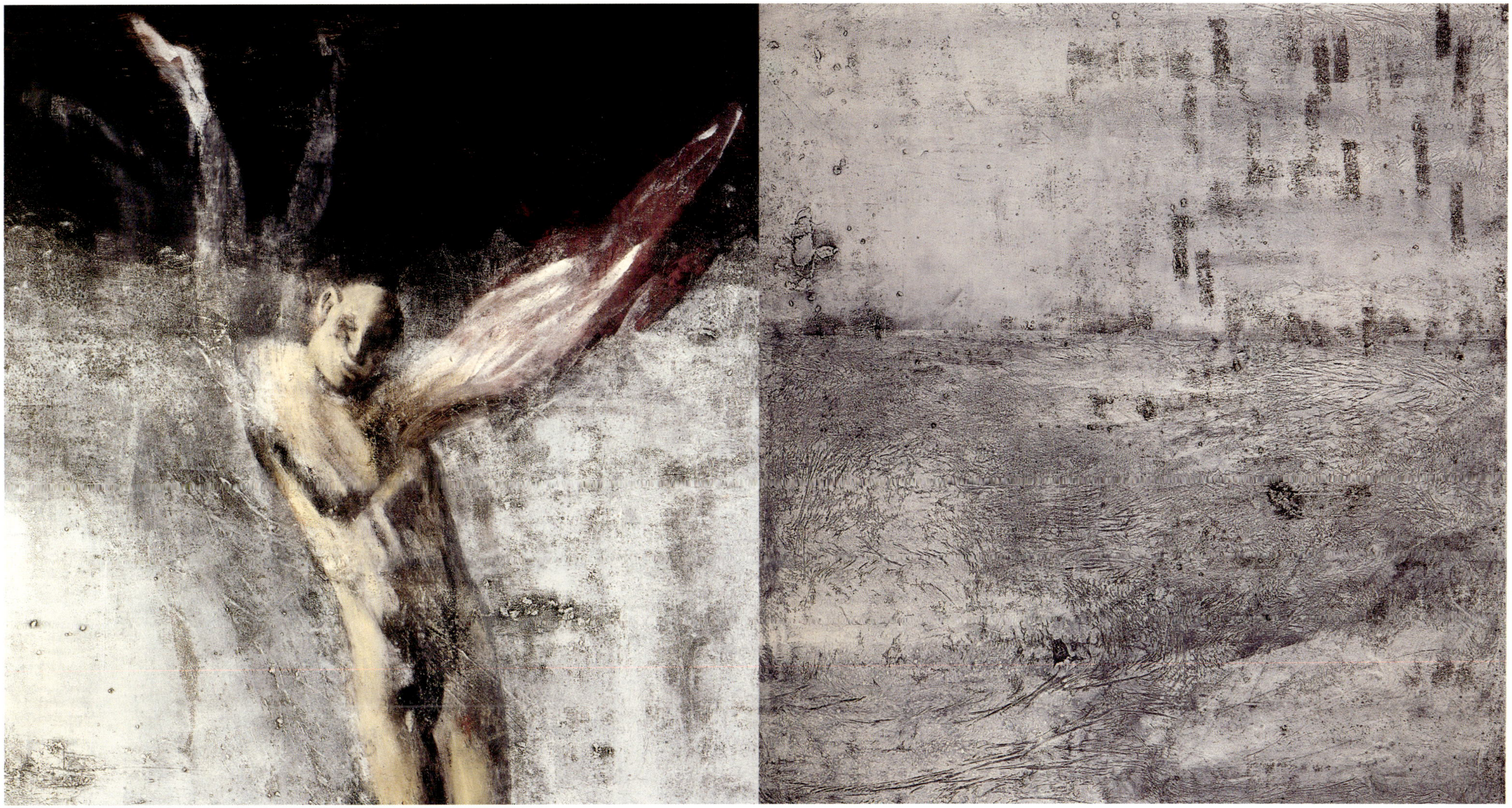

◀ Detail

Plate 59

Drowning in a Desert 1994.
Oil on Panel
72 × 134 inches

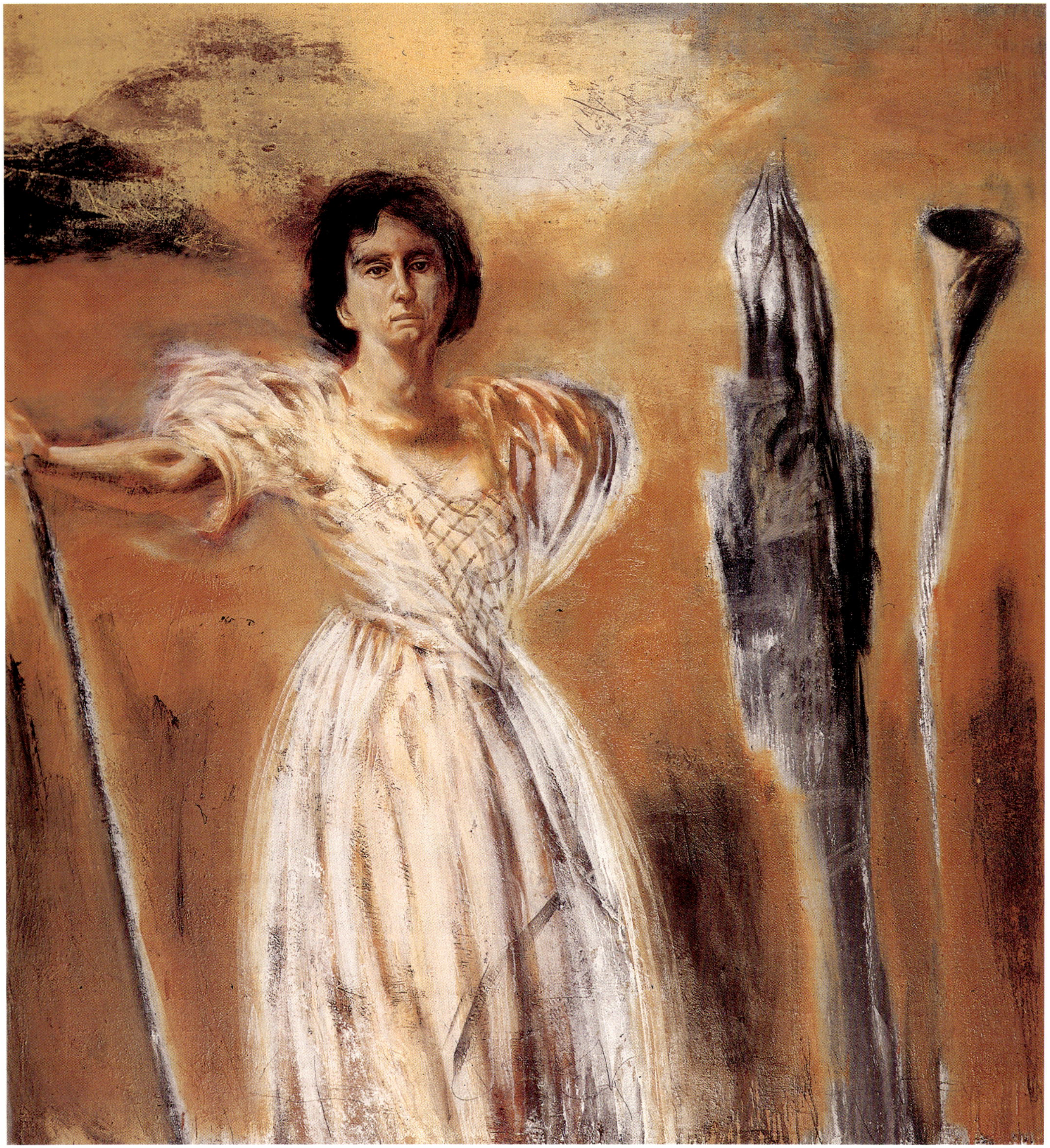

Plate 60

Cathedral 1994–95.
Oil on panel
72 × 67 inches

Biographical notes

1955 Born 8 September, Dar es Salaam, Tanganyika (Tanzania), third son of Tom and Colombe Wood.

1958 Tom Wood senior died of a heart attack on 31 August, aged 39.

1959 Colombe Wood moved with her three children to Liversedge, West Yorkshire, home of the Wood family.

1966–75 Attended Cardinal Hinsley Catholic Boys Grammar School, Bradford.

1975 Foundation Course, Batley School of Art.

1976–78 Sheffield School of Art.

1977 Married Elaine Barraclough.

1978 Working part-time at Batley School of Art. First meeting with Arthur Haigh, influential collector and patron.

1980 Started working part-time at Bretton Hall College. Visited Paris.

1981 June, daughter Laura born. Artist in industry fellowship at Redfern Glass, Barnsley. Artist in residence at the Piece Hall Art Gallery, Halifax. Awarded Elizabeth Greenshields Foundation Award.

1982 Awarded Gulbenkian Foundation Printmaker's Award and also commissioned by print publishers Woodward Roodhouse to make a large etching.

1983 April, daughter Elinor born. William Feaver selected work for touring show. Two man show at the Paton Gallery, London. Large commissioned portraits of Arthur Haigh, and Elaine Wood completed. Artist in Industry Fellowship at Vickers plc, Newcastle upon Tyne.

1984 Commissioned to do a large drawing of the engine room of the ship M.V. *Melampus*. Awarded second Elizabeth Greenshields Foundation Award. Commissioned by Bradford Art Galleries and Museums to do a large double portrait of Arthur Haigh and former *Yorkshire Post* Art Critic, W.T. Oliver. Retrospective exhibition at Cartwright Hall, Bradford.

1985 Awarded second prize in the John Player Portrait Award. Moved from Bradford to live and work in Halifax, West Yorkshire.

1986 Prizewinner, ninth International Print Biennale, Cartwright Hall, Bradford.

1987 February, daughter Saskia born. Commissioned through Public Arts to make a record of the Colne Valley. Artist in School Residency, Bradford. Moved to a studio in Dean Clough, Halifax. Portraits commissioned by H.R.H. The Prince of Wales and Bradford University.

1988 London Underground commissioned poster for The Museum of Mankind.

1989 Completed portrait and poster commissions. Work exhibited at Dean Clough, Halifax and Agnews, London. Artists Residency at the National Portrait Gallery. Awarded Honorary Fellowship by Sheffield Hallam University.

1990 Commenced association with Hart Gallery. Visited New York, Chicago, Toronto and Ottawa. Workshops at The McClellan Gallery, Glasgow. Portrait of Alan Bennett commissioned by

National Portrait Gallery, and portrait of Timothy Colman commissioned by Norwich Castle Museum and Art Gallery. Lectured at the Yale Center for British Art, New Haven and Yale University.

1991 Participated in symposium at Yale Center for British Art. Visited New York, Atlanta, Pensacola, Florida, Majorca and Amsterdam. Commissioned to work on the design of a bar to be installed in the Square Chapel Arts Centre, Halifax. Completed 'Lexicon', a boxed set of ten prints with printer Ralph Gratton, and worked on collaborations with rugmaker Peter Colgan and designer Alwyn Turner. Suite of prints commissioned by The Caring Arts for the new St Lukes Hospital, Bradford. Large monoprints commissioned by British Gas. Recieved RSA *Art into Architecture* award.

1992 Exhibited prints at Marlborough Gallery, London. Portrait of Professor Peter Brooks commissioned by Yale University. Met Jean Francois Lyotard. Visited New York.

1993 May, Colombe Camille Wood, mother, died. Skopos Professor at Bretton Hall College.

1994 Commissioned to paint portraits of Professor Sir Michael Thompson, Birmingham University and Professor Kenneth Morgan, University of Wales. Artist in Schools Residency, Bradford. Visited Los Angeles.

1995 Visited Madrid, Toledo, Geneva, Florida and Mombasa. Living and working in Halifax, West Yorkshire.

1996 Commissioned to paint portrait of Sir Colin Dollery, Royal Hammersmith Hospital.

Living and working in Halifax, West Yorkshire.

Collections

Arthur Andersen & Co.

University of Birmingham

University of Bradford

Bradford Art Galleries and Museums

British Gas plc

Calderdale Art Galleries and Museums

Calderdale School and Museums Resource Service

Dean Clough Contemporary Art Collection

H.R.H The Prince of Wales Collection

Kirklees Art Galleries and Museums

University of Leeds

Leeds Arts Education Loan Service

Leeds City Art Gallery Print Loan Collection

London Underground

National Portrait Gallery

Norwich Art Gallery and Museum

Ocean Trading and Transport plc

Octagon Marketing Group

Provident Financial Group plc

Rank Xerox

Redfern National Glass

Shaw Timber Ltd

Sheffield Art Galleries and Museums

Skopos Ltd

Vickers Defence Systems plc

Wakefield Art Galleries and Museums

Wakefield School and Museum Resource Service

Whitworth Art Gallery

University of Wales

Yale Center for British Art

Yale University

Group Exhibitions

1978 Seven Young Artists, Danefield Gallery, Bradford

1979 Two man show, Bankfield Museum, Halifax

1981 Six artists in industry, Cartwright Hall, Bradford

Anderson, Langton, Wood, St Paul's Gallery, Leeds

1983 Gulbenkian Award winners, Arnolfini, Bristol

Contemporary Printmaking, Air Gallery, London

Yorkshire Arts Touring, St Paul's Gallery, Leeds

Two man show, Paton Gallery, London

1984 Art At Work, Hatton Gallery, Newcastle

Look People, St Paul's Gallery, Leeds and National Portrait Gallery, London

Works on Paper, Freetown, Sierra Leone

British Artists, Dortmund, West Germany

1985 Critics Choice, Mappin Art Gallery, Sheffield

The Bestiary, Two man show, Arcade Gallery, Harrogate

Two man show, Linton Court Gallery, Settle

John Player Portrait Award, National Portrait Gallery, London

Just Drawings, Hawskworth Gallery, Ilkley

1986 The Irresistible Object: Still Life 1600–1985, Leeds City Art Gallery, Leeds

Art At Work, South London Art Gallery, London

Tradition and Innovation in Printmaking Today, Barbican Art Gallery, London

Ninth International Print Biennale Cartwright Hall, Bradford.

Art, Science and Industry, Imperial College, London

1987 Leicester School and Museum Resource Show, Leicester

Two man show, Hawksworth Gallery, Ilkley

New Art in Yorkshire, Leeds University Gallery, Leeds

Spirit of the Colne Valley, Huddersfield City Art Gallery

Artists Day Book, Smiths Gallery, London

1988 Two man show, Smiths Gallery, London

Graven Images: Art, Religion and Politics, Harris Museum and Art Gallery, Preston

Object and Image: Aspects of British Art in the 1980s, Stoke Museum and Art Gallery, Stoke-on-Trent

Hommage to the Square, Flaxman Gallery, London

Two man show, Leeds University Gallery, Leeds

Modern British Artist as Printmaker: The Post-War Years, Austin Desmond Gallery, London

1990 The Art Machine, McClellan Gallery, Glasgow and Barbican, London

Crown Pictorial, Yale Center for British Art, New Haven, USA

Leeds Art Fair

1991 Art London, Contemporary Art Fair, Olympia

Leeds Art Fair

Group show, Dean Clough, Halifax

1992 Art 92, London Contemporary Art Fair

Contemporary Prints, Marlborough Graphics, London

Edinburgh Contemporary Art Fair

1993 Art 93, London Contemporary Art Fair

Manchester Fine Art Fair

Chicago International Art Exposition

Bath Contemporary Art Fair

Art L.A., Los Angeles International Art Fair

'The Portrait Now', National Portrait Gallery, London

Family and Friends, Norwich Castle Museum

1994 Art 94, London Contemporary Art Fair

Twentieth Century British Art Fair, Royal College of Art, London

Dean Clough Artists, Bury Art Gallery

Manchester Fine Art Fair

1995 Art 95, London Contemporary Art Fair

Manchester Fine Art Fair

Group Show, Dean Clough, Halifax

Europ'art, Geneva

Twentieth Century British Art Fair, Royal College of Art, London

Lineart, Ghent

Recent Acquisitions, Whitworth Art Gallery, Manchester

Group Show, Escuela de Arte, Oviedo, Spain.

Solo Exhibitions

1980 Ilkley College, Ilkley
Bretton Hall College, West Bretton

1981 Mappin Art Gallery, Sheffield
Piece Hall Art Gallery, Halifax

1983 Northern Arts, Newcastle

1984 Cartwright Hall, Bradford
Huddersfield Art Gallery

1986 Lister Gallery, Bradford

1987 Langley Furrow, Rochdale
Hawksworth Gallery, Ilkley
Dean Clough Contemporary Art Gallery, Halifax

1989 Dean Clough Contemporary Art Gallery, Halifax
Agnews, London
Library Gallery, Cardiff

1990 Wakefield City Art Gallery, Wakefield
Hart Gallery, Nottingham
Gardner Kirby Gallery, Ottawa, Ontario

1991 Linton Court Gallery, Settle
Hart Gallery, Nottingham
Craft and Design Centre, Leeds

1992 King of Hearts Gallery, Norwich

1993 Craft and Design Centre, Leeds
Hart Gallery, Nottingham

1994 Hart Gallery, London
Leeds City Art Gallery, Leeds

1995 Bretton Hall College, West Bretton
Hart Gallery, London

1996 Hart Gallery, Nottingham

1997 Hart Gallery, London

Bibliography

Allen, Vic, 'Tom Wood', *Art Scene Yorkshire and Humberside,* November 1994

Bailey, Martin, 'The Prince and The Painter', *Observer Magazine,* 3 September 1989

Berryman, Larry, 'The National Portrait Gallery John Player Awards', *Arts Review,* 27 September 1985

Bumpus, Judith, 'Enter a Different World — Tom Wood's', *The Green Book Vol. 3 No. 10,* 1991

Burn, Guy, 'Prints', *Arts Review,* 24 June 1983

Collins, Judith and Gibson, Robin, *HRH The Prince of Wales: A Portrait Commission,* exhibition catalogue published by Smith Settle, Dean Clough Contemporary Art Gallery, Halifax, 25 October–18 November 1989 and Agnew's London, 28 November–15 December 1989

Crothall, Lucia, *Six Artists in Industry,* exhibition catalogue, Cartwright Hall, Bradford, 25 July–13 September 1981

Fuller, Peter, 'Putting The Prince in The Picture', *Modern Painters,* autumn 1989

Gayford, Martin, 'Painted Faces', *Telegraph Magazine,* 13 November 1993

Gibson, Robin, 'The Portrait Now', exhibition catalogue, National Portrait Gallery, 19 November 1993–6 February 1994

Gill, Allen, 'Putting Bennett in the Picture', *Yorkshire Post,* 10 June 1993

Hamilton, Robert, *Tom Wood Recent Work,* exhibition catalogue for 'The Bestiary', Arcade Gallery, Harrogate, 27 July–24 August 1985

Idem, 'The Bestiary' — Tom Wood Paintings, Mike Hughes Words, *Arts Review,* 2 August 1985

Hart, John, 'An Introduction to Tom Wood', exhibition catalogue, Hart Gallery, 1990

Hewitt, John, 'A Shiver Up My Spine'. *Bradford Telegraph and Argus,* 29 August 1978.

Idem, 'Tom Wood', *Arts Review,* 23 November 1984.

Idem, 'Turning Point of Painter's Career', *Arts Yorkshire,* November 1984

Idem, 'Review', *Bradford Telegraph and Argus,* 5 November 1993

Idem, 'Art', *Bradford Telegraph and Argus,* 16 November 1994

Heywood, Ian, 'The Spirit of Place', Paintings 1990–94, exhibition catalogue, Leeds City Art Gallery, November 1994

Hyatt, Derek, 'Tom Wood Richard Gray', *Arts Review,* 17 July 1978

Oliver, W. T., 'Paintings by Thomas Wood and Photographs by Barry Wood', *Yorkshire Post,* 22 August 1978

Idem, 'Paintings and Prints by Tony Summers, Gregory Townend and Tom Wood', *Yorkshire Post,* 5 March 1980

Idem, 'Paintings and Drawings by Tom Wood', *Yorkshire Post,* 23 October 1980

Idem, 'Paintings and Drawings by Tom Wood', *Yorkshire Post,* 10 November 1981

Idem, 'Tom Wood Paintings and Drawings', exhibition catalogue, Mappin Art Gallery, Sheffield, 1 August–2 September 1981

Idem, 'Haigh's Art', *Yorkshire Post,* 3 August 1981

Idem, 'Recent Work on paper by Tom Wood', *Yorkshire Post,* 1 December 1986

Idem, 'Work by Tom Wood', *Yorkshire Post,* 5 December 1987

McManus, Irene, 'Tom Wood', *Guardian,* 28 November 1984

Morris, Susan, 'Tom Wood Graeme Wilson', *Arts Review,* 8 April 1988

Ormondroyd, Diane, 'Six Artists in Industry', *Arts Review,* September 1981

Robertson, Alexander and Strickland-Constable, Miranda, *The Irresistible Objects: Still Life 1600–1985,* exhibition catalogue, Leeds City Art Gallery, 18 October–8 December 1985

Sara, Mary, 'The Mystery Plays of Light and Colour', *Yorkshire Post,* November 1994

Seddon, Richard, 'Prized Expressions', *Yorkshire Post,* 2 September 1985

Idem, 'Glory For Two in the Garden', *Yorkshire Post,* 18 April 1988

Sheeran, John, 'Tom Wood: Studio Visit', *The Artist,* April 1987

Smith, Nima, 'An Interior Journey', exhibition catalogue essay for *Tom Wood: Work — A Selection of Paintings, Drawings and Prints 1978–87,* Dean Clough Contemporary Art Gallery, Halifax, 21 November–19 December 1987

Idem, 'Tom Wood: Profiles in Thought', exhibition catalogue essay for *North of Watford — Recent Work by Graeme Willson and Tom Wood,* Smiths Gallery, London, 4–16 April 1988

Stubley, Trevor, 'The New St Paul's', *Arts Yorkshire,* August 1984

Sykes, Geraldine, 'Quiet by Design', *Huddersfield Examiner,* 8 October 1982

Vines, Ian, *Object and Image — Aspects of British Art in the 1980s,* exhibition catalogue. Stoke-on-Trent Museum and Art Gallery, 3 September–16 October 1988

Warner, Simon, 'An Inner African', *Halifax Evening Courier,* 14 December 1987

Idem, 'The Prince and The Painter', *Halifax Evening Courier,* 24 May 1988

Wood, Tom, Interview in 'Print Supplement', *Artist's Newsletter,* March 1983

Wood, Tom, *From The Face to The Fish,* exhibition catalogue, Cartwright Hall, Bradford, 3 November–9 December 1984

Wood, Tom, 'Artist's Diary', *Art Review,* November 1994